A TLS COMPANION

THE MODERN MOVEMENT

Edited and with an Introduction by
John Gross

HARVILL
An Imprint of HarperCollins*Publishers*

First published in 1992
by Harvill
an imprint of HarperCollins Publishers
77/85 Fulham Palace Road,
Hammersmith, London W6 8JB

1 3 5 7 9 10 8 6 4 2

A CIP catalogue record for this book
is available from the British Library.

ISBN 0 00 272673 4

Set in Garamond 156 by
Servis Filmsetting Ltd, Manchester
Printed and bound in Great Britain by
HarHartnoll Ltd, Bodmin, Cornwall ɔw

CONTENTS

James Joyce

T. S. Eliot

Wyndham Lewis

Virginia Woolf

W. H. Auden

II. INTERNATIONAL FOCUS

III. T. S. ELIOT AND VIRGINIA WOOLF
REVIEW ...

THE TLS AND
THE MODERN MOVEMENT

John Gross

As a literary term, "modernism" is open to some large objections. Everything was modern once. Everything ceases to be modern sooner or later. To single out the modernity of a work of art tells one very little in itself about its other qualities.

None the less the idea of "the Modern" remains one of the most potent in twentieth-century literature. In the 1920s it came to signify a drastic break with the past, as drastic as that accomplished by the Romantics. The period between the two world wars – the high summer of modernism – was an age of bold experiments and broken taboos; of new techniques, new sensibilities, new bearings, new directions; of Auden's "new styles of architecture" and Ezra Pound's *Make It New*. Everyone agreed, whether they approved of the phenomenon or not, that there was something called modern poetry – something roughly the equivalent of modern music and modern art. Fiction, too, had its strange modern gods. And the term still clings to works of the period – to *Ulysses*, say, or *The Waste Land* – long after it has ceased to overlap with "contemporary".

Modernism came in many varieties. One could argue for a long (and possibly tedious) time about what were its defining characteristics, about when it began and ended, about exactly who qualifies as a modernist. An anthologist, however, is forced to simplify, and in the present book I have judged it best to concentrate on a dozen key writers, eight of them writing in English and four of them in other languages. In each case I have tried to indicate something of how the *TLS* reacted to their work on its first appearance, and something of how it has come to be viewed in retrospect. I have also included separate review-articles on ten further writers, a number of miscellaneous items, and a selection of reviews by the two major modern writers who were also regular contributors to the paper, T. S. Eliot and Virginia Woolf.

*   *   *

"During the 1920s," the American critic Harry Levin once wrote, "the *TLS* took a dim view of much that was brilliantly going on." The reality, as I hope the following pages will show, was rather more chequered; but there can be no denying that in its early decades the paper had the reputation of being a bastion of literary conservatism. An austere format; the maintenance of anonymity; a heavy emphasis (not least in the correspondence columns) on traditional scholarship; a general flavour of club, common-room and parsonage; the link with *The Times* itself – in avant-garde eyes, these were the unmistakable stigmata of the Establishment. It must also be remembered that only a limited number of longer articles were devoted to imaginative literature – the paper, then as now, had many other interests to consider; and that when they were, it was almost always to the literature of the past. Contemporaries, whether they were modernists or not, had to be content with medium-length notices at best.

Within these limits, however, the *TLS* felt that it had an obligation to cover any significant new work. Bruce Richmond, the editor since the supplement's founding in 1902, was a man whose taste had been formed in the nineteenth century; he was a product of late-Victorian Winchester, All Souls and the "grand old fortifying classical curriculum". But he could hardly fail to be aware of changing literary currents – the review-copies turned up on his desk, the names were in the air; and towards the end of the First World War he began to employ a number of younger contributors who were far more attuned to what was happening than his own contemporaries. One key recruit was Middleton Murry, who began reviewing regularly in 1917, specializing in French literature. When Murry became editor of the *Athenaeum* in 1919, he was succeeded as chief French reviewer by Richard Aldington, but he continued writing for the paper throughout his career. (Between June 1938 and March 1939, for example, he contributed nearly forty reviews, ten of them full-page articles.) Aldington, too, was a prolific contributor. His work for the paper was his most regular source of income for much of the 1920s; he was also responsible for arranging the first meeting between Richmond and Eliot – the beginning of a notable editorial connection. And in due course other rising talents were brought aboard: Herbert Read, for instance (another of Aldington's friends) and the poet Edgell Rickword, a regular reviewer from

1921 until he helped to establish his own review, *The Calendar of Modern Letters*, in 1925.

At the same time Richmond continued to use his old reliables. There was no question of reserving "modern" books for "modern" contributors; they were at least as likely to be reviewed by someone like the Edwardian man of letters Arthur Clutton-Brock (a mainstay of the paper from its beginnings until his death in 1924), or by an in-house writer like Harold Child or A. S. McDowall – both men with an exceptional breadth of learning, both members of the staff of *The Times*.*

It was Child who acclaimed the self-renewing power of the middle-aged W. B. Yeats in his review of *Responsibilities* (1914). Twenty-five years later, by now in his seventies, he reviewed Louis MacNeice's study of Yeats – taking stock of the poet's achievement, puzzling over the masks he had adopted, drawing the line at all but the most obvious of his symbolism. In this last he was representative: few of the original *TLS* reviewers of Yeats's later work were willing to engage with its esoteric side. But they had no trouble recognizing its greatness, or acknowledging what an advance it represented over his early poems – the poems that most of them had grown up with. The most acute of these first-time-round commentators was Austin Clarke, the leading Irish poet of his own generation; it would surely have been appropriate to have waived the anonymity rule for once and to have let readers know that it was Clarke who was responsible for the tribute that was published following Yeats's death.

Ezra Pound made his first appearance in the *TLS* in November 1912, when the paper published a review of his translations of Guido Cavalcanti – commending them as "useful helps towards the study of the original", but comparing them unfavourably as poems with the versions of Cavalcanti by Rossetti. Two weeks later a surprisingly temperate reply from Pound appeared in the correspondence columns. He explained that his primary purpose had been to convey the force of Cavalcanti's personality, and that

---

*Child, who had begun his career as an actor, later became a leading authority on theatre history. In the course of his journalistic labours he also found time to contribute more articles to *The Cambridge History of English Literature* than any other writer apart from George Saintsbury. McDowall was a close friend of Thomas Hardy, and wrote a study of his work that is still well worth reading.

there was no clash between Rossetti's "aesthetic" method and his own "scholastic" one: "He was as avowedly intent on making beautiful verses as I am on presenting an individual."

Pound's own personality presented reviewers with something of a puzzle in the years that followed. They tended to alternate between being intrigued by his showmanship and bemused by his aggressiveness; they all found things to praise in his work – there was none of the spluttering indignation which legend might suggest – but their comments, right down to the 1930s and the early volumes of the *Cantos*, remained disappointingly skimpy. The most obvious missed opportunity was Aldington's review of the 1928 *Collected Poems* – an inexplicably lukewarm performance, given that the two men were still close friends at the time.

It was only after the Second World War that the paper set out to do justice to Pound, though at the price of largely ignoring his conduct during that war and the problems posed by his politics in general. The first large-scale celebration of his work, in 1950, was assigned to Peter Russell, who was his most dedicated British champion in the immediate post-war period. Ten years later Christine Brooke-Rose suggested that "his may be the only comprehensible poetry to the twenty-first century, under a new economic order" – a notion which looks even quainter now than it did then. By contrast, G. S. Fraser's account of Pound as a translator remains a model of its kind: an all-round man of letters (as opposed to a specialist or an acolyte) offering common-sense guidance to the common reader.

Pound himself only reviewed once for the *TLS*, in October 1916. (An excerpt from the review can be found on p. 293). The book in question – an odd choice – was an attack on Woodrow Wilson for failing to take America into the First World War; the author, Morton Fullerton, is better known today for having been the lover of Edith Wharton. Bruce Richmond plainly had no inclination to repeat the experiment, but then it is unlikely that Pound would ever have felt at home writing for him. In 1914–15 he had published a series of mocking extracts from the *TLS* in the magazine *The Egoist*: one instalment was headed "Inconsiderable Imbecilities".

He resumed contact of a sort forty years later, however, when he was moved to send the paper a number of letters for publication.

The one reprinted on p. 300 must surely rank as one of the craziest ever to appear in its pages.

No contemporary writer commanded more space in the *TLS* in the years between the wars than D. H. Lawrence, and for the most part the treatment he received was fair-minded and sympathetic. At first one is tempted to put this down to the Middleton Murry connection, and the unsigned tribute by Murry which was published after Lawrence's death – a startlingly personal piece, by the standards of the paper at the time – might seem to confirm such an idea. But the books of the 1920s and the posthumous books of the 1930s were in fact mainly reviewed by the old brigade, Child and the rest. While they were less fully committed to Lawrence than Murry, they responded to his genius, and they recognized that his faults were often the penalty he paid for struggling to break new ground. They did not simply content themselves (as McDowall's excellent review of the letters makes clear) with asking him to revert to the more traditional mode of *Sons and Lovers*.

Two reviews of the 1920s stand apart. Virginia Woolf's account of *The Lost Girl* not only makes some good points; it is also a fascinating example of two very different visions rubbing up against each other. (It shared a page, incidentally, with a review of Eliot's *The Sacred Wood*, and also – such are the vagaries of journalism – with a review of a book by Stephen Leacock called *Winsome Winnie*.) The angry and largely dismissive review of *Women in Love* is another matter. It turns out to be the work of Edmund Blunden: according to his biographer, Blunden claimed to have been put off Lawrence "by the memory of some of the sexually explicit material which had circulated among his wartime battalion".

Of the post-Second World War reviews, Middleton Murry on Leavis's *D. H. Lawrence: Novelist* is in a class by itself: a magisterial piece, which only Murry could have written. But Malcolm Muggeridge, looking at Lawrence in the light of common day, also said something which needed to be said in the piece he wrote in 1950 – something all the more telling because he did not deny Lawrence's "wonderful sense of life and beauty". This was the pre-television Muggeridge; later on his opinions became less nuanced.

In the case of James Joyce, the record is more patchy. When

Dubliners appeared, it naturally had to take its chance among the week's fiction: it received a mildly favourable notice from E. E. Mavrogordato, who was for many years tennis correspondent of *The Times*. Arthur Clutton-Brock, on the other hand, was deeply impressed by *A Portrait of the Artist as a Young Man*, even though he regretted that Joyce had not chosen subject-matter "of more distinction". ("He is stating the English preference for tawdry grandeurs," Joyce commented to Frank Budgen. "Even the best Englishmen seem to love a lord in literature.") In 1918 Clutton-Brock also wrote an enthusiastic review of *Exiles*, while ten years later his son Alan Clutton-Brock, who was art critic of *The Times*, had some kind words for *Anna Livia Plurabelle*. Most of the *TLS*'s early responses to the "Babylonian dialect" of *Finnegans Wake*, down to and including the appearance of the complete work, were in fact reasonably friendly. But meanwhile what should have been the centre-piece of the story was missing. There was no review of *Ulysses* when it was first published in 1922, in Paris (it was of course banned in Britain), and the brief review of the 1936 English edition can hardly be said to have made good the gap.

Nor can Joyce's ghost have been pleased by some of the big post-war discussions of his work which appeared in the paper's pages. In spite of praising this aspect or that episode, they often seem to have been largely animated by an urge to cut him down to size. The review of Richard Ellmann's biography (1959) is an exception – as far as Joyce is concerned, that is. Unfortunately the account it gives of the biography itself is quite inadequate; but I hope that the extract from Ellmann's interview with Craig Raine, first published in 1982, will go some way to restoring a proper sense of his virtues.

T. S. Eliot produced a graceful account of his dealings with Bruce Richmond on the occasion of Richmond's ninetieth birthday (see p. 263). Writing when he himself was in his seventies, he was rather vague about the circumstances of their first meeting; but Richard Aldington, who introduced them, supplies some further details in his autobiography. All three men had lunch together in a pub, and at the outset (if Aldington is to be believed) Eliot very nearly muffed his opportunity. He was looking "awful", "wearing, if you please, a derby hat and an Uncle Sam beard he had cultivated in Switzerland." Before long, however, he won Richmond over with the quality of his conversation, and as a result he was commissioned to write the leading article on Ben Jonson which appeared in November 1919. The following year he contributed an article on Philip Massinger; the year after that, three of his most significant essays – on Marvell, on Dryden and on the Metaphysical Poets; and he continued to review for the paper until well into the 1930s. His last substantial contribution, an article on John Marston, was published in July 1934.

There is a curious discrepancy between Eliot's importance to the *TLS* as a reviewer and the treatment meted out to his own work. The brief notices of *Prufrock* (1917) and *Poems* (1919), which appeared before he had met Richmond, both completely missed the point, and Richmond is said to have deeply regretted them; yet subsequent coverage of his poetry during Richmond's time, while it was always respectful, tended to be guarded and rather meagre.

The 1923 review of *The Waste Land* is a special case. The poem had already been commended in the *TLS* the previous year, in a note on the first number of the *Criterion*, where it had originally appeared; and in assigning it to Edgell Rickword, Richmond could reasonably have assumed that he was placing it in sympathetic hands. Rickword was a member of the young, modern-minded generation; the kind of topics he wrote about for the *TLS* – Donne and Baudelaire, for instance – were very much Eliot's own. In the event, however, he was perplexed by *The Waste Land*, and honest enough to say so. Two years later he wrote an appreciation of Eliot in *The Calendar of Modern Letters*, in which he rated the poem more highly. But he was still prepared to raise the same awkward questions, albeit in a more refined form.

Eliot's verse fared even less well during the editorship of D. L. Murray, who succeeded Richmond in 1937. One sometimes feels that there was a positive feeling against it around the office. Philip Tomlinson, who wrote the review of *East Coker* which provoked a letter from F. R. Leavis (p. 83), was a member of the staff. By all accounts he was a sensitive spirit: the words used to describe him in his obituary in *The Times* were "gentle, meditative, scrupulous".* On this occasion, however, he undoubtedly hit the wrong note – or

---

*He was the brother of the novelist H. M. Tomlinson, and a close friend of Edmund Blunden: Blunden's *Undertones of War* is dedicated to him.

a number of wrong notes. The review of *Little Gidding*, to take another instance, was more measured, but scarcely commensurate with the occasion: leaving aside the quotations, it came to less than 400 words. And in 1944, when the poems that make up *Four Quartets* were brought together in a single volume, the *TLS* did not review the book at all.

Such a decision would have seemed scarcely credible if it had been recalled at the time Eliot died in 1965 ("A Great Man Gone"). He went to his grave an acknowledged modern classic – for many, *the* modern classic. Since then, fashions have changed, more than once, and he has come under attack from numerous directions. Donald Davie's attempt to write him down as essentially "commonplace", a merely transient modernist, is one of the more interesting hostile accounts. But he has never lacked for distinguished champions, either.

The best-known of his own contributions to the *TLS*, apart from those already mentioned, include "Lancelot Andrewes", "Wilkie Collins and Dickens", "Francis Herbert Bradley", and his essays on Middleton, Heywood, Tourneur and Ford. (All of them are readily available elsewhere.) The other topics he wrote about, while mainly Elizabethan or Jacobean, ranged from Spinoza to the American critic Paul Elmer More. Only his early pieces, notably "The Metaphysical Poets" and "Andrew Marvell", have an immediate bearing on his own poetry, but most of the others cast light on his personality – not least on his willingness to assume (or perhaps parody) the tone of a conventional scholar. His sympathetic review of Lytton Strachey's *Elizabeth and Essex* is the most unexpected of them. Here and there, one feels that he would have done better to have left the book to a professional historian. But he makes an excellent point when he writes that "irony and mockery are not Mr Strachey's product, but merely his tools, which he uses slyly to allow us the luxury of sentiment without being ashamed of it."

Most of the early *TLS* reviews of Wyndham Lewis impress one with their open-mindedness. Arthur Clutton-Brock was first over the top, as so often, with a thoughtful account of *Tarr*. Subsequent reviewers, once they had got the hang of Lewis, tended to approach him with what might be called modified fascination. And it is easy to sympathize. The *idea* of *The Apes of God*, for instance, is endlessly fascinating; the experience of actually reading it – I can only speak for myself – is often closer to that recorded by Orlo Williams.* But there was plainly a place for more extended expositions of Lewis, by writers who were more in sympathy with him. They came after the Second World War, above all in a series of valuable reviews by Julian Symons.

Virginia Woolf, who was always acutely aware of criticism of her work, recorded in her diary that the *TLS* review of *To the Lighthouse* hung over her "like a damp cloud" – it was "gentlemanly, kindly, timid & praising beauty, doubting character, & leaving me moderately depressed." It also seemed to her to be "an exact copy" of the *TLS* reviews of *Jacob's Room* and *Mrs Dalloway* – as well it might have done, since all three pieces were the work of A. S. McDowall. We can agree with her about their lack of impact, and regret that Richmond did not cast his net more widely; but there is still a good deal of truth in what McDowall says, especially about *Jacob's Room*. The only piece about her in the paper that gave her unqualified satisfaction seems to have been Harold Child's review of *Kew Gardens* (which she thought was by Logan Pearsall Smith) – a review "in which as much praise was allowed me as I like to claim."

At the time of her death, her reputation was in decline. The *TLS* rose to the occasion, however, with a fine tribute, just as it did in the 1950s, when her fortunes were beginning to revive. That revival was to have its superficial gossipy aspects, and also, with the spread of feminism, its purely polemical ones; but Joan Bennett's lengthy review of *A Writer's Diary* (1953) concentrated firmly on her claim to be considered an important artist. It was also (as far as I know) the first occasion on which her work was discussed in the *TLS* by another woman.

Her own contributions to the paper would merit a study in themselves. The statistics alone are impressive enough. Her first *TLS* review (of two books on "the Dickens Country" and "the Thackeray Country") appeared in March 1905. She was soon

*Orlo (short for Orlando) Williams is also represented in this book by an extract from his excellent and notably unflustered review of *Lady Chatterley's Lover*, and by his obituary tribute to Virginia Woolf. A regular reviewer of the *TLS*, he was Clerk of Committees at the House of Commons, and the author of books on subjects ranging from parliamentary procedure to Italian literature. His other achievements included winning the school heavyweight boxing championship while he was at Eton.

writing seven, eight, a dozen reviews a year; then there was a tapering-off; then, beginning in 1916, an extraordinary burst of energy. In the course of 1917 she contributed no less than 35 reviews, many of them full-scale articles; in the course of 1918, an astonishing 43. How can she have found time to do anything else that year? And though from 1920 onwards she mostly wrote for other papers, she remained an occasional contributor as long as Richmond was editor. Her last article, on Congreve, appeared in September 1937.

Examples of her work for the *TLS* make up a large part of her various collections of essays. Of the three examples I have chosen, one, "Modern Novels", is an important statement of her artistic credo, and I think that her own conception of the novel is already implicit in the concluding paragraph of her review of Arnold Bennett's *Books and Persons*. The short piece on Edgar Lee Masters, which has never been reprinted, is a reminder that she was willing to take on some unlikely assignments, and that she almost always found something stimulating to say when she did.

Virginia Woolf's connection with the *TLS* meant a great deal to her. She often complained about the paper, and occasionally cursed it, but her last word about Bruce Richmond ought to be allowed to stand as her truest: "I learnt a lot of my craft writing for him: how to compress; how to enliven; & also was made to read with a pen & notebook, seriously."

W. H. Auden was first mentioned in the *TLS* in 1926, in a brief review of that year's *Oxford Poetry* which dismissed him as an "unsuccessful suitor" of the Muse – and the poem cited was admittedly a poor one. The first extended notice he received was in a review of his *Poems* (1931), which spent much of its space complaining about his obscurity. (The piece was the work of the literary journalist Hugh I'Anson Fausset, another *TLS* regular: in John Haffenden's *Auden: The Critical Heritage* it is wrongly attributed to F. R. Leavis.) Most of Auden's work in the years that followed was treated sympathetically, and often quite spryly. One only wishes that some of the writers could have been given more space – the reviewer of *Look, Stranger!* (1936), for instance, who had to make do with a mere three or four paragraphs at the bottom of the page. It was not until 1948 that the paper was ready to assess his cumulative achievement, in a review-article (pegged to the appearance of *The Age of Anxiety*) by a poet of a younger generation, Alan Ross. And it was another poet, Peter Porter, who took stock of his entire career eight years after his death, in 1981, in one of the best pieces about him ever written.

From early on the *TLS* prided itself on the attention it paid to foreign literature, above all literature in French. Works by Gide, Valéry and other major figures were duly reviewed on their first appearance; works by many minor figures, too. But the French writer who received the most thorough coverage was undoubtedly Proust.

It began with the admirable review of *Du Côté de Chez Swann* which appeared in December 1913, less than a month after the book had been published in Paris. The piece was long thought to be the work of the theatre critic A. B. Walkley – yet another of the innumerable false attributions to which anonymity gave rise; it was in fact written by Mary Duclaux (1857–1944), a veteran *TLS* contributor, and someone well worth a short study in her own right. She was born Mary Robinson, the daughter of a prosperous and cultured London architect; Walter Pater and John Addington Symonds were among her early friends; she married, in 1888, James Darmesteter, a distinguished French orientalist, and in 1901, after Darmesteter's death, Émile Duclaux, a no less distinguished scientist and the director of the Pasteur Institute. Living in France for most of her long life, she became best-known as an interpreter of French literature for English-speaking readers, although in her early days she had also enjoyed, with some justice, a considerable reputation as a poet. (Several examples of her work can be found in Christopher Ricks's recent *Oxford Book of Victorian Verse*, most memorably a poem called "Neurasthenia".) She was, in short, a woman of imagination as well as learning, and her review of *Swann* – given that she was coming to the book with no idea what to expect – shows exceptional insight. Proust himself was well pleased with it.

He was less satisfied with the reviews of *Pastiches et Mélanges* and *A l'Ombre des Jeunes Filles en Fleur* which the paper carried in 1919. He had hoped that Mme Duclaux, with whom he was in touch, would review him again, but by the time she asked Richmond for the books they had both been assigned to Richard Aldington. Not that he did not receive abundant praise in the two pieces, as he continued to do (in spite of various oddities and reservations) as the later instalments of *A la Recherche* made their appearance. And the tributes at the time of his death – the unsigned article by Middleton Murry, the text of the letter from English admirers to the *Nouvelle Revue Française* – were designed to set the seal on his reputation as one of the greatest figures of modern literature. The examples of the paper's subsequent treatment of his work which I have chosen show some interesting ups and downs. (Murry was much cooler in 1940 than he had been in 1923, for instance.) But their combined effect is to leave one with an even deeper sense of his genius.

Of the three German or German-speaking writers who have been singled out, Thomas Mann was a familiar name – to anyone who read *TLS* reviews of German books, that is – from the days of *Buddenbrooks* onwards. On their first appearance, however, his later works were often made to sound far too heavy for Anglo-Saxon tastes, and his reviewing history underlines how much English understanding of German literature owes to refugees from Hitler – Erich Heller, Michael Hamburger, J. P. Stern and others. Rilke was appreciated from early on; Kafka's hour came in the 1930s, although strong reservations – and not merely insular ones – have persisted.

The section on Marianne Moore, Anna Akhmatova and the other writers who are represented by one essay apiece can, I think, be left to speak for itself. Ernst Kaiser's 1949 article on Robert Musil might be singled out, however, as an impressive example of the international literary commerce to which the *TLS* has always aspired: an authoritative and, more important still, an attractive introduction to a major foreign writer who was virtually unknown in England at the time.

The final section of the book contains a brief sampling of letters and curiosities, and of poems that made their first appearance in the paper. The review of Tristan Tzara and the Dadaists is a reminder that some manifestations of modernism did indeed get the door slammed in their face: it was the work of a writer who was himself a minor modernist, in a subdued English fashion, the Imagist poet F. S. Flint. Wyndham Lewis's peculiar review-article about Matthew Arnold, published in 1954, was one of the very few occasions on which a contributor was permitted to breach the anonymity rule. In reading Lewis's comments on Thomas Arnold, we should perhaps bear in mind that he was educated at Rugby himself.

The practice of publishing poems in the *TLS* began under the editorship of D. L. Murray. Everyone agrees that Murray was a less distinguished editor than Richmond, but he did take some important steps towards brightening the paper up. Auden's poem on Edward Lear must have seemed a very jazzy departure indeed to older readers: it appeared on the cover of the Spring Books number in 1939, surrounded by a frieze of Lear drawings. Over forty years later Auden himself was to be commemorated in a poem – or lay – by Gavin Ewart. The publication of Wallace Stevens's "A Child Asleep in its Own Life" can in some measure be seen as an atonement for the long neglect of Stevens in this country, in the *TLS* as elsewhere; it appeared in an American number which was part of the much more enterprising coverage of American literature that marked the editorship (1948–59) of Alan Pryce-Jones. With Seamus Heaney's "Small Fantasia for W. B." we come full circle: "W. B." is the author with whom the present book opens.

* * *

When Bruce Richmond died in October 1964, at the age of 93, the *TLS* accompanied its announcement of his death with a single sentence: "He left behind him one cardinal rule: the right man for the right book." An irritatingly sententious observation. What literary editor would not ideally hope to abide by the same rule? What literary editor has ever succeeded? And the hint of olympian authority was even more objectionable in an era of unsigned reviews – for whatever virtues anonymity may have had, it also fostered a mystique which the facts did not warrant. When the mask is removed, *TLS* reviewers generally turn out to have been not so very different from other people's.

Yet the paper's scope, its traditions, its special interests, its foreign coverage, the number of books with which it deals, the amount of space it offers contributors – taken together, these do undoubtedly give it a unique character. And if the quality of contributions has inevitably varied, the standard aimed at has always been high. All the items in this book are worth reading as documents of literary history and changing literary taste, but most of them are also well worth reading on their own account.

JOHN GROSS

NOTE: The beginning and ending of excerpts are indicated by three dots. In other respects texts follow the original *TLS* texts exactly, which means that a number of errors have been preserved – the assumption, for example, that Thomas Mann's translator, H. T. Lowe-Porter, was a man.

I

———

TWELVE WRITERS REVIEWED

MR YEATS IN MIDDLE AGE

Harold Child

What lover of Mr Yeats's work – poetry, prose, or drama – ever thinks of him as other than a youth? Even the long spell of silence – during which he has given himself up to

> The day's war with every knave and dolt,
> Theatre business, management of men,

and, as author, to the rewriting of his own compositions – has never seemed to be more than a pause in a very far from complete development. Hugging jealously what Mr Yeats had done, we were still speculating eagerly what he was going to do, confident that this spring of beauty could not run dry, this spiritual energy slip into a pattern or cease to be. And that confidence will survive these two books, in which Mr Yeats comes before us deliberately as a middle-aged man, not so much stating as implying that his creative ardours are over. [...]

"The lying days of my youth" – the days when Mr Yeats was an enthusiast, a greedy romantic we learn much about them from the "Reveries." It is a fascinating book. Only in poetry can the poet reveal himself; but the middle-aged autobiographer, telling us with candour, now smiling and now the least bit wry-mouthed, about his youth, can help us some way on the road to understanding what the poems reveal. [...]

The end is sadness. The middle-aged man is "sorrowful and disturbed."

> It is not that I have accomplished too few of my plans, for I
> am not ambitious; but when I think of all the books I have
> read, and of the wise words I have heard spoken, and of the
> anxiety I have given to parents and grandparents, and of the
> hopes that I have had, all life weighed in the scales of my
> own life seems to me a preparation for something that
> never happens.

Responsibilities and Other Poems. Reveries over Childhood and Youth, by W. B. Yeats
[October 19, 1916]

It is not for the poet himself, but it certainly is for those who, to the best of their ability, absorb his work to point out, first, that the end is not yet; and then that something has happened; and something self-sufficient without further warranty.

Suddenly I saw the cold and rook-delighting Heaven
That seemed as though ice burned and was but the more ice –

is not that, in itself, something to have happened?

THE MEMORIES OF
MR YEATS

Arthur Clutton-Brock

In this book Mr Yeats gives us a history of his own mind in concrete and æsthetic rather than intellectual or abstract terms. He has, as he has often proved in prose and verse, the artist's power of realization: he can make things happen again, and revive people out of the past; and this book is alive with them, related always to Mr Yeats himself, but not egotistically. We see him in terms of them and we feel the growth of his mind in his account of them. That mind, though always keeping its own peculiar character and interests, has not lived always in one world, but has moved to and fro between an English literary and an Irish Nationalist society, remaining itself detached, mystical, experimental. Mr Yeats is a poet and a fanatic for the purity of literature, like other members of the Rhymers' Club, the tragic generation as he calls them; but, like Blake, he also wishes to prove something about and through poetry; the very fact that poetry exists and must be practised in its purity proves for him something about the nature of things, so that, even in the effort to be a pure poet, he too is proving something. He is not the, perhaps fabulous, artist who sings because he must, but a discoverer even in his music, a listener to another music not made by himself which, he believes, will tell him secrets hidden from our stiff-minded generation. [. . .]

The Trembling of the Veil, by W. B. Yeats [November 23, 1922]

MR YEATS'S DREAMS

Edward Shanks

[...] The development of his style has permitted the widening of his range and has allowed him to use subjects which he could not have attempted before. In his beginnings there was something dim, remote and trance-like about all he did. But now that with his stripped austere style he gives to his dreams the firm outline of real things, he can also on occasion write about real things themselves. Hence come the verses on the *Playboy*, on Sir Hugh Lane's pictures, and on the Easter Week Insurrection. Hence come also, it must be owned, somewhat pitiful followings of Milton or Wordsworth and such crawling lines as

> I think it better that in times like these
> A poet keep his mouth shut, for in truth
> We have no gift to set a statesman right.

But the good outweighs the bad; and, though Mr Yeats's occasional verses are not a large part of his work, yet any extension of range is good. He is now able also to exercise a certain human and graceful playfulness which would have been impossible to the mournful writer of "The Wind among the Reeds." [...]

If we consider the whole spread of Mr Yeats's lyrical work, we find in it a steady growth which, after all, not many of our lyrical poets have surpassed – not many of them, indeed, having had the opportunity to do so. The earlier poems are specially endeared to us by familiarity and hence, often, by their faults; the later are sometimes strange, difficult and disconcerting. But when we have had a little time we shall see the whole as an harmonious and self-consistent development.

Later Poems, by W. B. Yeats [December 28, 1922]

MR YEATS'S NEW POEMS*

Austin Clarke

When the later poetry of Mr Yeats had shown a complete abnegation of imaginative festivity, a deliberate poverty at table and gate, the dismissed reader was inclined to believe that the poet had mistaken mocking rags and an empty state for true austerity. Impatient with an earlier and lovelier mood that had never been easily won, Mr Yeats had seemed to choose too resentfully, as images against life, "all things uncomely and broken, all things worn out and old." Disturbing as that phase of disillusion had been, one believed that it would pass into contentment. Although there is no philosophic peace in this new book of poems, the acerbity has changed, as often as not, into intellectual anxiety and indignation: one becomes aware of a deeper sorrow at the roots of being that one cannot read of without being strangely moved. More constantly than in preceding books, perhaps, there is a quality in these poems which seems at variance with their personal disquiet, a freedom of the poetic elements, an imaginative and prosodic beauty that brings one the pure and impersonal joy of art. [...]

Personal discontents and the commotion of Irish public times mingle, indeed, in these verses, satirical or lyrical; but happily the imagination, despite its own inhibitions, remains as free and symbolic. [...]

THE COLLECTED POEMS
OF W. B. YEATS†

Alex Glendinning

Here are all Mr Yeats's poems, from "The Wanderings of Oisin" to "The Winding Stair." It is difficult to think of any adequate parallel

---

*The Tower, by W. B. Yeats [March 1, 1928]
†The Collected Poems of W. B. Yeats [March 8, 1934]

for the peculiar achievement which this collection represents. Covering a period of more than forty years, it records for us a long and hazardous journey – a journey from an enchanted twilight into the harsh light of our common day. Few poets have sought so eagerly as Mr Yeats to build and inhabit an imaginative "dream-world" remote from the ordinary world of affairs. His earlier poems have the quality of an incantation, and a very potent incantation it is. But, as Mr Eliot recently remarked of these poems: "You cannot take heaven by magic, especially if you are, like Mr Yeats, a very sane person." This realization finds its way gradually into the poems; a poetry of harder outlines and more athletic rhythms succeeds the drowsy richness of "The Wind Among the Reeds." Already, in "Responsibilities," Mr Yeats has discarded his "embroidered coat" and determined on "walking naked." In the poems which follow, the bitterness and regret of disillusion are evident:–

> The holy centaurs of the hills are vanished;
> I have nothing but the embittered sun;
> Banished heroic mother moon and vanished,
> And now that I have come to fifty years
> I must endure the timid sun.

But how little of resignation or defeat there was in Mr Yeats's endurance "The Tower" and "The Winding Stair" will testify. In these poems his genius asserts itself with renewed passion and vigour; and Mr Yeats, in his old age, is once more an active influence on the younger generation of poets. [...]

YEATS'S INNER DRAMA

Austin Clarke

[...] The most striking characteristic of Yeats's later poetry, and one which immediately holds the attention, is the intense and brilliant personality which both dominates and informs it, giving unity to its very contradictions and bringing into full circle the many contrasted moods. And the presence of this dominating

[Article] [February 4, 1939]

personality, which is divided against itself, lends to all this later work its inner drama. But it is essentially a poetic personality and in its expression is posited the plight of the poet in modern times, whether we regard Yeats as the last of the great Romantics, a lonely thinker concerned with ultimate questions of time and the soul's circumstance, or as one who ventures to peer into the mortal future. It is this dramatised plight of the poet, moving between moods of arrogance and humility, concerned with the problems of his strange profession – it is this dramatised presentation which has attracted a young generation caught between repressed emotion and distressing necessity. These poems, long and short, complex or simple in their lyrical purity, are, in fact, charged with experience and personality. This gives them their compelling power.

The poet was fortunate inasmuch as his new manner brought him into accord with our times. The development of an intricate and metaphysical poetry, the renewed interest in difficulties and obscure by-ways, rendered possible the immediate acceptance of his newly evolved style and manner. In this new style a living, natural speech was not incompatible with traditional eloquence, and cunning simplicity could blend with the far-fetched and strange. Undoubtedly the poet, after a lifelong devotion to poetic discipline and technique, achieved an art of display which conceals itself. Without such an art of selection and display the intellectualism of his later work could not have been so readily assimilated. But in this new mode the poet found what other and younger writers were seeking. In this medium, which is also a synthesis, he was able to hold as in a natural equivalence, and without distressing incongruity, every variety of temper, from lyrical innocence blended with experience to the starkness of old age contemplating itself, from passing querulousness to a rich formal content of intellectualised image and figuratively pointed abstraction. It was this new freedom in discipline which enabled him to range from the passing theories of Spengler to the formative cycle of Vico, or to pass from an obscure astrology to the attractive subjectivism of Berkeley with its eighteenth-century brilliance of dialect. Like Valéry and other modern poets, he seemed to have acquired a European range, traversing a cultured world of myth and imagery, drawing here and there upon what took his fancy, and if at times his verse were encyclopaedic – and we use that word in the strict sense – the variety was not incompatible with our times. [. . .]

THE MYSTERY OF YEATS

Harold Child

[...] Art is not "liberated from life" by being made unintelligible; and any symbol the interpretation of which is known only to the few initiated is death, not to the despised common life, but to the poetry. Far from purifying it, such things corrupt it. Mr Macneice anticipates the contention that "Yeats's cat-headed figures or hounds with one red ear are no more *spiritual* than the everyday figures or objects met with in the Greek Anthology or in Burns or Wordsworth." They are, indeed, or may easily become, less spiritual – mechanical contrivances for the expression of esoteric meaning at the expense of the exoteric meaning; and thus they obstruct the response of the spirit to the appeal of the poetry. Some of them, like a dog with one red ear, have the taint of the ridiculous which lurks in so many of the Irish legends. (Conchubar, we read in Yeats's note to "The Secret Rose," had been struck by a ball made out of the dried brains of an enemy and hurled out of a sling; and this ball had been left in his head, and his head had been mended with thread of gold because his hair was like gold, and thus he lived for seven years.) Others are delightfully decorative:–

> Their legs long, delicate and slender, aquamarine their eyes,
> Magical unicorns bear ladies on their backs.

It is to the good – to the good of us, the readers – that from these Irish myths Yeats should have drawn, especially in his earlier years, a set of values in which the dream life is truer than the waking life – values which may correct our too much absorption in the day-to-day material traffic of life. We may read the little poem of "Fergus and the Druid," or "The Man who Dreamed of Faeryland," or the crown of all this sort of work in Yeats, the play of *The Shadowy Waters*, and be spiritually the richer. But as Yeats's life-long search for his spiritual home went on and he added Oriental to Irish lore, and adventured into mysticism, into spiritualism, into astrology, into metaphysics, he acquired more and more symbols which appeared to him to be means of self-expression but were, in fact,

The Poems of W. B. Yeats, by Louis Macneice [March 29, 1941]

devices for self-concealment. His human sympathies had begun to widen before Lady Gregory drew him into the popular atmosphere of the theatre; but to the very end he suffered from a sort of hang-over from the fastidious contempt for ordinary life that had kept him "reclining on a yellow satin sofa" in his days of aesthetic languor.

> John Synge, I and Augusta Gregory, thought
> All that we did, all that we said or sang
> Must come from contact with the soil, from that
> Contact everything Antaeus-like grew strong.
> We three alone in modern times had brought
> Everything down to that sole test again,
> Dream of the noble and the beggar-man.

The corollary, says Mr Macneice, is that the aristocrats must be kept on their pedestals and that the peasants (which would include the beggar-man), "finally, must remain where they have nothing to lose." That is a sociological rather than a poetical concern (and the relation between poetry and sociology is a matter on which Mr Macneice writes in another chapter with vigour and good sense); but, sociology apart, such a view of society is obviously arbitrary and artificial. [. . .]

YEATS IN YOUTH AND MATURITY

Joseph Hone

[. . .] Yeats's first important book was the *Wanderings of Oisin and Other Poems* (1889). He preserved the long title poem – said to have set the tone of the Irish literary revival – through the years while subjecting it to constant and severe revisions. But well over half of the "Other Poems" were to be summarily rejected, and rightly; indeed a glance at the discards sets us wondering whether any other great poet ever wrote so many mediocre poems in his youth. On

The Variorum Edition of the Poems of W. B. Yeats, edited by Peter Allt and Russell K. Alspach [March 7, 1958]

the other hand, a consideration of what he retained from the *Wanderings* and from the *Countess Cathleen and other Legends and Lyrics* – such verses as "The Stolen Child," "Down by the Salley Gardens," "When you are Old" (the imitation of Ronsard), "The Man who Dreamed of Faeryland" – suggests that much of his early poetry deserved the acclaim with which it was greeted in the 1890s.

This is not to object, as was the habit of the Irish companions of his youth, to Yeats's amendments of his early work, which sometimes amounted to the complete reconstruction of a poem. It is permissible to enjoy "The Sorrow of Love" (from the *Countess Cathleen* volume) in the original version, and yet to admit that it was ultimately transformed into something richer and rarer. This poem, he told Robert Bridges in 1901, was one of which he was "never very proud," but it was not until the 1920s, a great period of radical revisions, that Helen of Troy first made her appearance in it. Every line was then altered. In the autobiographical fragment, *Dramatis Personae*, he referred to the introduction of certain prosaic words into his verse, so as to "give the impression of an active man speaking," and in "The Sorrow of Love," "a climbing moon upon an empty sky," is substituted for "a curd pale moon, the white stars in the sky," and "all that famous harmony of leaves" for "the loud song of the ever singing leaves." The same motive is evident in the final lines of the "Lamentation of the Old Pensioner," savagely changed from "All the old faces are now gone," "And the fret lies on me" into "I spit into the face of time, That has transfigured me." His theme, the sentiments of an aging man, remained the same, but was given a more vigorous expression. The reviewer remembers how, with Yeats in mind, Allt used to quote a passage from the funeral oration on the Vicomte de Turenne: "Il a eu dans la jeunesse toute la prudence d'un âge avancé, et dans un âge avancé toute la vigueur de la jeunesse." More questionable is the behaviour of the Loves in the final version of that interesting early poem, "The Two Trees." It is hard, as Mr Arland Ussher has observed, to admire them "gyring, spiring to and fro."

Sometimes, however, as in the "Dedicatory Verses to a Collection from Irish Novelists" (1890), the material remained refractory; "Even in its rewritten form," Yeats wrote of this poem in 1924, "it is a sheaf of wild oats." Maybe he only preserved the poem in order to signalize the distance that separated him from the sentimental patriotism of his youth. Ireland is now seen as –

That country where a man can be so crossed;
Can be so battered, badgered and destroyed
That he's a loveless man.

A certain biographical interest attaches to a narrative poem that never appeared in book form, "How Ferencz Renyi kept Silent." It relates an incident in von Haynau's brutal suppression of the Hungarian rising in 1848, and was written for an Irish-American magazine in 1887, the year that young Chief-Secretary Arthur Balfour arrived in Ireland to combat the Plan of Campaign. Except for the Irish exordium

We, too, have seen our bravest and our best
To prisons go, and mossy ruin rest
Where homes once whitened vale and mountain crest . . .

it might have come from the pen of some competent versifier, stirred to utterance by the repression of Hungary two years ago. The surprising thing is that Yeats should have resurrected the verses in 1901 – he had by then a reputation to protect – as a gift to AE for the Christmas number of his agricultural journal, the *Irish Homestead*.

The history of the poem which prefaced the volume *Responsibilities* (1914) is also curious. In the original version of this Apology to ancestors "a Butler and an Armstrong" fight for their "bad master" James at the Boyne. It was not often that Yeats submitted to facts, but in this instance he had no alternative. The poem had no sooner been published than his sister Lily, the authority on family history, informed him that the two forefathers in question were Williamites; in all subsequent printings "a Butler and an Armstrong" withstand "James and the Irish when the Dutchman crossed." [...]

Yeats's urge to better his work never ceased, but three great poems of his maturity were to remain untouched, apart from punctuation: "Among School Children," "Sailing to Byzantium" and "Byzantium." (A like indulgence was extended to the best-known of his early poems, "The Lake Isle of Innisfree," which however he failed to include in the selections from his own work in his *Oxford Book of Modern Verse*.) He *did* rewrite the first line of "Sailing to Byzantium" when shortly before his death he was in London rehearsing for Broadcast programmes. His rehearser Mr

Clinton-Baddeley, who has told the story in "Reading Poetry with
W. B. Yeats" (*London Magazine*, Dec. 1957), having observed that –

This is no country for old men the young –

would be difficult to speak, he shouted down the talk-back, "It's
the worst piece of syntax I ever wrote," and returned the same
evening to Broadcasting House with a new line that was never
printed:

Old men should quit a country, where the young

However slight the textual variations in many of the poems of
Yeats's maturity may be, the close student of this volume will not
miss their importance: *e.g.* the change in the prophetic "Second
Coming" (a poem occasioned by events during the Irish civil war
and first published by the Cuala Press in 1921), "Somewhere in
sands of the desert" for "A waste of desert sand," and "Reel
shadows" for "wind shadows," and in "Leda and the Swan," "A
sudden blow; the great wings beating still" for "A rush, a sudden
wheel, and hovering still." In "The Spur" in *Last Poems* (1936–39)
"dance attendance on my old age" becomes "dance attention," a
change made in the last year of the poet's life. [...]

SOME RECENT VERSE

Harold Child

[...] Mr Ezra Pound's originality is of a different kind. He begins
with a challenge –

When I behold how black, immortal ink
    Drips from my deathless pen – ah, well-away!
Why should we stop at all for what I think?
    There is enough in what I chance to say.

Do you bite your thumb – or, rather, do you cock your hat – at me,
Sir? He ends with a poem headed "From a thing by Schumann."
They are fine, careless fellows, these poets. And in between come

Ripostes, by Ezra Pound [December 12, 1912]

brilliant examples of cleverness, magical use of words, proofs of sound learning, metrical triumphs – mixed up with more cockings of the hat, "things" that remind us of nothing so much as the defiant gestures of retreating small boys, and essays in what we will call by the gentle name of wilfulness. At the Post-Impressionist exhibition some spectators may be seen dancing with fury, others quaking with laughter, others indiscriminately worshipping, and a few using their brains coolly. Mr Ezra Pound's book will have the same effect, no doubt, upon its readers. Now and then it is hard not to join the first group. Perhaps, on reading "From a thing by Schumann," it is safer to pass by, as one might pass by a bust in its third stage by Matisse, with the polite reflection that we do not understand its aim and therefore cannot see the art or the beauty of it. There is enough, we understand, in what Mr Pound chances to say; but why should a poet have chanced to say this "thing," when he can write such "things" as the poem to Swinburne, "Salve Pontifex," or the fine, harsh "Seafarer," or the exquisite "Thou keep'st thy rose-leaf" – each of which has its little bursts of wilfulness to give flavour to beauty, but is not the cocking of a hat, not a vulgar gesture of defiance? [...]

POEMS FROM CATHAY

Arthur Clutton-Brock

We do not know from the title of this little book [...] whether Mr Pound has translated these poems direct from the Chinese or has only used other translations. But for those who, like ourselves, know no Chinese, it does not matter much. The result, however produced, is well worth having, and it seems to us very Chinese. [...]

There is a strong superstition among us that a translation should always seem quite English. But when it is made from a literature very alien in method and thought, it is not a translation at all if it seems quite English. Besides, a literal translation from something strange and good may surprise our language into new beauties. If we invite a foreigner of genius among us, we don't want to make

Cathay: Translations by Ezra Pound [April 29, 1915]

him behave just like ourselves; we shall enjoy him best and learn most from him if he remains himself. So we think Mr Pound has chosen the right method in these translations, and we do not mind that they often are "not English." The words are English and give us the sense; and after all it is the business of a writer to mould language to new purposes, not to say something new just as his forefathers said something old. So it is the business of the reader not to be angry or surprised at a strange use of language, if it is a use proper to the sense. [...]

THE POEMS
OF MR EZRA POUND

Arthur Clutton-Brock

[...] His verse is not ordinary speech, but he aims in it at the illusion of ordinary speech; and, though this illusion gives an air of liveliness to his poems, it seems to us to be bought at too high a price. Certainly the original poems as well as the translations show that he has talent – one can read them all with some interest – but why should he use it to express so much indifference and impatience? Why should he so constantly be ironical about nothing in particular? He seems to have private jokes of his own which he does not succeed in making public. He seems to be always reacting against something; and the very form of his verse is a reaction against exhausted forms. But nothing can be made of mere reaction or a habit of irony. The world may not be serious, but the universe is. One suspects a hidden timidity in this air of indifference, as if Mr Pound feared above all things to give himself away. A poet must be ready to give himself away; he must forget even the ironies of his most intimate friends when he writes, no less than the possible misunderstandings of fools. [...]

Lustra, by Ezra Pound [November 16, 1916]

DIVERSITIES AND
PROVOCATIONS*

Arthur Clutton-Brock

[. . .] He says that he takes no great pleasure in writing prose about æsthetic, and that one work of art is worth forty prefaces. But he continues to write prefaces and prose about æsthetic as if he liked doing it; and we confess we like reading him. He has learning, a grasp of principle, and a strong, wilful taste of his own; and it is amusing to watch the conflict between his principles and his wilfulness. He would like to curse Milton and Wordsworth altogether, but he cannot do it; he knows that they are great artists. He knows also that it is worth while to write prose about æsthetic, if it is well done, though he affects the careless impatience of the artist when he does it. He is himself part artist, part philosopher, part fanatic; and each of these elements in him is apt to inhibit or impede the others. He sees so clearly what the perfect poem would be, and then writes poems that are reactions against all kinds of sham poetry, and sometimes nothing more. And then he writes criticisms that are reactions against sham criticism, remembering all the time that he is himself an artist and anxious to avoid the wordiness and vagueness of the professional critic. He seems to be angry with a number of tiresome people, named or unnamed, all the time; we wish he would forget them, and say what he has to say as if he were talking to a friend who understood him, not as if he were answering a cross-examining counsel in the witness-box. [. . .]

AN AMERICAN POET†

Richard Aldington

[. . .] Reacting rather violently from the Romantic delicacy of his earlier manner, he made truculent efforts to be "modern," and the

Pavannes and Divisions, by Ezra Pound [September 19, 1918]
†*Personae: The Collected Poems of Ezra Pound* [January 5, 1928]

change was not always happy. Affectation takes the place of naive Romanticism, and the poet quite fails to obtain the desired effects of strength, virility and modernity by a neglect of good manners and discipline. It is not funny to comment upon Mr Chesterton's person, and Mr Pound's reiterated "Instructions" to his personified "songs" rather lose point when the songs somehow fail to get written. However, a new use for his stylistic gifts was found when Mr Pound paraphrased with felicity Professor Fenollosa's literal renderings of Chinese poetry.

From distant Cathay Mr Pound now returned to the more familiar fields of Provence, with a brief excursion into the Greek Anthology and a still briefer visit to Ferney, where three of Voltaire's poems were paraphrased. Yet once again Mr Pound showed his talent for writing "allusions" by his original re-working of Propertius. Wilful anachronisms and not always wilful misreadings of the text should not blind the reader to the curious felicities and quaint energy of these Propertius poems. While they must shock the classical scholar, they are a spirited effort to bring a Roman poet up to date and in harmony with Transatlantic manners. And in the Envoi (1919), built upon a hint from Waller, Mr Pound once more huddles on his singing-robes, and takes his leave with a beautiful stanza, just to show that he can do it when he chooses. [. . .]

MR EZRA POUND

Alex Glendinning

[. . .] The "Cantos" rely too much and too pedantically on material which is referred to rather than knit into the texture of the poem; and unevenness of accomplishment adds to the difficulty of realizing their design. There is writing in the "Cantos" which has all the sensitive compulsion and precision that we look for in poetry. There is also writing which is exemplary only for its badness, as in the overwrought invective of Cantos XIV and XV. A less obtrusive weakness is apparent in Mr Pound's handling of

A Draft of XXX Cantos, by Ezra Pound [December 28, 1933]

contemporary rôles, in his often laboured imitations of dialect and
his naive clowning:–

> And one day in Smith's room,
> Or may be it was that 1908 medico's
> Put the gob in the fireplace
> Ole Byers and Feigenbaum and Joe Bromley,
> Joe hittin' the gob at 25 feet
> Every time, ping on the metal
>> (Az ole man Comley would say: Boys! ...
>> Never cher terbakker! Hrwwkke tth!
>> Never cher terbakker!

Final judgment must wait for the complete work. At present Mr
Pound's poem leaves us where it left Mr Yeats, grateful for some
scenes "of distinguished beauty" which isolate themselves in the
mind, not as components of a whole, but as fragments. [...]

HOMAGE TO
PROPERTIUS

N. C. Smith

[...] Opinions will differ as to the relative verisimilitude of the
various ghosts whom Mr Pound has from time to time summoned
to drink the dark blood from the pit of his insatiable curiosity: and
there is probably no one whose range of studies coincides with that
of Mr Pound sufficiently for a sound comparison. What is obvious
enough is that they are all, as he calls them, "*personae* of Ezra
Pound" rather than the *Dramatis Personae* which his first readers
may have expected from the evident and acknowledged influence
of Browning on the young poet. Browning could not keep himself
altogether out of his impersonations; Mr Pound, while neglecting
no means that learning and artistry afforded of steeping himself in
his subjects, has always seemed primarily self-conscious and
desirous of communicating his own personality – a personality

Homage to Sextus Propertius. A Draft of Cantos XXXI – XLI, by Ezra Pound
[October 17, 1935]

before the War of a fairly cheerful *fin de siècle* hedonist, but since the War increasingly bitter and cynical.

The "Propertius" is much less bitter than the "Mauberley" or the "Cantos," partly, no doubt, because of the keen aesthetic and intellectual pleasure inseparable from reading Propertius, even when your object is not so much to understand him as to make him a vehicle for your own moods.

THE FIFTH DECAD OF
CANTOS*

Hugh I'Anson Fausset

[. . .] Mr Pound has in recent years become more and more esoteric. Needless to say there are fragments of vivid colour and fiery satire, *disiecta membra poetae*, imbedded in the compost of scrap learning, scrap lingoes, elaborate incoherences and other miscellanea of Mr Pound's mature style. And one can sympathize with the denunciation of usury, which is the principal theme. But how much more effective are the Minor Prophets!

THE POEMS
OF EZRA POUND†

Peter Russell

[. . .] All too often Mr Pound's reputation rests on the shorter poems made familiar to the public by the *Selected Poems*, with an introduction by Mr T. S. Eliot (1928), and its many reprints. Those who have based a considered estimate of Mr Pound's work on his most important achievement, namely "The Cantos," are very few indeed. To judge his status by his shorter poems is as silly as to judge Spenser without consideration of *The Faerie Queene*. [. . .]

The Fifth Decad of Cantos, by Ezra Pound [July 17, 1937]
†*Selected Poems*, by Ezra Pound [January 13, 1950]

The form of his epic poem, if we may term it such, is that of an immensely long monologue. But, unlike Browning's dramatic monologues and indeed his own earlier poems, "The Cantos" is not so much a monologue about the speaker, as a monologue in which the speaker is now rhapsodizing, now reminiscing, now haranguing an imaginary audience, on the whole field of history and criticism. At first sight the poem seems a series of unconnected pieces of poetry, some obviously of great power and beauty, others colloquially dogmatic or pedantic, and the reader might form the idea that each section would be better as a separate poem. However, on better acquaintance it becomes quite clear that the coherence of the many styles and the single-mindedness of its author before such diverse subject-matter bind it into a single whole. This could not ever be said of the *Selected Poems*, which, as the name implies, is a collection of separate pieces. In "The Cantos" theme after theme reappears, reinforcing its previous significance and throwing new light on other themes. The whole poem reminds one of a tapestry where threads of blue or green or brown disappear behind the canvas and reappear some inches farther along, making the whole composition even in texture and colour, though scrappy when seen from close up. As in all long poems, there are dull patches. Some of the battle scenes in the later books of the *Aeneid* are dull enough, after all, and parts of *Paradise Lost*, if they keep the attention of the reader at all, keep it by their theological or psychological interest rather than by purely poetic vitality. Until Mr Pound's epic is finished – and eighteen cantos out of one hundred remain to be written – it will be too early to judge the whole poem with any certainty, but unless there is a radical alteration (and this is unlikely, considering the homogeneous nature of the eighty-two cantos already published) a fair idea of the structure and meaning of the whole can already be gained.

The Pisan Cantos themselves are the latest instalment of the poem, and were written while the author was detained in a prison camp at Pisa during the spring and summer of 1945. These cantos are more directly personal (though never in any sense introspective) than any of Mr Pound's other work. They move away from the scene of the imprisoned propagandist only for short periods, whereas earlier cantos changed scene very rapidly if they had a scene at all. Those who have always distrusted his frequent quotation from learned sources as an exhibitionist show of spurious learning will be disappointed to find that Mr Pound, in spite of his serious mental breakdown and the deprivation of all books save a volume of Confucius in Chinese, is able to quote and misquote just as easily as ever from Greek, Latin, Provençal, Italian, Spanish, Chinese and even Persian. Whether this need alter in any way the reader's attitude to his method is another matter. It can only be said that Mr Pound does indeed have "an acquaintance with things that are profoundly moving." Not only has he this acquaintance, he also communicates it with passion, now dramatic and forceful, now reminiscent and nostalgic, now with humour. This section of the poem is a mine of anecdotes of distinguished literary figures of our time, as well as a moving record of the affliction of one who, whether he were guilty or innocent of the crime of treason, evidently believed with unswerving faith that he had worked for thirty years by his pen to preserve peace and promote prosperity. *The Pisan Cantos* were awarded the Bollingen Prize of $1,000 for the best poetry of the year published in the United States.

THE POET AS
TRANSLATOR

G. S. Fraser

There are several current views, favourable and unfavourable, about Mr Ezra Pound's gifts as a translator. The most favourable view (but one which depends for its favourableness on an excessive disparagement of Mr Pound's gifts as an original poet) is that expressed with his usual force and pungency by Mr Percy Wyndham Lewis in *Time and Western Man*:

> ... [Mr Pound] is a crowd: a little crowd. People are seen by him only as types. There is the "museum official," the "norman cocotte," and so on. *By himself* he would seem to have neither convictions nor eyes in his head ... Yet when he can get into the skin of somebody else, of power and

The Translations of Ezra Pound [September 18, 1953]

renown, a Propertius or an Arnaut Daniel, he becomes a
lion or a lynx on the spot . . .

The verdict there on Mr Pound's original poetry is, it will seem to
many readers, a harsh one. Admirers of *Hugh Selwyn Mauberley*, that
splendid documentary poem, which seems to sum up a whole
literary period, and of the moving passages of personal reminiscence in *The Pisan Cantos*, would probably violently disagree with
Mr Wyndham Lewis's statements that "there is nothing that [Mr
Pound] intuits well, certainly never originally" and that "when he
writes in person . . . his phrases are invariably stagey and false, as
well as insignificant." On the other hand, Mr Pound's achievements as a translator have sometimes offered easy targets for
academic critics, who would perhaps like to attack his original
poetry, but hesitate to do so. The gist of such attacks is that (apart,
perhaps, from his versions from Provençal, French, and Italian) Mr
Pound often shows signs of not knowing properly the languages
he is translating from. Even where he must be presumed to know
the sense of his originals, such critics declare, Mr Pound often, for
his own rhetorical purposes in English, distorts it in a wilful and
unnecessary way.

   The work by Mr Pound which has laid itself most open to this
kind of attack, *Homage to Sextus Propertius*, is not included in the
volume of collected translations under consideration here. At the
same time, though it is strictly not a translation of Propertius so
much as what a Restoration poet would have called an "Allusion to
Propertius" or "Imitation of Propertius," it perhaps provides the
best starting-point for a general consideration of Mr Pound's
achievements as a verse translator. The academic critics of this
poem are right, of course, in discovering howlers in it. They could
discover comparable howlers in Marlowe's very beautiful versions
of Ovid, and it may be admitted that Mr Pound's knowledge of
Latin is nearer to that of an eager undergraduate (an undergraduate
impatient with grammar and in love with the *idea* of poetry) than to
that of a university lecturer. At the same time, the academic critics
of *Homage to Sextus Propertius* have largely missed Mr Pound's
point. We can see what he is doing in this poem most clearly if we
look at passages where there are no howlers, but where, for the
sake of bringing out a latent irony in Propertius, Mr Pound
deliberately distorts his strict sense. Thus the elegiac couplet,

>   a valeat, Phoebum quicumque moratur in armis!
>   exactus tenui pumice versus eat,

which is literally, in Butler's version, "Away with the man who keeps Phoebus tarrying among the weapons of war! Let verse run smoothly, polished with fine pumice," becomes in Mr Pound's variation:

>   Out-weariers of Apollo will, as we know, continue their
>   Martian generalities.
>   We have kept our erasers in order.

Mr Pound obviously here does understand the literal sense of the Latin. But for his own purposes, he is "pointing up" that sense. He is not using Propertius as a *mere* stalking-horse. He is, in the lines just quoted, striving by a slight distortion of the literal sense of his original to bring over much more vividly than Butler does its tone and feeling. He brings in "Martian" to remind us that after all it is a Latin poet he is starting from. On the other hand, he brings in the modern word "generalities" and the word "erasers" (which probably suggests typewriter erasers to us more immediately than fine pumice) to remind us that the reason why he is imitating, or alluding to, Propertius, is that Propertius has contemporary relevance. We are to reflect not only that Propertius did not want to write war-poetry but that Mr Pound did not fancy himself as a poet of the school of Newbolt and Kipling. The distortion for the sake of Mr Pound's own emphasis becomes even more obvious when, later on in this passage from *Homage to Sextus Propertius*, the lines

>   multi, Roma, tuas laudes annalibus addent,
>   qui finem imperii Bactra futura canent;
>   sed, quod pace legas, opus hoc de monte Sororum
>   detulit intacta pagina nostra via,

which, again in Butler's version, are literally, "Many, O Rome, shall add fresh glories to thine annals, singing that Bactra shall be thine Empire's bound; but this work of mine my pages have brought down from the Muses' mount by an untrodden way, that thou mayest read it in the midst of peace," become, effectively but certainly very surprisingly:

Annalists will continue to record Roman reputations,
Celebrities from the Trans-Caucasus will belaud Roman
                                                celebrities
And expound the distentions of Empire,
But for something to read in normal circumstances?
For a few pages brought down from the forked hill
                                                unsullied?

   This is the sort of passage that gets the academic critics all agog,
wondering, for instance, whether it is just possible that Mr Pound
thinks "annalibus" means "by annalists." It is obviously, however,
not a version but a gloss. The "celebrities from the Trans-
Caucasus" who "will belaud Roman celebrities" are a bright
notion of Mr Pound's own, suggested, perhaps, by the single word
"Bactra." To "expound the distentions of Empire" is a deliberate
"pointing up" again to the verge of caricature of the very faint note
of mockery that is perhaps latent in "qui finem imperii Bactra
futura canent," just as "But for something to read in normal
circumstances?" is a very brilliant expansion indeed of the three
words, "quod pace legas." A critic judging *Homage to Sextus
Propertius* merely as a version (or even, possibly, merely as a rather
expansive paraphrase) might justly complain that Mr Pound here
seems much more certainly to be projecting a mood of his own into
Propertius than drawing out a mood that is really implicit in the
Latin poet. Propertius seems to be saying modestly, if we take him
literally, that war poetry and patriotic poetry are not his sort of
thing: no doubt it is partly a mock-modesty, and he does make it
clear earlier and later that he thinks his own sort of thing very
original and interesting. But the violent satirical contempt with
which the idea of Imperialism is treated in *Homage to Sextus
Propertius* does seem to be almost entirely Mr Pound's own
contribution. If when Mr Pound wrote of "out-weariers of
Apollo" and their "Martian generalities" he had perhaps Kipling
and Newbolt in mind, when he wrote of "celebrities from the
Trans-Caucasus" he may have had in mind derivative and old-
fashioned patriotic poetry from, say, Australia or New Zealand (or
even from Ceylon or Nigeria). Propertius at such moments does
become largely a pretext for an indirect expression of what Mr
Pound feels about the literary, social, and political situation of
England. If we bear this in mind, we shall begin to wonder whether

Mr Pound is, indeed, as Mr Wyndham Lewis asserts, a poet with "no convictions," or whether his translations are indeed essentially the work of "a man in love with the past." It may be rather that he is a man who finds it easiest to express both his contemporary "convictions," and his deepest personal feelings, indirectly – through assuming a mask.

Homage to Sextus Propertius is, as has been said, a very special case, but nevertheless the case that gives us most clues to Mr Pound's general attitude as a translator. He is deliberately playing up a certain aspect of Propertius – the latent humour and irony – and playing down another, the conventional rhetoric which is to be found in all Latin elegiac poetry; and which is to be found, for instance, in the elegies of James Hammond, of which Dr Johnson thought so little:

> Panchaia's odours be their costly feast,
> And all the pride of Asia's fragrant year;
> Give them the treasures of the farthest East,
> And, what is still more precious, give thy tear.

Dr Johnson was no doubt right when he observed of such lines that "he that courts his mistress with Roman imagery deserves to lose her: for she may with good reason suspect his sincerity." Nevertheless, a stanza like this of Hammond's does give a reader who has no Latin a fairly clear notion of what the average texture and feeling of Roman elegiac poetry is like: *Homage to Sextus Propertius*, for all its greater brilliance, fails to give the reader with no Latin this notion. It is likely to leave him thinking of Propertius as primarily a poet of abrupt transitions, harsh colloquialisms, and witty parodies of the "grand manner," a poet who might have written for the Roman equivalent of *Blast*, a poet closely resembling the young Mr Eliot or the young Mr Pound himself. It makes Propertius the type, like the young Mr Pound, of the eager and irreverent innovator. And it is notable that Mr Pound has been drawn as a translator very largely to poets like Guido Cavalcanti or Arnaut Daniel or Charles d'Orléans, who strike him as representing the "first spritely runnings," the springtime, of a tradition; a reader who knows his tastes will not expect him to attempt to render a Virgil or a Petrarch or a Racine. The maturity of a culture bores him. Both his strength and his weakness as a poet lie in the fact that all through his life (and he is now a man in his sixties) he has retained the temperament of his "first hard springtime," the freshness and the ruthlessness of an eager undergraduate or even an eager schoolboy – of the young man from the Middle West, who seeing the riches of the European past spread out before him, has been tempted almost to exclaim like Blücher looking down on London: "What a place to plunder!" Perhaps the importance of Mr Pound's translations, then, lies less in their accuracy, or even in the faithfulness with which, sacrificing mere literalness, they convey a mood or a cadence, than in the fact that translating is for Mr Pound a way of writing his *own* poems.

Their reliability, merely as versions, obviously varies. When Mr Pound wrote *Cathay* in 1915 and worked up Fenollosa's notes on, and versions of, the Noh play in 1916 he did not, in a sense that any scholar would recognize, "know" either Chinese or Japanese. Fenollosa was primarily a scholar of Japanese, and the names both of poets and places in his notes were given in their Japanese form. Thus even a reader who has a mere smattering of knowledge about Chinese and Japanese should recognize that Rihaku is a Japanese name and that the place-name in the beautiful line,

Ko-Jin goes west from Ko-kaku-ro,

must be Japanese, because Chinese words and names are monosyllables or combinations of monosyllables, and because there is no *r* in Chinese phonetics, just as there is no *l* in Japanese. This is not a matter of real importance. A young American scholar, Mr Roy Teele, who has written an extremely thorough monograph on the translation of Chinese poetry into English from the eighteenth century onwards, thinks that *Cathay* is both more literally accurate, and nearer to the mood and spirit of Chinese poetry, than many versions by writers with an infinitely more impressive scholarly equipment, like Giles. Mr Pound, working from Fenollosa's notes, was very much in the position of a Japanese scholar who does not really "know" either French or English, but who is working from the rough notes of another Japanese scholar who knew French well, and had made a rough prose Japanese version of Shakespeare's sonnets from a French translation of these. It is almost incredible in the circumstances that *Cathay* should not be wildly inaccurate, but apparently it is not so, and it has not been replaced as a window for English-speaking readers into the classical Chinese world even by the scholarly and genuinely poetical versions of Mr

Waley. And in *Cathay*, as in *Sextus Propertius*, we may feel that Mr Pound is at his very best when the theme of his original brings some of his own deeper feelings into play:

> What is the use of talking, and there is no end of talking.
> There is no end of things in the heart.
> I call in the boy,
> Have him sit on his knees here
> To seal this,
> And send it a thousand miles, thinking.

The sense of exile, the memory of the meeting and parting of friends, the remembering of friends at a distance are also some of the most insistent themes, and the most movingly handled, in the *Pisan Cantos*. What a poet of Mr Pound's power and originality perhaps ultimately does find in the poetry of other times and languages is his own preoccupations, his own vision, himself.

It is doubtful, therefore, if from Mr Ezra Pound's very special case any general deductions can be made about the role of the poet as translator. The best of his translations have entered into our tradition in their own right. When we read these lines, with their breath-taking magnificence, from his version of the Anglo-Saxon *Seafarer*,

> Days little durable,
> And all arrogance of earthen riches,
> There come now no kings nor Caesars
> Nor gold-giving lords like those gone.
> Howe'er in mirth most magnified,
> Whoe'er lived in life most lordliest.
> Drear all this excellence, delights undurable!
> Waneth the watch, but the world holdeth.
> Tomb hideth trouble. The blade is layed low,

we feel that we should be merely pedantic if we pointed out either that, if Mr Pound wants us to pronounce "Caesars" as "Kaisers" he should spell the word in that fashion, and not rely on our having learned the modern pronunciation of Latin at school; or that though the splendid line,

> Waneth the watch, but the world holdeth,

wonderfully represents the sound of its original, it completely misrepresents the sense, which is, "The weak live on, and hold the earth." Mr Pound's *Seafarer* is a more actual influence on modern poetry than (unfortunately, or otherwise) its original is ever likely to be. We read, as Mr Eliot once pointed out in this connexion, the great Tudor translators more as part of the English literature of their own age than as a guide to the books they translated. The seeming transparency of some great translations can never be more than a contemporary illusion. It is as a durable addition to, and influence upon, original poetry in the English language in this century that Mr Pound's translations will be finally valued. They are poems, not cribs.

HIS NAME
IN THE RECORD

Christine Brooke-Rose

Mr Ezra Pound is still often regarded as a crank, a great poet with a bee in his bonnet about usury, who has ruined his poetry with Chinese ideograms and recondite references which one may skip for the sake of the "good" bits, because, of course, he can "rise" to occasional passages of magnificent poetry.

. This view simply will not do. It might be worth recalling that Mr Pound has said, in another context (at the end of the *Money Pamphlets by £*),

> I hope the reader has *not* "understood it all straight off". I should like to invent some kind of typographical dodge which would force every reader to stop and reflect for five minutes (or five hours), to go back to the facts mentioned and think over their significance for himself.

Facts – "a sufficient phalanx of particulars" – are Mr Pound's material, and the juxtaposing or ideogrammatic method of presenting them is the "typographical dodge" he has invented to make us stop and reflect. Even in his prose he does not argue in an

Pavannes and Divagations. Thrones: 96–109 de los cantares, by Ezra Pound [June 10 1960]

Aristotelian manner but ideogrammatically. If it makes most people slide over the very facts he wishes them to stop and reflect on, that is his risk, and their loss. For the Cantos, read properly, can give a sheer poetic enchantment not to be found elsewhere, even to those who do not accept the didactic value that Mr Pound places on his facts. [...]

Many have argued that Mr Pound shows colossal arrogance in expecting his readers to be familiar not only with everything he has ever written (e.g., among the various oddments collected as *Pavannes and Divagations* there is the interview with Ford Madox Ford in which he said the above) but also with every book he has ever read. Yet the objection collapses if one thinks of the number of these and articles on the books which anyone great enough, from Chaucer to Mr Eliot, must have read, or on what Chaucer or Shakespeare do with their sources; and of the long, painstaking footnotes on Villon's personal friends. His friends are dead, but Villon is read.

There is a timeless, apocalyptic quality in Mr Pound's poetry which one suspects even his adverse critics find disturbing, but which most poets respond to, even if they do not understand. Who knows, his may be the only comprehensible poetry to the twenty-first century, under a new economic order, undreamt of now. We may, for that matter, all be speaking Chinese in western Europe then, and thinking ideogrammatically, with nothing left of older civilization but the fragments he has shored against our ruin. It might just possibly be he who will "have his name in the record... Thrones, courage."

SONS AND LOVERS

W. J. Lancaster

In one aspect Mr D. H. Lawrence's close and intimate history of a struggling family in the colliery districts of the Midlands, SONS AND LOVERS (Duckworth, 6s.), may be summarized as a long crescendo of realism. We finish Part I with a strong feeling of admiration for the success of Mr Lawrence's resolute reliance upon cumulative

Sons and Lovers, by D. H. Lawrence [June 12, 1913]

detail. He knows his countryside and the conditions of hard-worked life in it, inside and out, and when he plunges without preamble into the early married life of the Morels, pity, interest, anticipation are rapidly kindled. [...] The rest of the book is a complex study of warring loves and passions, containing much beauty, but often overwrought. Paul's relations with Miriam Leivers, of Willey Farm, and, afterwards, with Clara Dawes constitute an enigma which 250 pages do not suffice to solve. All that we fully understand of the cause of his agonized struggle against his love for the gentle, devoted Miriam is that she seems to him, as to his mother, a spiritual vampire who would leave his soul no rest; but if we read her aright that is a most hapless obsession. His attraction to Clara, her foil and antidote, is passionate only, and in describing it Mr Lawrence might well have spared us the constant reiteration of a kind of detail lacking in at least the finer reticence. But the sincerity of the book is unquestionable. The sheer hard matter of living is vividly presented; the toil of existence in village and town, the solace of Nature, the joy of occasional respite from labour admirably realized and rendered.

POSTSCRIPT OR PRELUDE

Virginia Woolf

Perhaps the verdicts of critics would read less preposterously and their opinions would carry greater weight if, in the first place, they bound themselves to declare the standard which they had in mind, and, in the second, confessed the course, bound, in the case of a book read for the first time, to be erratic, by which they reached their final decision. Our standard for Mr Lawrence, then, is a high one. Taking into account the fact, which is so constantly forgotten, that never in the course of the world will there be a second Meredith or a second Hardy, for the sufficient reason that there have already been a Meredith and a Hardy, why, we sometimes asked, should there not be a D. H. Lawrence? By that we meant that

The Lost Girl, by D. H. Lawrence [December 2, 1920]

we might have to allow him the praise, than which there is none higher, of being himself an original; for such of his work as came our way was disquieting, as the original work of a contemporary writer always is.

This was the standard which we had in mind when we opened "The Lost Girl." We now go on to trace the strayings and stumblings of that mind as it came to the conclusion that "The Lost Girl" is not an original, or a book which touches the high standard which we have named. Together with our belief in Mr Lawrence's originality went, of course, some sort of forecast as to the direction which that originality was likely to take. We conceived him to be a writer, with an extraordinary sense of the physical world, of the colour and texture and shape of things, for whom the body was alive and the problems of the body insistent and important. It was plain that sex had for him a meaning which it was disquieting to think that we, too, might have to explore. Sex, indeed, was the first red-herring that crossed our path in the new volume. The story is the story of Alvina Houghton, the daughter of a draper in Woodhouse, a mining town in the Midlands. It is all built up of solid fabric. If you want a truthful description of a draper's shop, evident knowledge of his stock, and a faithful and keen yet not satiric or sentimental description of James Houghton, Mrs Houghton, Miss Frost, and Miss Pinnegar, here you have it. Nor does this summary do any kind of justice to the variety of the cast and the number of events in which they play their parts. But, distracted by our preconception of what Mr Lawrence was to give us, we turned many pages of very able writing in search for something else which must be there. Alvina seemed the most likely instrument to transmit Mr Lawrence's electric shock through the calicos, prints, and miners' shirts by which she stood surrounded. We watched for signs of her development nervously, for we always dread originality, yet with the sense that once the shock was received we should rise braced and purified. The signs we looked for were not lacking. For example, "Married or unmarried, it was the same – the same anguish, realized in all its pain after the age of fifty – the loss in never having been able to relax, to submit." Again, "She was returning to Woodhouse virgin as she had left it. In a measure she felt herself beaten. Why? Who knows . . . Fate had been too strong for her and her desires. Fate which was not an external association of forces, but which was integral in her own nature." Such phrases taken in conjunction with the fact that Alvina, having refused her first suitor, wilted and pined, and becoming a midwife mysteriously revived in the atmosphere of the Islington-road, confirmed us in our belief that sex was the magnet to which the myriad of separate details would adhere. We were wrong. Details accumulated; the picture of life in Woodhouse was built up; and sex disappeared. This detail, then this realism, must have another meaning than we had given them. Relieved, yet a trifle disappointed, for we want originality as much as we dread it, we adopted a fresh attitude, and read Mr Lawrence as one reads Mr Bennett – for the facts, and for the story. Mr Lawrence shows indeed something of Mr Bennett's power of displaying by means of immense industry and great ability a section of the hive beneath glass. Like all the other insects, Alvina runs in and out of other people's lives, and it is the pattern of the whole that interests us rather than the fate of one of the individuals. And then, as we have long ceased to find in reading Mr Bennett, suddenly the method seems to justify itself by a single phrase which we may liken to a glow or to a transparency, since to quote one apart from the context would give no idea of our meaning. In other words, Mr Lawrence occasionally and momentarily achieves that concentration which Tolstoy preserves sometimes for a chapter or more. And then again the laborious process continues of building up a model of life from saying how d'you do, and cutting the loaf, and knocking the cigarette ash into the ash tray, and standing the yellow bicycle against the wall. Little by little Alvina disappears beneath the heap of facts recorded about her, and the only sense in which we feel her to be lost is that we can no longer believe in her existence.

So, though the novel is probably better than any that will appear for the next six months, we are disappointed, and would write Mr Lawrence off as one of the people who have determined to produce seaworthy books were it not for those momentary phrases and for a strong suspicion that the proper way to look at "The Lost Girl" is as a stepping stone in a writer's progress. It is either a postscript or a prelude.

WOMEN IN LOVE

Edmund Blunden

[...] But let us yield to Mr Lawrence's reading of love, and forget
how we loathe it; and after we have mastered its implications let us
leave out the further passages of expansion. Mr Lawrence has a
right to his opinions, but he has no right to produce a tedious book
– and stripped of all the dogma of ether-erotics, life-motion, and so
on, "Women in Love" is a dull, disappointing piece of work. It
ambles, it meanders extravagantly through sets and scenes of the
most flaccid type. Blind-alleys envelop some of the characters, and
those to whom we feel most attracted. The book is a succession of
chapters, certainly, but scarcely a story; it is true that we begin with
Ursula and Gudrun Brangwen and have them with us at the end,
and yet there are unwieldy interruptions to the narrative of their
relationships in love. And even those are told with painful
elaboration. [...]

The satirically treated figure of Hermione stands out as,
probably, the one thing in the whole work which was worth Mr
Lawrence's powers and time or the reader's. She has the same effect
on us as she has on the people whose meetings with her are
described; there is something of immense dignity in her which,
though her foibles bring her to the very verge of ridicule, carries
her past triumphantly. She, in the midst of all her artificiality, in all
her masks and postures, is sincere. Most of the other characters, for
all their hot passion and desperate fleshiness, are little better than
"shadows of life and artificial flowers." They doubtless have some
counterpart in existence; but their impossibility on paper is Mr
Lawrence's failure, for whatever a novelist's purpose his work
must compel us to an eager interest in its world.

Women in Love, by D. H. Lawrence [June 9, 1921]

AARON'S ROD*

Harold Child

[. . .] Mr Lawrence, giving us a thorough shaking-up, forces us to preach back at the preacher. But the new novel, AARON'S ROD (Secker, 7s. 6d. net), is not all a sermon at a Black Mass. It is the story, picaresque in form, of a man – a miner by occupation, a musician in soul – who wandered away from all ties except that of his friendship for another man, in search of himself. Perhaps in form it is a little too picaresque. It has no end. Judged by the old rules, the idea-plot is too strong for the action-plot; and, looking back, we see episodes of wonderful beauty or ugliness like the curves of a river that runs into the sand. We must have more evidence before we can believe that it is not the sand but the sea. Aaron Sisson goes to Italy. We are glad of that, because it enables Mr Lawrence to give a description of Florence that is one of the finest of his many fine things; although perhaps Italy was not necessary to the tale of Aaron's peregrination among a dozen strange, angry, talkative men and one or two of those strange, lustful, dominating women by whom Mr Lawrence and Strindberg are obsessed and frightened. There is very great power in this angry genius. He can disturb one more in a chapter, than Mr Bernard Shaw in a whole play. Yet the final result is to leave one feeling rather old and wise. He sees and feels intensely; he will have no comfortable illusions. But he knows so little! And he will never begin to learn until he learns first not to be afraid.

ST MAWR†

A. S. McDowall

Mr D. H. Lawrence, with his gospel of the dark power within us, the apartness of the real self and the demoralization of our civilized

Aaron's Rod, by D. H. Lawrence [June 22, 1922]
†*St Mawr*, by D. H. Lawrence [May 28, 1925]

selves, often seems like an oddly transmuted Rousseau. We may grow impatient of these ideas; why should such rare creative power be led away into abstractions? Yet we can scarcely wish them away, for they are part of his feeling and his inner fire; we only wish him to express them through characters and symbols rather than arguments. In his shorter stories, like "The Ladybird," it is less easy to digress, and for that reason they are perhaps the most artistic of his fictions. But St Mawr (Secker, 7s. 6d. net) is significant in a more vital way. For the title-story, itself a little novel filling three-quarters of the book, is not only rich with irony and poetry, but it succeeds, perhaps more completely than Mr Lawrence has yet done, in expressing those ultimate perceptions of his through a group of living symbols. He has not shunned extremes to find them. St Mawr, decidedly a character, is a horse: a magnificent bay stallion who seems to belong to the heroic age, with a dark fire in his eyes and a remote power that make Lou, the heroine, cry after she first sees him. The two grooms come next in primitiveness; "Phoenix" the half-breed, something of a lost savage, and Lewis, an intensely enigmatic, self-contained little Welshman with whom Mr Lawrence shows a tacit sympathy. The probings of consciousness are for their American employers; and there is an amusement in the icily disillusioned Mrs Witt, and an attraction in her daughter Lou, also disillusioned, though more wistfully, with the present race of men, including her charming and rather futile young husband.

Sex, throughout the story, "in prison lies," and there is only a fleeting shadow of a passion. Mr Lawrence has drawn isolated and frustrated souls, and defined them against an ideal, or mirage, of natural perfection. But on the underlying blankness or despair he weaves subtle characterizings, by turns humorous and moving; and the greater part of the story is vivid with these contrasts and with the satirical entertainment which England yields to Mrs Witt. When the scene shifts finally to New Mexico there is a prevailing mystery and beauty. All that wild splendour has sunk into Mr Lawrence. Whether he is painting the wonder of the vast landscape, or the squalor bristling in the mountain glory, or the mingled enmity and beauty, it calls up his astonishing magic of phrase. [...]

This ruthlessly wild nature is the final symbol. Whatever we may think of the conceptions in the story, whether they lead to anything or refute each other, we have to admit that they are perfectly conveyed. We can read it like a parable, though its characters and actions move with the wayward spontaneousness of life. [...]

D. H. LAWRENCE

John Middleton Murry

I should like to put down in haste a few of the most enduring personal impressions which a close friendship with D. H. Lawrence, lasting (alas! with catastrophic interruptions) over sixteen or seventeen years, has left upon me. I regret that I must put them down in haste; but I desire (if I can) to correct the impression, which is widespread, that D. H. Lawrence was a madman of genius, savagely bent on violating sanctuaries, and bruising the finer conscience of his fellow-men.

To defend Lawrence's passionate convictions is no part of my hasty undertaking. These do not need to be defended, only to be understood, and understood in the light of an experience extraordinary in its depth and comprehensiveness. And again I am not invoking the beauty of his personality to excuse his work. It is right that I should make it clear that I do not consider his work needs any excuse. If it was wrong, it was passionately wrong; and to be passionately wrong is far better than to be coldly right. What I have to say concerning Lawrence the man could easily be corroborated from his work, if it is read by sympathetic and discerning eyes. But who knows how long sympathy and discernment may be in coming?

Lawrence was the most remarkable and most lovable man I have ever known. Contact with him was immediate, intimate and rich. A radiance of warm life streamed from him. When he was gay, and he was often gay – my dominant memory of him is of a blithe and joyful man – he seemed to spread a sensuous enchantment about him. By a natural magic he unsealed the eyes of those in his company: birds, beasts and flowers became new-minted as in Paradise; they stood revealed as what they were, and not the poor objects of our dull and common seeing. The most ordinary

[Article] [March 13, 1930]

domestic act – the roasting of a joint of meat, the washing-up of crockery, the painting of a cottage room – in his doing became a gay sacrament. He surrendered himself completely to whatever he had in hand; he was utterly engrossed by it. And the things he took in hand were innumerable. In bare record they may seem fantastic, as when for weeks together he decorated little wooden boxes, or, years later when, during his last Christmas in England, he fashioned a marvellous little Adam and Eve beneath the tree in Eden, made of modelling clay and painted; but those who shared in these makings will remember them for some of the most simple, happy hours in their lives.

As his happiness was radiant, so his gloom was a massive darkness in which his intimates were engulfed. I see him sitting crouched and collapsed on a wooden chair when the long horror of the War had begun to gnaw his vitals – forlorn, silent, dead. One could not speak against the numbness of that sheer desolation. But sometimes, in those bitter days – out of which sprang his lifelong passion of rebellion against the European consciousness, and his unresting search for a land and a way of life to which he could surrender himself – sometimes, in those days, he would rise to the surface with a flickering smile and begin to sing:–

> Sometimes, I feel like an eagle in the sky ...
> Sometimes, I feel like a moaning dove ...

With the first line he soared; with the second he sank, down, down, down.

He was completely generous. At a moment when there were not ten pounds between him and destitution he thrust five of them upon a friend and, because the friend refused them, flew into a transport of high-pitched rage. Friendship was to him a blood-brotherhood, an absolute and inviolable loyalty, but not to a person, but to the impersonal godhead beneath. I do not believe that he ever found the friendship after which he hungered; and perhaps this was the tragedy of his life. The men he knew were incapable of giving that which he demanded. It was not their fault, though in his heart of hearts he believed it was.

He had an infinite capacity for making warm human contacts. In whatever part of the world he found himself in his quest for newness of life, he left his mark and memory among the common people. Whatever may be our intellectual judgment of the theories he built upon his immediate experience, no one who knew him well has any doubt whatever that he had a mysterious gift of "sensing" the hidden and unconscious reality of his fellow human beings. He did not sentimentalize about them, but he did *know* them, in ways more direct and ultimate than any of which ordinary men have experience. What is vague and dimly apprehended instinct with most of us was in him an exquisitely ramified sensibility, responsive to realities which elude our blunter organizations and for which our common language has no appropriate expression. Hence the seeming violence which Lawrence, a native master of the delicate and creative word, did to the conventions of style and morality. His sacrifice of "art" was quite conscious, and quite deliberate; he was not concerned with it any more. "Fiction," he said in a letter, "is about *persons*; and I am not interested in persons."

Perhaps he never clearly understood how extraordinary were these gifts of his for making contact with the life that is prior to personality. No doubt for a man of genius such as his to admit that he is in some sense radically unlike his fellows – a queer creature, an animal of a different species – is almost impossible. Such absolute isolation is not to be endured. Because Lawrence found his friends and mankind at large lacking in faculties which were native to him, he inclined to believe that they had deliberately buried in the earth a talent which was never theirs. So he was often, in his later years, induced to think men perverse and wicked when they were merely dull; and he grew exasperated with them.

APROPOS OF LADY CHATTERLEY'S LOVER

Philip Tomlinson

"Lady Chatterley's Lover" was the last novel by D. H. Lawrence. It is not known to the public at large. A certain number of copies were printed by the author, and there are some others, for pirates were prompt to take advantage of its unprotected state. It has been described as a gross book, full of obscene words, for in it Lawrence

From *My Skirmish with Jolly Roger*, by D. H. Lawrence [July 3, 1930]

rejects all circumlocution, no matter what the subject. Here is what Swift called "the plain Billingsgate of calling names." The argument for and against such licence is interminable. Logically the law-breakers may have the better of it, but something ultimate and beyond the risk of reason forbids. But this matter is touched upon only lightly in this essay, which Lawrence describes as "a postscript or afterthought" to the novel. Yet it would appear that he did set out with the intention of defending what most people regard as offensive. "The words that shock so much at first," he writes, "don't shock at all after a while. Is this because the mind is depraved by habit? Not a bit. It is that the words merely shocked the eye, they never shocked the mind at all." It would be interesting to follow this farther, but it was not Lawrence's way to argue a matter out. His mind buzzed with ideas, not thoughts. He threw them out in picturesque profusion. Soon we are being asked to consider a more fundamental question: whether fidelity in marriage is better than promiscuity. Now we find Lawrence emphatically on the side of the Church, in its inhibitory decrees against faithlessness, if not in its initial sanction. And for a moment, until he drops his argument in another side-track, or spoils it by a false illustration (as when he appeals to a recent notorious law case, which he entirely misrepresents), this is Lawrence at his most persuasive and at the height of his power in rhetoric.

He is moving in his protest against the modern loud and sentimental counterfeit of the emotions of love in their higher manifestations, "from genuine desire to tender love, love of our fellowmen, and love of God." He finds in fidelity the deepest instinct in the complex called sex: "All the literature of the world shows how profound is the instinct of fidelity in both man and woman, how men and women both hanker restlessly after the satisfaction of this instinct, and fret at their own inability to find the real mode of fidelity." Marriage, he pleads, is a permanent sacrament. Where he will find disagreement, although, granting his premise he is right, is in his argument that marriage is no marriage that is not basically and permanently sexual. To prove his point he appeals to physiology. He feels that Christianity's great contribution to the life of man was in making marriage a sacrament: "marriage sacred and inviolable, the great way of earthly fulfilment for man and woman; in unison, under the spiritual rule of the Church." No Churchman would disagree if Lawrence were content to leave the matter there. But he despoils the Churchman and the unorthodox, too; for he will not admit the marriage of true minds; the marriage must be a sexual alliance only. Just as if the old tragic struggle had not arisen out of the boredom and tyranny of such unions.

LADY CHATTERLEY'S LOVER

Orlo Williams

It would be idle to pretend that D. H. Lawrence's novel LADY CHATTERLEY'S LOVER (Secker, 7s. 6d. net) has not been emasculated by the omissions that have been made in what is called the "authorized abridged" edition. [...]

The asterisks which replace the scenes in question certainly purge these pages of much that might be injurious to immature minds, for which they were never intended; but they sadly weaken the contrast that throughout Lawrence was concerned to draw between the warm fruitfulness of a sexual union in which nothing of feeling or emotion is held back on either side and the cold, selfish unions between men and women that breed bitterness and death in the soul.

Nevertheless, even in this form, whether it strikes the reader as ugly or beautiful, it remains unmistakably the work of a genius. In a sense it is almost wholly painful, for it is inspired with so intense a rage against the unhuman, unloving, sordid and unheroic life of our day. Lawrence observed not only a chill in the relations between men and women, a numbness in their cores which superficial pleasures and money-making could not heal, but also the overlaying of an England robust and whole – aristocratic England – by an industrial growth that was purely mechanical, producing no happiness, nothing but money, pleasure-seeking and discontent. [...]

Lady Chatterley's Lover, by D. H. Lawrence [February 25, 1932]

LETTERS OF
D. H. LAWRENCE

A. S. McDowall

[. . .] His intuitiveness extended to persons as well as things, though it goes sometimes unrecognized in his novels because he did not devote himself to character. His own way did not necessarily involve the rejection of "art," even if it implied a recasting of fiction:–

> That which is physic – non-human, in humanity, is more interesting to me than the old-fashioned human element – which causes one to conceive a character in a certain moral scheme and make him consistent. The certain moral scheme is what I object to. In Turgenev, and in Tolstoi, and in Dostoievsky, the moral scheme into which all the characters fit – and it is nearly the same scheme – is, whatever the extraordinariness of the characters themselves, dull, old, dead. . . . I don't so much care about what the woman *feels* – in the ordinary usage of the word. That presumes an *ego* to feel with. I only care about what the woman *is* – what she IS – inhumanly, physiologically, materially – according to the use of the word; but for me, what she *is* as a phenomenon (or as representing some greater, inhuman will), instead of what she feels according to the human conception. . . . You mustn't look in my novel for the old stable *ego* of the character. There is another *ego*, according to whose action the individual is unrecognizable, and passes through, as it were, allotropic states which it needs a deeper sense than any we've been used to exercise, to discover are states of the same single radically unchanged element. (Like as diamond and coal are the same pure single element of carbon.)

It sounds an impracticable method. The study and play of character has been one of the surest foundations of the novel, at least of the

The Letters of D. H. Lawrence, ed. by Aldous Huxley [September 29, 1932]

English novel. And Lawrence had begun by writing successfully in the traditional pattern; "Sons and Lovers" is a great book, and there are many who will always hold it easily his finest. Yet part, at least, of the verdict has been inspired by conservatism as much as criticism. Though he could not keep control in his novels, he achieved a new point of view, using what was possible in his own prescription. He did not build up character – there are few figures in his work that one remembers as characters, in the usual sense – but by an undeniable divination he could render the essence of persons in a vision that was physical and yet went much farther than the senses. He saw, as Vernon Lee is said to have remarked, more than a human being ought to see. His people are fluid because they live in their flow of feelings – often Lawrence's feelings – and above all in their attitudes to one another. There his awareness of them creates in them an extraordinary awareness of each other; and though their conversations and behaviour are improbable the hidden current of their rapports, attractions and conflicts becomes a visible reality which is perhaps his chief contribution to the novel. [...]

But he was also his own nemesis. When we are told of his conviction that art should be fugitive, his dislike of perfection, they seem like a self-uttered sentence on his work. Our experience often repeats it as we read him. The "thought-adventure" of debate in his novels, at first so vivacious in its interest, looks arid to re-traverse; the drone of the dark gods and the pulse of the blood, once thrilling in his hypnotic prose, becomes at last a hardly tolerable boredom. The wastage and wilfulness were certainly immense. And what of the emphatic and yet dubious message? There seems to be almost every reason why Lawrence should not live; but it is equally impossible to think that such vitality should die. When so many prophets have erred, it will not matter much, perhaps, if he was wrong; and we are hardly yet at the point to judge how completely he was wrong in his search for a way of renovation. As an explorer, at any rate, of the malaise of our time he went farther than most. How little he was really seduced by a primitive mindlessness seems revealed when, in his letters, he declares his belief in "the living extending consciousness of man." The rest will burn away to the core, which was his own passionate experience. His relation of that and his rare perceptiveness of life must always have value.

PORTRAIT OF
D. H. LAWRENCE

Malcolm Muggeridge

[...] It is essentially as an embodiment of the spirit of the age that Lawrence emerges from Mr Aldington's biography. The *Zeitgeist* blew through him – a dry, desolate, fabulous wind, signifying:

> The end of democracy, the end of the ideal of liberty and freedom, the end of the brotherhood of man, the end of the idea of the perfectability of man, the end of the belief in the reign of love, the end of the belief that man desires peace, harmony, tranquillity, love and loving kindness all the while. The end of Christianity, the end of the Church of Jesus. The end of Science, as absolute knowledge. The end of the absolute power of the Word. The end, the end, the end.

Like Hitler, Lawrence gives an impression of proceeding somnambulistically – arms outstretched, vision confident but unseeing, footfall certain because unconscious. Many of his ideas, indeed, particularly in his last years, were decidedly Hitlerian; much in *Apocalypse* could have gone straight into *Mein Kampf*. According to Jessie Chambers, in every misunderstanding he "took refuge in an arrogance" which was nothing more than "a mask for his own wretchedness"; he would shriek and howl his antagonism, wanting to kill his enemies in millions, and how easy it is to imagine Rosenberg writing:

> My great religion is a belief in the blood, the flesh, as being wiser than the intellect. We can go wrong in our mind. But what our blood feels and believes and says is always true.

At the same time, underneath this fury of the will, this dreadful declamation of the ego wanting to occupy the universe's whole space, or, alternatively, failing that, to lose its identity and be obliterated, there was a wonderful sense of life and beauty which,

Portrait of a Genius, But ..., by Richard Aldington [March 31, 1950]

Mr Aldington writes, Lawrence "can transmit more than anyone else of his age." The lambs "stand and cock their heads at one, then skip into the air like little explosions"; the fir trees "are like presences in the darkness: each one only a presence. A sort of hush: the whole night wondering and asleep: I suppose that's what we do in death – sleep in wonder." [...]

DR LEAVIS ON
D. H. LAWRENCE

John Middleton Murry

Dr Leavis's study of D. H. Lawrence's novels opens with the words: "This book carries on from *The Great Tradition*." Readers of that book will regard the statement as something of a warning. For the treatment of the novelists dealt with in it was highly selective. Dickens barely scraped his second class, and that solely on the strength of *Hard Times*. And only portions of the three placed in the first class – George Eliot, James and Conrad – were awarded highest honours.

Lawrence is now admitted among them, and only Lawrence among their successors. But his entry is triumphal. Though Dr Leavis does not say so in so many words, from his tone it is evident that he regards him as the greatest of them all. Never has he been so prodigal of eulogy; never quite so pugnacious in downing the opposition, which consists, for Dr Leavis, not only of those who have been in any way publicly critical of Lawrence's work but even of the novelists who have had the misfortune to be contemporary with him.

Nevertheless, he applies to Lawrence the same selective method. One hundred pages of his book are devoted to *The Rainbow* and *Women in Love;* another fifty to *St Mawr* and *The Captain's Doll;* and since, excluding two appendices, there are only 300 in all, and many of these are spent on unnecessary polemic, the treatment of the rest of Lawrence's prose fiction is distinctly eclectic. Dr Leavis has his defence. "I want the stress to fall unambiguously on *The Rainbow*,

D. H. Lawrence, Novelist, by F. R. Leavis [October 28, 1955]

Women in Love, and the tales." These two novels, according to him, are of a much higher order than the others which Lawrence wrote; and they have had "essentially no recognition at all." But they are, in fact, the "supreme creative achievement" in "the great tradition" of the English novelists since Jane Austen, who are "the successors of Shakespeare."

It is a thankless task to criticize such enthusiasm; but in the interest of a just appreciation of one who, taken all in all, is the most significant English writer of the twentieth century, a caveat must be entered. Lawrence can be made to fit into "the great tradition" of the English novel, as Dr Leavis understands it, only by a great deal of manipulation. Take, for instance, *The Rainbow*. Concerning the earlier part of it, Dr Leavis has much that is wise and illuminating to say; he makes just and revealing comparisons to Lawrence's advantage with George Eliot. But when he comes to deal with the later and more baffling part of the book – the story of the relations between Ursula and Anton – he passes hurriedly over it.

> A more serious criticism, perhaps, bears on the signs of too great a tentativeness in the development and organization of the later part; signs of a growing sense in the writer of an absence of any conclusion in view. Things very striking in themselves haven't as clear a function as they ought to have. Above all, the sterile deadlock between Ursula and Skrebensky – a theme calling, we can see, for the developments it gets in *Women in Love*, but cannot have here – seems too long drawn out.

Considering the importance of this relation between Ursula and Anton, Dr Leavis's perfunctory treatment of it amounts to evasion. For the difficulty is not that the sterile deadlock is too long drawn out, but it is presented in terms which, even to the eager and sympathetic reader, are incomprehensible. It may be that what is arcane to them is lucid to Dr Leavis. But if ever exegesis was required, it is surely here. What is it that happens in the scene in the stackyard in Chapter XI, or on the seashore in Chapter XV? We have Lawrence's word for it that Ursula apparently unwittingly became for Anton "the darkness, the challenge, the horror"; that she "consumed and annihilated" him and that the annihilation was permanent; but the process by which it was accomplished, though described in detail and with vehemence by Lawrence, remains entirely mysterious. Yet this is the major psychological or spiritual happening in the second half of *The Rainbow*. Dr Leavis does not explain it at all.

Neither does he do so in his detailed exposition of *Women in Love*. In that novel, the theme of Ursula's destructive relation to Skrebensky is taken up again in the relation of Gudrun and Gerald; while Ursula finds a man whom she cannot annihilate and to whom she must surrender, in Rupert. Lawrence's descriptions of the crucial moments in both relations are as mysterious as they were when the book was first published. Again Dr Leavis passes them over: this time not quite in silence, for he quotes one of them and comments:

> I see here a fault of which I could find worse examples in *Women in Love*, though it is a fault that I do not now see as bulking so large in the book as I used to see it. It seems to me that in these places Lawrence betrays by an insistent and over-emphatic explicitness, running at times to something one can only call jargon, that he is uncertain – uncertain of the value of what he offers; uncertain whether he really holds it – whether a valid communication has really been defined and conveyed in terms of his creative art.

That is all. The difficulty is dismissed. But it has not been overcome. Consequently Dr Leavis gives the impression of expounding and exalting a different novel from that which Lawrence actually wrote: a version bowdlerized, or at least mitigated *in usum Delphini*.

It is easy enough to understand Lawrence's intention in *Women in Love*: to present first the contrast between a man who immolates himself to the mechanism of modern civilization and one who is in dynamic revolt against it; and also to present the fatal influence on the man-woman relation of the inward sterility of Gerald, and the gleam of hope in the "love" that is based on Ursula's response to the vitality with which Birkin conquers his own despair. The theme is profound and prophetic. But much of its working out is mysterious. Again we ask what it is that happens in the crucial scene where Ursula enters into the "full mystic knowledge" of Birkin's "suave loins of darkness." If it is true, as Dr Leavis suggests, that Lawrence was uncertain of the value of what he offered, uncertain whether he really held it, it has a vital bearing on the convincingness of the novel: for Ursula's relation to Birkin is certainly offered as the way out of the spiritual impasse of contemporary civilization. It is presented as "normative," to use Dr Leavis's word.

Dr Leavis's method of isolating the two novels from their important context does real injustice to Lawrence's achievement: for the subsequent novels are full of implicit and explicit criticism of what he had previously "offered," or at least of re-adjustment of it to further experience. So that to dispose of the subsequent novels as a preliminary to the consideration of the two that preceded them seems, in the literal sense of the word, preposterous. It is as a whole – as the unique record, and imaginative projection of the life and thought adventure of a man prophetically sensitive to the deep inward decay of a civilization – that Lawrence's achievement is so astonishing. It is at once greater and less than Dr Leavis represents it. He is understandably indignant with those who merely allow Lawrence a certain magic of style; but in his effort to vindicate for him the position of the supreme artist – let us put it bluntly, since Dr Leavis plainly implies it – of the same order as Shakespeare, he unduly exaggerates the perfection of some, and unduly depreciates the merit of other of Lawrence's work. Thus he dismisses *The Plumed Serpent* as "a bad book and a regrettable performance." Even if that were a sound judgment (as it is not) the phenomenon would call for explanation, for there is no doubt that Lawrence himself considered it as serious an undertaking as any novel he ever wrote.

Of his contrary tendency to impute perfection to work with serious defects his extreme eulogy of *St Mawr* is a striking example. *St Mawr*, it will be remembered, is the story of how a stallion comes to reveal to a woman the utter insufficiency of her husband and her marriage, and the sterility of the polite semi-artistic world in which her life has been caught. Lou, in contemplating the stallion, receives a revelation of the reality of the life-power that has been suppressed and destroyed in men of the modern civilization and she imagines a "new man" in whom the vivid instinctive life of the animal should be completed by a kindred swift intelligence. Dr Leavis admits that this ideal is not presented in any character of the story.

But it is, nevertheless, irresistibly present in *St Mawr* the dramatic poem; it is no mere abstract postulate. It is present as the marvellous creative intelligence of the author.

Is this argument more than ingenious? Can an author's intelligence, however creative and pervasive, really take the place of a created character of the kind posited? From *The White Peacock* onward Lawrence made many attempts to present such a character, the last being Mellors in *Lady Chatterley's Lover*. But, significantly, none of them has Dr Leavis's approval. So he subtly, and perhaps unconsciously, shifts his ground. Lou repudiates her mother's cynical insinuation that she wants a cave man.

> He's a brute, a degenerate. A pure animal man would be as lovely as a deer or a leopard, burning like a flame fed straight from underneath. And he'd be part of the unseen, like a mouse is, even. And he'd never cease to wonder, he'd breathe silence and unseen wonder, as the partridges do, running in the stubble. ... Ah no, mother, I want the wonder back again, or I shall die.

On which Dr Leavis comments:

> Lawrence can make "wonder" ... seem so much more than a vaguely recoiling romanticism, because for him it is so much more. He can affirm with a power not given to poor Lou, who is not a genius, and there is nothing merely postulated about the positives he affirms.
>
> The power of the affirmation lies, not in any insistence or assertion or argument but in the creative fact, his art; it is that which is an irrefutable witness. What his art *does* is beyond argument or doubt. It is not a question of metaphysics or theology. ... Great art, something created and *there*, is what Lawrence gives us. And there we undeniably *have* a world of wonder and reverence, where life wells up from mysterious springs.

For all its surface plausibility, this burkes the real issue. In so far as it is relevant to Lou's demand for a "new man," it amounts to no more than implying that Lawrence himself was such a man. And Lawrence himself, in a remarkable sequence of novels with which Dr Leavis does not really grapple, dealt with astonishing honesty

with that possibility, or hypothesis, and demonstrated where it
failed. The wonder, which Lawrence the writer felt and so
marvellously communicated, of the animal and natural world, does
not extend to the human being – except in the case of his fictional
presentation of himself.

But that, it might be said, is because the "wonder" is not in
civilized man or woman. It has departed. That assuredly was
Lawrence's conviction. But Dr Leavis does not adopt it. Instead he
asserts that such figures as Rico and Mrs Witt are triumphs of
creative art. Surely he is hypnotizing himself. He is apparently not
quite unaware of the danger.

> Lou's vision is of a flood of evil enveloping the world. Rico
> "being an artist," and bent on kudos and "fun," might
> seem to be too much of a figure of comedy to play the major
> part assigned to him in so portentous a vision. It is a mark
> of the wonderful success of the tale in its larger intention
> that, irresistible as it is in its comedy, we are not moved to
> anything like that criticism: the significance represented by
> the visionary role inheres potently in the Rico we have been
> made to realize. He is, in the first place, we may say,
> Bloomsbury. . . .

A half-page of denunciation follows. A sense of anti-climax is
irrepressible. Whether or not Rico is a plausible embodiment of
Bloomsbury – and one would say he was not – he cannot carry the
weight of apocalyptic significance with which Dr Leavis would
invest him; neither can Mrs Witt, with her enjoyment of the
churchyard, carry hers. With characteristic gravity Dr Leavis
warns us:

> Mrs Witt's note is not so much merely light as it sounds.
> The churchyard, with its funerals, becomes an insistent
> theme. It isn't, for Mrs Witt, an obsession with death as the
> terrifying and inescapable reality, but a fear that death will
> prove unreal. Reported in this way, the case may not seem
> to carry much in the way of convincing poignancy. But this
> is what we are actually given; the thing is *done*, in its
> inevitability an astonishing triumph of genius; and since
> the success – the convincing transmutation, in Mrs Witt, of
> hard-boiled ironic destructiveness into agonized despair –

is crucial to the success of the whole, a long quotation will
be in place.

The long quotation cannot be copied; but to the present writer's
sense it simply does not substantiate Dr Leavis's claim. And the
shrillness of his superlatives which culminate in the dictum that
"one would have said that the kind of thing hadn't been done
and couldn't be done outside Shakespearian dramatic poetry"
seems to be a means of drowning the still small voice of critical
sanity.

St Mawr is a significant story; but not a supreme one. Dr Leavis's
criticism of it has been dealt with in some detail, because his
method of intense and highly selective concentration on parts of
Lawrence's prose fiction admits no other mode of questioning. To
account for his aberration – and his emphatic endorsement of Rico
as a convincing apocalyptic character can be reckoned no less – we
should invoke his unnecessary divagation against Bloomsbury,
and his previous invective against the successors of Bloomsbury.

> In the period in which Auden was so rapidly established as a
> major poet and remained one for so long, and Spender
> became overnight the modern Shelley, it was not to be
> expected that the portrayer of Rico would receive the
> sympathetic attention denied him in the emancipated
> twenties.

Dr Leavis has, in fact, made Rico a symbol of his critical
detestations. Rico's illusory magnitude and convincingness as a
character are a function of his own private universe. They are not
intrinsic to the character presented by Lawrence. Here we touch
upon a real and pervasive weakness of Dr Leavis's championship
of Lawrence. For all his genuine reverence for Lawrence's genius,
he cannot refrain from using him as a weapon of offence against
those whom he regards as literary enemies. What in Lawrence
himself was light-hearted becomes weighted with a deadly
seriousness in Dr Leavis's commentary: Lawrence's casual dismis-
sals are transmuted into excommunications.

It is an exaggeration to represent Lawrence as neglected since his
death. He has been continually in the consciousness and on the
conscience of literate England for at least twenty-five years. And if
he has not yet been accepted as the only inheritor of "the great

tradition" of the English novel, it is largely because he was, essentially, something more important than that – more revolutionary, more truly new, more challenging, more disturbing – which refuses to be accommodated in our conventional categories. Dr Leavis, by virtue of his profession, has made a heroic effort to subsume all that he can of this unique being under the category of "supreme artistic intelligence." He has made a brave and stimulating effort to separate Lawrence's art from his doctrine; but in order to do it he has been compelled to a tacit expurgation. The doctrine is always there.

A MAN IN HIS SENSES

Rayner Heppenstall

[. . .] One should perhaps regard *Lady Chatterley's Lover* as, essentially, a "social" novel, perhaps the most perceptive since Disraeli. Its directly literary progeny has been strange. No doubt many readers have been led to compare it with Charles Morgan's *The Fountain*, inspired, one may feel, by pity for Chatterley, together with a notion that Mellors, though he had experienced the Army, had not experienced war; together, it may be, with a southern middle-class feeling that the Trent basin was neutral like Holland. A less-noticed comparison may be made with Mr L. P. Hartley's *The Go-Between*. When this book was published, it enjoyed great success as a serious work. From some of Mr Hartley's other writings, a cosily tucked-in private joke might have been suspected, but, it seems, none was. Its literary derivation seems clear. The sire was *Lady Chatterley's Lover*, the dam *Cold Comfort Farm*. Grandma had seen "something horrid in the woodshed". What had she seen? Mr Hartley tells us. She had seen one of the love passages in *Lady Chatterley's Lover* being enacted. Mr Hartley's mistake was to allow *his* Connie to be a virgin. He lacked Lawrence's social sense, to say the least. Lawrence had abandoned even *The Virgin and the Gipsy*, where the class thing was not a quarter so much involved.

It is not easy to find a simple formula for *Lady Chatterley's Lover*.

Lady Chatterley's Lover, by D. H. Lawrence [November 4, 1960]

A failure by a dying man very much in his senses might be one attempt, it being understood that to be out of his senses had been one thing which helped to make D. H. Lawrence a great – as well as sometimes a very bad – writer. As for the passages which have been so much debated, the worst thing to be said about them is that they sometimes make one laugh. [...] The actual "description of the whole act" is done with great sweetness, with, moreover, many of the pitfalls clearly and helpfully indicated. Young persons of either sex are the last out of whose hands anybody should think of keeping this book. The worst it could do to them would be to make them a little oversolemn.

FRIENDS AND ENEMIES

A. H. Gomme

[...] Belief was the real living clue for Lawrence – "religious in the most vital sense": belief in "the Eternal God, not to be seen or known, so bright in his fire that all things pass away, evanescent at its touch", in "the great impersonal which never changes and out of which all change comes", "trust in life's sacred spontaneity", a responsibility transcending all individuals. It is something that finds any number of revealingly different expressions in the letters; and Lawrence discusses it at length in the previously suppressed parts of a remarkable letter to Cynthia Asquith (14/5/15). In 1915 he had insisted on the need for a society built "around a religious belief that leads to action". Throughout the war he would say over and again, "We must now begin with our deepest souls, to bring peace and life into the world". Then, when it was over, he saw nothing but unbelief:

> the young are so disconcerting in that they have no centre of belief at all. No centre of real affirmation. They have epicurean and stoic qualities – courage and a certain endurance and honesty – very hostile to any form of tyranny or falsity – and then, nothing: a sort of blank.... It's rather hard lines, really, they *inherited* unbelief: like

The Collected Letters of D. H. Lawrence, ed. by Harry T. Moore [April 27, 1962]

children who expected to be left rich, when their parents
died, and find themselves paupers.

Lawrence could never stop at negation; and when he said, "I *loathe*
humanity, and see the Spirit of Man a sort of aureoled cash-
register", it is very different from the negative disgust of Swift. "I
like people as people anywhere", he said with obvious truth.
People as people: only the fixed, conquering will, the social self, the
cash-nexus were what he hated; and he wanted instead a society of
really free men, true to their essential selves. "God above, leave me
single and separate and unthinkably distinguished from all the
rest", he exclaimed in a letter to Koteliansky (23/9/17) – the
unthinkable distinction (*disquality*) he insisted that all had and that
all should reverence.

He must go down into a separate grave and rise again in
pure singleness. *Then* you will be happy together, you and
he. It only needs to have faith which is unshakable against
everything, a faith in the creative unknown.

That Lawrence had a right to say this cannot be doubted by anyone
who has followed him through the death and rebirth of which the
early letters are so poignant a witness. [...]

DUBLINERS

E. E. Mavrogordato

[...] "Dubliners" may be recommended to the large class of
readers to whom the drab makes an appeal, for it is admirably
written. Mr Joyce avoids exaggeration. He leaves the conviction
that his people are as he describes them. Shunning the emphatic,
Mr Joyce is less concerned with the episode than with the mood
which it suggests. Perhaps for this reason he is more successful
with his shorter stories. When he writes at greater length the issue
seems trivial, and the connecting thread becomes so tenuous as to
be scarcely perceptible. The reader's difficulty will be enhanced if
he is ignorant of Dublin customs; if he does not know, for instance,
that "a curate" is a man who brings strong waters.

Dubliners, by James Joyce [June 18, 1914]

WILD YOUTH*

Arthur Clutton-Brock

[...] Mr Joyce does not talk about futilities because he cannot make anything happen in his story. He can make anything happen that he chooses. He can present the external world excellently, as in the quarrel over Parnell at a Christmas dinner at the beginning of the book. No living writer is better at conversations. But his hero is one of those many Irishmen who cannot reconcile themselves to things; above all, he cannot reconcile himself to himself. He has at times a disgust for himself, a kind of mental queasiness, in which the whole universe seems nauseating as it is presented to him through the medium of his own disgusting self. That perhaps is the cause of those improprieties we have mentioned. What an angel he would like to be, and what a filthy creature, by comparison with that angel, he seems to himself! And so all men and women seem to him filthy creatures. So it was with Hamlet. There is nothing good or bad but thinking makes it so; and thoughts pass through his mind like good or bad smells. He has no control of them. [...]

POMES PENYEACH†

Alan Clutton-Brock

[...] Mr Joyce is not afraid to write such a couplet as this –

> Whose soul is sere and paler
> Than time's wan wave.

For this occasional poetry lives always upon the heights, and if it had not to express the most elevated emotions it would not be written at all. Any other but such high and turbulent emotions Mr Joyce would probably have expressed in his prose writings. [...]

A Portrait of the Artist as a Young Man, by James Joyce [March 1, 1917]
†*Pomes Penyeach*, by James Joyce [November 10, 1927]

MR JOYCE'S
EXPERIMENT

Alan Clutton-Brock

The dissatisfaction of the Irish with the English language and their efforts to change and revivify it make one of the most curious chapters in the history of English letters, but none has ever gone so far and made so many changes as Mr Joyce. He is not content with an Irish dialect or with the simpler primitive tendencies of Irish writers, but he has attempted to change the whole face of the English language. "Anna Livia Plurabelle" is a fragment of a work on which he is now engaged, and here, as Mr Colum explains in an appreciative preface, he is still writing about Dublin. But while his subject is akin to that of "The Dubliners" and of "Portrait of the Artist as a Young Man," the treatment is altered out of all knowledge, though doubtless it is a development out of Mr Joyce's intervening work. There is the same kind of poetry in prose, but it would seem that this has needed the stimulus of new language and new technical devices to prevent its exhaustion. "Anna Livia Plurabelle" is written in an outlandish dialect; the roots of English words can be recognized, sometimes after thought, but often the endings and the spelling are much changed. One is at times reminded of the devices of manufacturers in their trade names, when they spell words phonetically or change "f" into "ph." Undoubtedly, though inexplicably, this has a value in advertising, but it needs great boldness to find in it something of value for poetry or for poetical prose. "Frostivying tresses dasht with vireflies" is a good example of this device in Mr Joyce's work. In addition to this there is every kind of euphuism, foreign words are used, and much alliteration and rhyme.

Certainly this is a new literary dialect, and it is possible to read it, though with more trouble than Chaucer demands; and one can see that if Mr Joyce's real gifts of fantasy and poetry were in danger of exhaustion the invention of a new dialect is a conceivable means of restoring them. Mr Joyce is, in fact, desperately and with

Anna Livia Plurabelle, by James Joyce [December 20, 1928]

remarkable courage trying to bring back the English language to a period like the Elizabethan, when each neologism was a happy discovery and the spout of words flowed freshly and with exuberance. [...]

A GUIDE TO "ULYSSES"*

Alex Glendinning

[...] The fact that we disagree with Mr Gilbert at the outset, that we do not think "Ulysses" is "antisentimental," nor that Mr Joyce has that serene detachment with which Mr Gilbert credits him and which is so necessary to the condition of "static beauty," need not affect our judgment of his study, which is not after all, in its main purpose, critical. Mr Gilbert makes his pronouncements, and, having made them, takes "Ulysses" to pieces for us and leaves us to decide for ourselves in how far the complex harmony of its parts achieves "a static perfection." [...]

MR JOYCE'S EXPERIMENTS†

Alex Glendinning

[...] Ingenuity as well as an extensive knowledge of Dublin and its history are necessary to understand Earwicker's pompous recital of all that he has done for the city and for his Anna. Its implications are occasionally obvious, to Dubliners at least, as in the reference to streetnames in

> my nordsoud circulums, my eastmoreland and westland-more, running boullowards and syddenly parading ...

Read aloud, as Mr Joyce's work should be, the prose of this fragment has a stateliness appropriate to its matter, in ponderous,

*James Joyce's Ulysses, by Stuart Gilbert [June 19, 1930]
†Haveth Childers Everywhere, by James Joyce [December 18, 1930]

masculine contrast to the streamlike melodies of "Anna Livia Plurabelle."

INTERPRETATIONS OF "ULYSSES"*

Alan Clutton-Brock

[...] There is, of course, a deliberate attempt to impose order on the incoherence of "Ulysses" by making all its events belong to a single day and by making the same episodes and characters appear and reappear in the kaleidoscope. But when one chapter contains a succession of masterly parodies of English prose in chronological order, from "Beowulf" to modern slang, when another is an amusing and satirical excursion on the Irish literary movement, another an irresistibly funny transcription of a young girl's daydream in terms of the novelettes she has been reading, then the use of the same characters and episodes has the appearance of a merely conventional link between all the sections of the book. No doubt the link has a certain use in helping the reader along, but there is no reason to suppose that it makes the book a coherent whole from which no part can be removed without disaster. It is of no use to look for secret connexions, for in a work of art if the relations of the parts are not apparent enough to be felt, then the parts are not artistically related. [...]

THE PROGRESS OF MR JOYCE†

R. A. Scott-James

[...] It has often been said of Mr Joyce that he was a writer in revolt against the conditions that prevailed in his country – religious,

Ulysses, by James Joyce [January 23, 1937]
†[Article] [May 6, 1939]

social, intellectual. But that might equally have been said thirty years ago about Mr Shaw or Mr Wells, who have little in common with him. Revolt has no significance unless it has a positive and constructive side to it – and Mr Shaw and Mr Wells were concerned about social or moral reconstruction, which is utterly alien to Mr Joyce's purpose in literature. On the contrary, "Finnegans Wake" shows him as almost savagely satisfied with the thrilling spectacle of life as he sees it in all its sordidness, its restless emotionalism, its inconsequence, its somnambulant absurdity. He does not desire to reform it, but to gratify his creative spirit in the expression of his impressions of it. His constructive purpose is to find a way satisfactory to himself of expressing the movement of life as he sees it, changing its texture and hue from moment to moment, a flux of sensations whose reality cannot be appreciated without a sense of the flux. [. . .]

MR JOYCE EXPRESSES HIMSELF

R. A. Scott-James

[. . .] That he should have wrapped up his vision in a maze of words which his fantastic invention has distorted from their familiar shapes, and that he should have heaped these words together in tangled skeins which can only be unravelled in proportion as we are capable of following the playful gambols of his impressionable mind, these are drawbacks which will deter some intelligent people from reading him, and prevent any of them from fully understanding him. He has set some pretty jig-saw puzzles for sophisticated people to talk about, and since the book is "holusbolus authoritative" they may derive intellectual profit from it as well as credit. But heaven forbid that it should be imitated. This is Mr Joyce's individual mode of self-expression, and therefore nobody can do anything properly comparable with it without doing something quite different.

Finnegans Wake, by James Joyce [May 6, 1939]

THE SIGNIFICANCE OF
JAMES JOYCE*

Philip Tomlinson

[...] It is a strange feast "Ulysses" invites us to, abundantly, brilliantly, boringly, obscenely, intellectually, bewilderingly mixed, a phantasmal expedition into the conscious and the sub-conscious. There are hypnotic qualities, scenes of genius in it – and long stretches of dullness and pretence. The reproductions made by his uncanny gift of visualizing are sometimes perfect, but often they are too trivial to be worth the effort. There are things beyond praise, uproarious Rabelaisian patches, and things beyond damnation. There are enticing pages of prose with the effect of music, and pages that are not prose nor anything recognizable as literature. [...]

EXAGMINATION OF
JOYCE†

Anthony Powell

[...] Bloom himself remains a somewhat confused conception. We are told the most intimate details about him, but at the end of it he is not such a graphic figure as Fagin or Monsieur Nissim Bernard: nor does one feel that a fuller physiological account of either of the two latter would have resulted in more photographic portraits. The fact is that the presentation of Bloom suffers from the usual difficulties of attempting to record in great detail the mental processes of a character other than the author's projection of himself – in this case Stephen. As Bloom's thoughts are, in fact, Joyce's thoughts (even though at the remove of being Joyce's

*[Article] [January 25, 1941]
†*The Essential James Joyce*, with Introduction and Notes by Harry Levin [October 30, 1948]

thoughts of what Bloom's thoughts might be) Bloom ends by giving the impression of being more like Joyce than the romantically conceived Stephen, who is always treated as if he necessarily belonged to a higher plane than those who surround him. After seven hundred pages we do not have a sense of knowing Stephen better than, say, Benjamin Constant's Adolph after fifty. Joyce was not a writer with the imaginative potency of Dickens and Kipling on the one hand; or James and Proust on the other; and he does not, perhaps, set out to create character in the sense in which this phrase is often used; but all novelists are to some extent to be judged by the vitality of their creatures, and in this direction his abilities are not seen at their most outstanding; though minor figures like Mr Deasy suddenly emerge with vividness. [...]

THE MASTER BUILDER

Anthony Cronin

"Joyce holds his place of eminence under fire; he is much more assailed than writers who are evidently his inferiors," says Mr Ellmann, with truth. Among the curiosities of to-day is the ambivalent attitude adopted in some quarters towards the revolutionary works of the century, the progenitors of what is also assumed to be a victorious "modernity." The *Cantos* and *Finnegans Wake* are still, it is fairly safe to say, regarded as pretty dubious ventures.

A little while ago it was alleged that the task of "experiment" was accomplished and over; and the common cry was for a "consolidation of gains." Yet, although it is often reluctantly conceded that there is something wrong with the orthodox novel as a form, *Ulysses* is pointed to if at all as a still and rather brackish backwater. At the same time, by the law of ambiguity that surrounds these matters, it is alleged that its influence has been over-extensive. In fact it can be argued with more truth that it has been nil. By English criticism at any rate Joyce is still received with a mixture of awe, bemusement, indifference and even hostility. The awe is accorded to the relentlessness with which his conceptions

James Joyce, by Richard Ellmann [November 20, 1959]

were carried through, but is nearly always accompanied by the suggestion that these nocturnal peregrinations through blind alleys are enormous eccentricities in which serious people concerned with the political, scientific and philosophical preoccupations of the modern world – the sort of people who read C. P. Snow, for example – can scarcely be expected to take much interest. [...]

Not surprisingly, the ambiguous but discernible hostility with which Joyce's work is now regarded in England can be seen since the publication of his letters, his brother's account of his early life, and now Mr Ellmann's biography, to extend to the man as well. And not only to the myth or to the man as archetype of certain attitudes towards creation, but to the man himself, of whom it is alleged in almost the same breath that he was both too human and in some way less than human. His single-mindedness, his remoteness, his lack of opinions about, or indeed interest in, the "ideas" of his time have all come under fire.

The very weight, size and undiscriminating nature of Mr Ellmann's record of his life will probably cause these prejudices to persist. [...]

We need to see Joyce again in the whole context of the modern movement, a context in which Mr Ellmann's extremely informative record somehow fails to place him. In the history of the modern consciousness – the specifically modern consciousness – Joyce is at least as important as Baudelaire or Flaubert. With Pound and Eliot – the achievement of the three is in many ways inseparable – he attempted in the English language the expression of a more total, a more unified and a more honest view of human nature, soul and body, than was characteristic of the literature that immediately preceded them. *Ulysses* was and remains the first great masterpiece of anti-heroic literature; if the novel has survived it, there is yet an uneasy feeling abroad that it has not recovered from the shock. The indifference to "ideas" and philosophical theorizing with which critics charge Joyce is part of his fidelity to the certainties of human life, comparable to the fidelity to the object of certain great painting. He extended enormously the recorded area of human experience and extended, it is not too much to say, the scope of literature itself. In the ordinary, the debased, the degraded, and the comic he discovered a fitting subject for contemplation. "The trouble with me is I have no imagination," he remarked ruefully, yet he knew that true imagination is the intensity with which the familiar is contemplated, and in contemplating it he demonstrated not only the sustaining comic power of life itself but what he had called as a young man translating Aquinas's word, the "radiance" of things.

His life was triumphant or sorry according to the point of view. Mr Ellmann somehow contrives to create the impression of a sadness greater than the facts he gives or Joyce's essentially sociable nature would warrant. It is a pity that while he was so busily putting so much in (and we should be grateful for it all) he appears also to have left something out.

ULYSSES RETURNS

Rayner Heppenstall

[. . .] What the reviewer has gathered from the communications of practising novelists suggests that a painful accidie normally supervenes a little over halfway through a book and that the acceptance and conquering of this ordeal is what principally distinguishes a novelist from a failed novelist. If Joyce, exerting his will, had persisted in his original intention, he would then have written a very good novel, fairly homogeneous in style, rather more than half the length of the *Ulysses* we know. Joyce, however, taking the book up again, contrived to push on only by treating each subsequent episode as a separate problem. The circumstance of serial publication also determined this injured, conceited man to keep his American readers agog. Each episode henceforward should be a virtuoso performance of a new kind.

The "Sirens" episode in the Ormond Hotel is a bridge passage. The sad thing is that, in itself, without the intruded fragments of tedious word-play (written and put in subsequently?), it would have been one of the best scenes in the old vein. Miss Douce and Miss Kennedy, Dedalus's father and Ben Dollard, are first-rate. The plot, insofar as it consists in willing cuckoldry, here reaches its crux. Blazes Boylan could not be more vividly glimpsed on his vile seducer's way. But we are fidgeted by all that feeble, pre-*Finnegan*

Ulysses, by James Joyce [June 24, 1960]

word-play. From now on there is both worse and better in store.
[...]

The Joyce cult flourishes among the London Irish, who rejoice in the Dublin street names, the surviving hotels and the seashore. It survives, of course, among the relics of the Left Bank *entre deux guerres*. It is a useful adjunct to the Irish tourist industry, though Joyce could hardly be thought a typical Irishman, unless it is typically Irish to spend most of one's life abroad, unpublished in Ireland. The rest of us must take *Ulysses* as we find it. Because of its complexity, it is critics' (and professors') meat. The pastiches of its last two thirds vary in merit, but we may take *Ulysses* as a text-book, with examples, of narrative prose method. As a model to intending writers, the first third would do better. But Joyce was a prose virtuoso. After *Ulysses*, he gave us nothing but virtuoso performances. The acclamation of Anglo-American moneyed highbrows egged him on to ever dizzier heights. He had, in any case, nothing left to communicate, once he had dealt with Dublin and his own youth. The capacity for new human experience or for any but linguistic thought had been used up.

AN OLD-FASHIONED
RADICAL

Richard Ellmann and Craig Raine

In preparing his BBC Radio 3 programme James Joyce: A Touch of the Artist, *which was produced by Judith Bumpus, and broadcast last week for the centenary of Joyce's birth, Craig Raine recorded an interview with Richard Ellmann, who has been working on a revised edition of his biography of Joyce, to be published this autumn by Oxford University Press. The following transcript of parts of the interview which were not broadcast is printed by kind permission of the BBC.*

[...] *Raine:* Eliot said, "When a great poet has lived, certain things have been done once and for all and cannot be achieved again. But on the other hand, every great poet adds something to the complex material out of which future poetry will be written." If we apply

[BBC interview] [February 5, 1982]

this to Joyce, would you say that his work has been a literary cul-de-sac? That, say, *Ulysses* can't be imitated any more than *Tristram Shandy*? Or do you think that his work has been a strong and useful influence, and if so on whom?

Ellmann: Well, that's a large question. But I think I would have to say that Joyce seems to me the most radical writer of the century. By that I mean that he's down at the roots of consciousness, including the unconscious. He's down at the roots of art, and also at the roots of language. We all assume, or would like to assume, that language is fixed and stable, but in fact of course it's very fluid and Joyce is the first, I think, to make this clear. Now as far as his experiments in language are concerned, there haven't been many people who have followed those, though one finds bits of *Finnegans Wake*-ese in Sean O'Casey's autobiography. So far as his development of consciousness, his exploration of consciousness, is concerned, why, everyone seems to be following him in that. And so far as his exploration of the roots of art and his experiments with all kinds of different narrative points-of-view, unreliable narrators and the like are concerned everybody seems to be following them too. So I would say that he's been a very important influence, that that is one of the signs of his greatness as perhaps the principal innovator in twentieth-century literature and perhaps in the literature of a much longer period than that.

Raine: What you're suggesting is a general diffusion.

Ellmann: Yes. But I would be willing to name more specific instances too, if you want those.

Raine: Well I wondered, for instance – one can obviously pick on small things: the O'Casey you've mentioned; Orwell, absolutely fatally, in my view, copies the "Circe" episode in *A Clergyman's Daughter* and never tries it again – but I was thinking of someone like Nabokov, who seems to me to bear the imprint of Joyce's influence. There are some very clear verbal parallels. This is from *Lolita*: "She lit up" – a cigarette – "and the smoke she exhaled from her nostrils was like a pair of tusks." Now in "Circe", one of the whores spouts "walrus smoke" through her nostrils. Exactly the same image. Do you think Nabokov is influenced by Joyce?

Ellmann: I'm sure he was, and we've recently had a book of his lectures on Joyce, which he gave at Cornell. The book which seems closest to Joyce is *Pale Fire*, where the character of Kinbote and Shade is very Joycean, very much reminiscent of the "Cyclops" episode. Kinbote is a thorough-going villain and this is never made clear because we hear it always from his point of view, just as we hear it all from Thersites' point of view in the "Cyclops" chapter.

There are some rather pleasant incidents of their friendship – because they *did* know each other. Perhaps the most telling one is that Nabokov once had to give a lecture on Pushkin, and he knew that there would be no audience whatsoever, except the Hungarian football team, which the Hungarian consul was forcing to attend. But when he went to speak at the hall, fearing that it would be otherwise entirely empty, he saw that one at least of the seats was occupied by the principal writer of his time who had come, feeling sympathetic to his situation and wanting him not to be left all alone in this lecture hall.

You know, as far as the question of influence is concerned, I am always amused when Anthony Burgess talks about Joyce, because he always insists that Joyce has had no influence whatsoever. But one has only to look at *Enderby*, or any other of Burgess's novels, and they always turn out to be full of Joyce. I don't mean that Burgess doesn't have his own flair, but he certainly has read Joyce carefully.

Raine: We agree about this, that Joyce's influence is everywhere. Yet oddly, Joyce himself didn't think of himself as a pattern-book for other writers. There's a letter to Harriet Shaw Weaver, in 1919. He says "Each successive episode dealing with some province of artistic culture – rhetoric or music or dialectic – leaves behind it a burnt-up field. Since I wrote 'Sirens' I find it impossible to listen to music of any kind." So he really thought of himself as exhausting a particular patch. But I don't think he did.

Ellmann: Music has probably survived him, yes.

Raine: What about his politics? In 1915, Pound writes to Joyce – they're talking about the possible publication of *Portrait of the Artist* – "It would be better if possible to publish in England. France is very much occupied with the War, news of which may have reached you." This kind of thing seems to be the received idea about Joyce and politics, that he was so completely the artist, he was absolutely uninterested in politics. Frank Budgen says that Joyce never talked politics. And when you look at the books – you look at *Ulysses* and the Russo-Japanese War gets two mentions, I think, in the entire work? There isn't much to build on. But "Ivy Day in the Committee Room" in *Dubliners* dismisses the idea of politics, really. It's for sentimentalists.

There's nothing in the work itself, the texts as they stand, to build a great theory of Joyce's politics on, but what about the letters? Is there more evidence which has come to light there?

Ellmann: There is some evidence in the letters, and I think there is a little in the books too. Joyce undoubtedly disapproved of the excessive nationalism that he saw so popular in Ireland at the time. On the other hand, he was a nationalist in his fashion. And at the end of *A Portrait of the Artist*, you remember, Stephen Dedalus, says, "I go to encounter for the millionth time the reality of experience and to forge in the smithy of my soul the uncreated conscious of my race". And earlier in the book, he asks how can he touch the hearts and minds of young Irish women so that they'll bring forth a race less ignoble than their own. It seems to me that a great deal of his work is directed towards an improvement of the Irish situation.

Raine: But that's only political in the most elastic sense, isn't it? I mean if you go to the *Portrait*, Davin's sentimental attraction to Fenianism, for instance, is dismissed out of hand. McCann's petition for peace, Stephen won't sign it. Basically what he's doing in *A Portrait* is opting out of all commitment except this very, very large one. And would it be really true to say that that's political?

Ellmann: Well, one can define politics in many ways. Clearly it did not mean voting. I don't suppose Joyce ever voted in an election. He couldn't have voted after he left Ireland. And he probably didn't vote in the year or two when he might have voted there. But on the other hand, as we learn from "Ivy Day in the Committee Room", voting was practically useless in Ireland at that time. It was one of those watersheds when nothing was happening in the country.

Joyce undoubtedly was much moved by the death of Parnell when he was a child. And he has a moving description of Parnellites and anti-Parnellites in the Christmas Dinner scene of *A*

Portrait of the Artist. In *Ulysses* he goes to the next stage, which I suppose is the question of ultra-nationalism, and he's very much against that. On the other hand, there is one Irish leader of that period, of the post-Parnellite period, whom he speaks of with great respect, repeatedly in *Ulysses* and that is Arthur Griffith. Griffith became President of the Irish Free State in 1922; the first President, and Joyce felt that there was some sort of conjunction between their two careers, in that Griffith was achieving by political means what Joyce was attempting to do by cultural means. Then of course he became somewhat less pleased with the new government. Griffith died, and it became repressive in its turn. In 1932 Joyce commented that the new Irish state appeared to reduce individual liberty even further than had been done under the British occupation, and there certainly hadn't been much individual liberty at that time.

But I like to remember that in 1914, just after the War was declared, Joyce decided that he would put together a group of seven articles which he had written for the Trieste newspaper, the *Piccolo della Sera*, about the state of Ireland and about Home Rule and about John O'Leary, the old Fenian, and related subjects. And he said to this Italian publisher in Rome. "I would like to publish these. I think that while they have no literary value whatsoever, they give a full picture of that situation and it is just at the moment when Ireland is coming into the news." The book was not published, but it seems to me a pity it wasn't, because it would have shown that Joyce was interested in the future of his country in a very particular way and was quite well informed about it.

I think he started out as a socialist – he called himself that – and gradually he became an anarchist. He began to disapprove of all governments increasingly as he got older. But he always retained a political feeling in that he was always for the Blooms of the world, the simple people, always for individual liberty, always very much against tyranny, always contemptuous of Hitler and Mussolini and always eager to do what he could to help refugees from Nazi Germany.

Raine: So it's really the personal life he believes in. There's actually a very useful quotation which sums up what you've been saying. This is a letter to Stanislaus in 1907 in which he says that he's lost all interest in socialism: "Yet I have certain ideas I would like to give form to. Not as a doctrine, but as a continuation of the expression of myself, which I now see I began in *Chamber Music*. These ideas, or instincts, or intuitions, or impulses, may be purely personal. I have no wish to codify myself as an anarchist or socialist or reactionary."

Ellmann: Yes, I think, though, that there are other remarks which indicate that he recognized that to be totally oblivious to politics would be a defect. I remember one letter in which he says that the thing which distinguishes Turgenev from lesser writers in Russia is his political awareness. And I think Joyce felt that he had political awareness, even though he was not active in politics in the way that we expect people to be in our present-day political scene.

BLOOMSDAY 1982

Eric Korn

"James Joyce, is it? That gobshite they threw out of the country for his dirty writings?" asked the taxi-driver, giving me the perfect opening (but you don't believe me) for an account of Bloomsday celebrations in Dublin in Joyce's centenary year.

Others spoke more generously. "It is time to repay some of the honour and fame he has brought to Dublin", said the President of the Republic, unveiling a bust by Marjorie Fitzgibbon on Stephen's Green. "He's got a fine head on him", said a bystander appreciatively as the covers came off, for all the world as if he were a glass of Guinness ("James's Choice", say the adverts). But the bust's grandson noted sourly that the monument was paid for by American Express, and stayed in Paris. Other absent invitees (or invited absentees) were Norman Mailer, Marguerite Duras and Samuel Beckett, but Sir William Empson and Dennis Potter and Tom Stoppard and Burgess and Borges were there, and Simon and Garfunkel, though perhaps on a different errand, and Hugh Kenner and Salman Rushdie and "I think I have been talking to Lech Walesa", mumbled a name-numbed citizen at the State reception.

[Article] [July 2, 1982]

"Here Comes Everybody", they called the Symposium, all too truly, and here too came I, in a trainload of Scandinavian Scouts and Scoutesses (integrated of course) filling the corridors with canoe paddles and reading something called *Dublinbör*. I'd chosen my travelling edition of The Words with a dandy's care ("not the vellum, I suggest, Sir, it might seem a trifle *parvenu*"): a stout two-volume paperback of *Ulysses*, Hamburg 1933, Stuart Gilbert's authorized revision, in the sought-after second impression, with the first literals repaired and no time for entropy to do its ugly work, the correctest edition, supposedly, until a perfect text issues from Munich next year; and I carried a neat tranny, so that Radio Telefís Eireann's thirty-one hour reading, every word from Stately to Yes uninterrupted by sleep or weather forecasts, could go whithersoever I went.

So I came Bloomsberrying into what seemed an indifferent city, until I observed that all the magazine covers featured Joyce's features, and *The Inside Guide to Dublin* had filled its odd corners with encouraging titbits: "Did you know that James Joyce invariably overtipped?", "Did you know that James Joyce's favourite wine was white?" And the bookshop windows were Joyceful with Finnegan Calendars and Biographies of Bloom, with *The Wake* annotated at IR£25.48, and maps and vade mecums and pilgrims' guides to the Stations of the Odyssey, with postcards and every text imaginable, and (fairly unimaginable) a book by a Jesuit, *James Joyce's Schooldays*. (He has a sensational find: the punishment book from Clongowes, with no mention of four on the hand with the pandybat for breaking his glasses and being a lazy idle schemer: but instead J. Joyce four for vulgar language, a mild dose compared with Lynch's eighteen for not knowing Virgil and Nasty Roche's ten for "constant lateness at duties".)

Literature began breaking in: at Newman House they were collecting signatures in the entrance hall for the Tsar's petition against War, though some cack-handed scholar had just put his elbow through the photograph ("he has the face of a besotted Christ") frame; and David Norris, Chairman of the Centenary Committee, was complaining gloatingly that in the morning, when Hugh Kenner had gone to put a plaque on 52 Upper Clanbrassil Street, where Leopold Bloom would have been born if he had been, know-better neighbours had gathered round to tell him he'd got it all wrong, the Blooms hadn't lived there at all, you must be thinking of Lower Clanbrassil, we knew them well, decent folk. There was a marvellous exhibition on Joyce's student days, giving flesh and feature and family to those epiphanic glimpses of his fellows in *Stephen Hero*; and all kinds of good things like the Minute Book of the Literary and Historical Society and J. J.'s copies of Ibsen, and the reviews from *The Irish Booklover* ("no clean-minded person could possibly allow it to remain within reach of his wife") and one of the most memorable throwaways in all literary reminiscence, from William Bulfin's *Rambles in Eirinn* (M. H. Gill, 1907):

> We intended riding to Glendalough and back, but were obliged to modify this programme before we reached Dalkey, owing to a certain pleasant circumstance which might be termed a morning call. As we were leaving the suburb my comrade said casually that there were two men living in a tower somewhere to the left who were creating a sensation ...

And there was a copy of Lamb's *Adventures of Ulysses*, used as a class book in the College. I was nudged. "It's published, do you see, by BROWN AND NOLAN, BRUNO NOLAN", said a stranger, temporarily deranged by paronomasia.

I went and listened to the Home Team, as it were, having a little quiet fun at the expense of cosmopolitan critics so full of symbols and structuralism they don't know who actually won the Gold Cup in 1904. Chuckles were had at references to the dangers of foot and mouth disease causing sterility in bullocks, and how this represented all kinds of sterility, references made by unworldly academics who don't know that bullocks are generally infertile. The critic who says that the crucial symbol is Stephen's refusal of the coffee, representing Communion, was collated with the critic who says that the crucial symbol is Stephen's acceptance of the cocoa, representing Communion, to their mutual disadvantage. The moral seemed to be that you must understand Ireland to understand *Ulysses*, and while you are all welcome and we need your advice ("I think of Mathew Arnold; I think of William Wordsworth; I think of all those great critics, none of them, alas, Irish ..."), you needn't think a week in Dublin will give you the insight that is our birthright. [...]

Bloomsday itself began with a various and chilly crowd of

devotees at Sandycove, some swimming at Forty Foot ("If I had a scrotum it would surely have tightened", remarked an Irish author of the female persuasion), others shaving on the gunrest, absurdly with electric razors, or toasting the day in Buck's Fizz in honour of plump Buck Mulligan – well you couldn't eat Mulligan Stew at that hour.

But even before that the radio began the reading, a vivid and respectful performance with an immense and accurate variety of Dublin voices (though Bloom was too unIrish for some) and innumerable obscurities illuminated (Roland McHugh, called in as textual adviser on the curious grounds of his familiarity with *Finnegans Wake*, complained of the problems of assigning narrative to the optimum number of narrators without creating false boundaries, a little like colouring a map with three inks). I carried it everywhere, feeling absurd at first, but no one objected except a pernickety Faculty wife from Ohio, and so many people were doing the same that gradually the air of Dublin began to fill up with Joyce's words. The time of the narrative moved sometimes ahead of, sometimes behind the sun: miraculously, it marched precisely with it at 2.55 when a hundred-odd costumed characters from the Mayor of Dublin (playing the Viceroy) to various unofficial improvisers, took to the streets to recreate the "Wandering Rocks" sequence. It was moving, absurd and delightful. Spectators rushed hither and yon along the crowded quays, or struggled with an oversized map to decide whether to catch Dilly Daedalus upbraiding her improvident father along Bachelor's Walk and watch Bloom and Blazes Boylan pass, or dash to the Dublin Bread Company in Dame Street where Buck Mulligan sees Parnell's brother-in-law. There was rather a surplus of ladies in Edwardian underwear for strict textual accuracy, though this is not a complaint, and while some of the minor characters showed extraordinary conscientiousness (old Ben Dollard, flies agape, explained his domestic problems over and over again to Father Cowley for all to overhear) some of the principals reacted to the anachronistic excitement of cameras. Leopold waved his copy of *Sweets of Sin*, enthusiastically; the blind stripling kept getting helped across a road he wasn't meant to cross; "Would that be Mrs Daedalus?" shouted a bemused camerawoman, and in the benign confusion many innocent passers-by were interviewed.

The Ormond Hotel, where most of the cast find themselves at

the end of the hour's peripeteia (except of course Father Conmee SJ, away in Mountjoy Square, and Molly and Blazes at it in what remains of no 7, Eccles Street) added to the confusion by letting slip that their share of the celebrations would be to sell beer at 1904 prices, although a secondary rumour, that they were only accepting pre-decimal currency, had earlier started a run on the piggy banks; a thirsty crowd, not all literary scholars, blocked the approaches and caused a traffic jam that may still be reverberating.

There was more street theatre later, when David Norris took the keys of 35 St George's Street, a crumbling mansion once Signor Maginni's Dancing Academy, as the future home of a museum and poetry centre. "Why spend money on the dead when there is none for living artists?" shouted a passing figure, presumably that of a living artist, and did not stay for the swift riposte: "We always have begrudgers and Brendan Behan had the word for them."

Brendan Behan's word, I'm informed, was "Fuck the begrudgers", but it was a more elegant toast that Borges offered at the Bloomsday Banquet later; once again the sound system, and an ironic samba from the next ballroom, victimized the speaker, but a wonderful Borgesian phrase snatched my ear: "If these books last long enough – and I think they may last for ever . . .". Dublin had done its best to ensure this. The costumes and the critics, the devotion and the exploitation, together had scraped a little hole in the surface of reality, through which the myth could shine.

And it is early on this second Bloomsday morning, and they are grilling kidneys in Bloom's Hotel, and in Jury's Hotel and the Clonakilty Hilton, the fine tang of faintly scented urine (page 56 line 5) faintly falling on the Royal Tara China Bust (£287 + p and p), on Davy Burns, and farther westward, on the Chapelizod Bridge, renamed the Anna Livia, and faintly falling, like the descent of their last end, upon all the living and the Dead.

PRUFROCK AND OTHER
OBSERVATIONS*

F. T. Dalton

Mr Eliot's notion of poetry – he calls the "observations" poems – seems to be a purely analytical treatment, verging sometimes on the catalogue, of personal relations and environments, uninspired by any glimpse beyond them and untouched by any genuine rush of feeling. As, even on this basis, he remains frequently inarticulate, his "poems" will hardly be read by many with enjoyment. [...]

A NEW BYRONISM†

Arthur Clutton-Brock

[...] Art presumes that life is worth living, and must not, except dramatically or in a moment of exasperation or irony, say that it isn't. But Mr Eliot writes only to say that it isn't; and he does not do it so well as the author of Ecclesiastes, who at least keeps the momentum and gusto of all the experiences he pretends to have exhausted. For Mr Eliot: –

> Midnight shakes the memory
> As a madman shakes a dead geranium.

There we are reminded a little of his countryman Poe, and "The Lovesong of J. Alfred Prufrock" is like Poe even in its curious and over-conscious metrical effects. They seem to be, as so often in Poe, independent of the poem itself, as if the writer could not attain to a congruity between the tune beating in his head and any subject-matter. In this poem he is really, with the poet part of him, questing for beauty, but the other part refuses it with a kind of nausea:–

Prufrock and Other Observations, by T. S. Eliot [June 21, 1917]
†*Ara Vus Prec*, by T. S. Eliot [March 18, 1920]

Shall I part my hair behind? Do I dare to eat a peach?
I shall wear white flannel trousers, and walk upon the beach.
I have heard the mermaids singing, each to each.
I do not think that they will sing to me.
I have seen them riding seaward on the waves,
Combing the white hair of the waves blown back,
When the wind blows the water white and black.
We have lingered in the chambers of the sea.
By sea-girls wreathed with seaweed red and brown,
Till human voices wake us, and we drown.

So it ends. Human voices for Mr Eliot drown everything; he cannot get away from his disgust of them; he is "fed up" with them, with their volubility and lack of meaning. "Words, words, words" might be his motto; for in his verse he seems to hate them and to be always expressing his hatred of them, in words. If he could he would write songs without words; blindly he seeks for a medium free of associations, not only for a tune but also for notes that no one has sung before. But all this is mere habit; art means the acceptance of a medium as of life; and Mr Eliot does not convince us that his weariness is anything but a habit, an anti-romantic reaction, a new Byronism which he must throw off if he is not to become a recurring decimal in his fear of being a mere vulgar fraction.

POETRY AND CRITICISM

Arthur Clutton-Brock

Mr Eliot is a critic with principles which have not been assumed hastily for the purpose of writing but which have grown out of his experience of literature. These he expresses calmly and with precision; he does not try to write prose-poetry about poetry, to make his criticism the poor relation of poetry. Criticism for him is an important and independent activity with its own procedure; it ought, he thinks, to be without caprice, raptures or tantrums, or

The Sacred Wood. Essays on Poetry and Criticism, by T. S. Eliot [December 2, 1920]

egotism. It is science rather than art – though we are apt to make too sharp a division between these – and ought to have the manners of science. Since he has an experience of literature perhaps more wide than intense, a keen intelligence and the power of expressing it precisely in language, his criticism is always worth reading and often of great value. But he has also certain perversities, instinctive rather than rational, of which one gradually becomes aware, concealed though they be even from himself by the air of reason which he consciously and rightly maintains. Against these one must be warned so that one may profit by his wisdom. [. . .]

In fact Mr Eliot is more grudging of praise than blame; often, indeed, he seems to grudge us our enjoyment, as if he took a pleasure in rubbing the gilt off the gingerbread, when really it is not gilt at all or mere gingerbread. And because of this we are tempted to read him with resentment, to resist even the many good things which he says. That he should provoke this resistance, that he should so often resemble the wind rather than the sun, is, we think, a proof that he is malicious without knowing it, and that this malice leads him sometimes into a practice contrary to those excellent principles which he states so well.

A FRAGMENTARY POEM

Edgell Rickword

[. . .] The poetic personality of Mr Eliot is extremely sophisticated. His emotions hardly ever reach us without traversing a zig-zag of allusion. In the course of his four hundred lines he quotes from a score of authors and in three foreign languages, though his artistry has reached that point at which it knows the wisdom of sometimes concealing itself. There is in general in his work a disinclination to awake in us a direct emotional response. It is only, the reader feels, out of regard for someone else that he has been induced to mount the platform at all. From there he conducts a magic-lantern show; but being too reserved to expose in public the impressions stamped on his own soul by the journey through the Waste Land, he

The Waste Land, by T. S. Eliot [September 20, 1923]

employs the slides made by others, indicating with a touch the difference between his reaction and theirs. So the familiar stanza of Goldsmith becomes:

> When lovely woman stoops to folly and
> Paces about her room again, alone,
> She smoothes her hair with automatic hand,
> And puts a record on the gramophone.

To help us to elucidate the poem Mr Eliot has provided some notes which will be of more interest to the pedantic than the poetic critic. Certainly they warn us to be prepared to recognize some references to vegetation ceremonies. This is the cultural or middle layer, which, whilst it helps us to perceive the underlying emotion, is of no poetic value in itself. We desire to touch the inspiration itself, and if the apparatus of reserve is too strongly constructed, it will defeat the poet's end. The theme is announced frankly enough in the title, "The Waste Land"; and in the concluding confession,

> These fragments I have shored against my ruins,

we receive a direct communication which throws light on much which had preceded it. From the opening part, "The Burial of the Dead," to the final one we seem to see a world, or a mind, in disaster and mocking its despair. We are aware of the toppling of aspirations, the swift disintegration of accepted stability, the crash of an ideal. Set at a distance by a poetic method which is reticence itself, we can only judge of the strength of the emotion by the visible violence of the reaction. Here is Mr Eliot, a dandy of the choicest phrase, permitting himself blatancies like "the young man carbuncular." Here is a poet capable of a style more refined than that of any of his generation parodying without taste or skill – and of this the example from Goldsmith is not the most astonishing. Here is a writer to whom originality is almost an inspiration borrowing the greater number of his best lines, creating hardly any himself. It seems to us as if the "The Waste Land" exists in the greater part in the state of notes. [...]

The method has a number of theoretical justifications. Mr Eliot has himself employed it discreetly with delicious effect. It suits well the disillusioned smile which he had in common with Laforgue; but we do sometimes wish to hear the poet's full voice. Perhaps if the reader were sufficiently sophisticated he would find these echoes suggestive hints, as rich in significance as the sonorous amplifications of the romantic poets. None the less, we do not derive from this poem as a whole the satisfaction we ask from poetry. Numerous passages are finely written; there is an amusing monologue in the vernacular, and the fifth part is nearly wholly admirable. The section beginning

What is that sound high in the air ...

has a nervous strength which perfectly suits the theme; but he declines to a mere notation, the result of an indolence of the imagination.

Mr Eliot, always evasive of the grand manner, has reached a stage at which he can no longer refuse to recognize the limitations of his medium; he is sometimes walking very near the limits of coherency. But it is the finest horses which have the most tender mouths, and some unsympathetic tug has sent Mr Eliot's gift awry. When he recovers control we shall expect his poetry to have gained in variety and strength from this ambitious experiment.

MR ELIOT'S NEW ESSAYS

Geoffrey West

[...] Undeniably the modern tendency is not to blame a man for his failings and failures – but Mr Eliot has already in "Lancelot Andrewes" declared for medieval as against modern. He denies the ability of the individual to stand alone; destroy communion with God, he asserts, and the most enlightened humanism can yield only disappointment. All these issues are brought to a head in the final essay, which is in purpose a questioning of Mr Babbitt's philosophy of secular humanism from the viewpoint of one accepting a religion of revelation and dogma. Can such humanism, he asks, ever provide an alternative to Christianity – save perhaps temporarily and on a basis of Christian culture? Is not the humanist, suppressing the divine, "left with a human element which may quickly descend again to the animal"? Has humanism ever

For Lancelot Andrewes: Essays on Style and Order, by T. S. Eliot [December 6, 1928]

achieved more than a sporadic accompaniment to a continuous Christianity? Can it, in short, be more than parasitical, secondary to religion? And he replies:–

> To my mind, it always flourishes most when religion has been strong; and if you find examples of humanism which are anti-religious, or at least in opposition to the religious faith of the place and time, then such humanism is purely destructive, for it has never found anything to replace what is destroyed.

The characteristic modern refusal to receive anything upon an authority exterior and anterior to the individual he rejects decisively:–

> Unless by civilization you mean material progress, cleanliness, &c. – which is not what Mr Babbitt means; if you mean a spiritual and intellectual co-ordination on a high level, then it is doubtful whether civilization can endure without religion, and religion without a church.

The essay in its parts and as a whole leads "to the conclusion that the humanistic point of view is auxiliary to and dependent upon the religious point of view. For us, religion is of course Christianity; and Christianity implies, I think, the conception of the Church."

Here, certainly, is nothing new, but from the author of "The Waste Land" it is at first sight astonishing, to say the least. We ourselves can only conceive of Mr Eliot's "act of violence" as consequent upon a dynamic fusion of the need for an object of belief with the desire – the increasing desire – for a universal and continuous rather than a living tradition. He has discovered at once a respite and a continuity. But it is our view that by accepting a higher spiritual authority based not upon the deepest personal experience (for that we must still turn to the poems), but upon the anterior and exterior authority of revealed religion, he has abdicated from his high position. Specifically he rejects modernism for medievalism. But most of us, like Mr Babbitt, have gone too far to draw back. It is to the country beyond the Waste Land that we are compelled to look, and many will consider it the emptier that they are not likely to find Mr Eliot there. Recently he recorded his conviction that Dante's poetry represents a saner attitude towards "the mystery of life" than Shakespeare's. Not a saner, we would say, but simply a different attitude, and to the majority, the great majority, to-day no longer a vital one.

AMONG THESE ROCKS*

Edmund Blunden

[...] Once again, then, Mr Eliot as poet stands as a modern Ecclesiastes, employing symbols and concepts which will not be found easy even by the minds of the time that are fitted by temperament and experience to ascertain their full reference. The scheme of the sequence, which has been shadowed out in this notice, is even now unusual. A fresh generation rises from the ashes. The energies of the human spirit press ahead to joyful illusion, brilliant fancy; and the subtle tones of our poet's consciousness, the pale flowers that spring from this soil of dejection, will remain as "evidence of character" for a period which looked so earnestly to Mr Eliot for poetic wisdom.

AFTER STRANGE GODS†

Alan Clutton-Brock

[...] Mr Eliot's own book may well seem to many readers, even to those who find his orthodoxies entirely acceptable, not the least eccentric sample of modern literature. We may not have any very imposing tradition, but surely we have enough "inherited wisdom of the race," wisdom acquired by learning from mistakes, to be rather shy of attributing to the devil opinions with which we do not agree.

---

*Ash-Wednesday, by T. S. Eliot [May 29, 1930]
†After Strange Gods: A Primer of Modern Heresy, by T. S. Eliot [April 19, 1934]

MR ELIOT IN SEARCH OF
THE PRESENT*

G. Buchanan

[...] *The Family Reunion*, to some extent, reflects the state of the modern theatre, both in its treatment and story. Old appearances are kept up, but always there is a sense of another thing, in this case horrible, ready to explode beneath. At intervals a choric frankness breaks forth, and the Eumenides are sighted for a second in a window embrasure. We realize it is inevitable that the surface will break completely, in the end, and that is all: a negative approach. The general effect is static and descriptive. We had imagined a dynamic and cursive drama, learning from the Greek, but moving away from it too. This is the contrary. Characters are erected like statues (made at Madame Tussaud's) here and there about the desiccated stage. They are the statues of an intellectual commentary, not bold complete figures in Greek sunshine, but tenebrous with nineteenth-century Gothic guilt. [...]

MR T. S. ELIOT'S
CONFESSION†

Philip Tomlinson

"East Coker" is not a pastoral in the Somerset dialect, nor in the dialect of "pure poetry," which Mr Eliot, not for the first time, scorns as a device outworn, the pretty plaything of times when poets had nice manners but only trivial themes – such as *Hamlet* and *Lear* and "Paradise Lost," poems basically misconceived because the motives were insufficient. Hamlet, for instance (no notice need be taken of God and the Devil and the fall of man) not having had sufficient ground for his tragic indecision in such day-to-day

The Family Reunion, by T. S. Eliot [March 25, 1939]
†*East Coker*, by T. S. Eliot [September 14, 1940]

incidents as the murder of his father, the betrayal of his mother and the suicide of his lover. We live in more critical days when there is motive enough to set going poets double Shakespeare's size. What is made of it by Mr Eliot, whose proportions are not of that dimension, but are considerable, considerable enough to create a following, a clique, even a claque – who, it should be acknowledged to him, earn his amused disdain? [...]

Mr Eliot despairs of our days and deeds. And he remains a poet in spite of his efforts to break up his splendid incantations with passages of the prosiest of prose:–

> So here I am, in the middle way, having had twenty years –
> Twenty years largely wasted, the years of *l'entre deux guerres* –
> Trying to learn to use words, and every attempt
> Is a wholly new start, and a different kind of failure
> Because one has only learnt to get the better of words
> For the thing one no longer has to say, or the way in which
> One is no longer disposed to say it.

This is indeed bare enough of poetry, but it is also a confession that he will never try to achieve an *opus consummatum* – a rebuke to the sad ghost of Coleridge who could make only excuses and promises. Mr Eliot has given a fresh and effective cadence to dramatic, lyrical and psychological poetry; and it fails in the long run to satisfy because for the most part it is used as a trick of defiance, an impish gesture, to show he knows all about that kind of thing. And it is unnecessary to say of Mr Eliot, with his rare knowledge of the best that has been done in verse, and his own considerable achievements and bold experiments, that he does know. Even when deploring his "different kinds of failure" he excites the reader with sudden felicities:–

> What is the late November doing
> With the disturbance of the spring
> And creatures of the summer heat,
> And snowdrops writhing under feet
> And hollyhocks that aim too high
> Red into grey and tumble down
> Late roses filled with early snow?
> Thunder rolled by the rolling stars
> Simulates triumphal cars

> Deployed in constellated wars
> Scorpion fights against the Sun
> Until the Sun and Moon go down
> Comets leap and Leonids fly
> Hunt the heavens and the plains
> Whirled in a vortex that shall bring
> The world to that destructive fire
> Which burns before the ice-cap reigns.

The reader has only just visited East Coker when he is lifted with pleasure into this. But he gets no farther, for Mr Eliot immediately apologizes. "That," he says (and there is no need, in view of the pressure on our space, to split the lines up into a visual appearance of poetry, as Mr Eliot does), "that was a way of putting it – not very satisfactory: A periphrastic study in a worn-out poetical fashion, Leaving one still with the intolerable wrestle With words and meanings. The poetry does not matter."

It does not. Poetry is worn out and is hereby consigned to the relics of a romantic past. We need consider only the bare bones, what "the poetry points out." Mr Eliot is disdainful of many things, of most things. His poetry is the poetry of disdain – disdain of the tragic view of life, of the courageous view, of futile sensualists, of poetry, and now even of himself. He is becoming more and more like an embalmer of the nearly dead; he colours their masks with expert fingers to resemble life, but only to resemble. On all their lips is the twisted smile of Prufrock. "In the beginning is my end," says the poet, and "in the end is my beginning." The knowledge gained from experience has only a limited value. We are in a dark wood, in a bramble, our foothold never secure.

> The only wisdom we can hope to acquire
> Is the wisdom of humility: humility is endless.

Humility is noble, and it is noble to come to it and to proclaim it as a faith. There is a grandeur in the humility of the English religious poets, but there is a lack of their ecstasy in "East Coker." Where Vaughan, whose days were as troubled as our own and little less violent, saw eternity the other night and bright shoots of everlastingness, Mr Eliot sees only the dark. "They all go into the dark," all the people in his vision of a world of bankers, men of letters, statesmen, committeemen, contractors, labourers, who eat and work and go to bed and get out of bed. All are for the dark,

> And we go with them, into the silent Funeral,
> Nobody's funeral, for there is no one to bury.

This is a hymn of humility, but a sad one, and somewhat incongruous. For in spite of the animation of his powerful incantations there is more satire than poetry in Mr Eliot's headshaking over a terrible bleak, meaningless world of hollow men, with smell of steaks in passage ways, and satire and humility go strangely together. This is the confession of a lost heart and a lost art. These are sad times, but we are not without hope that Mr Eliot will recover both, finding even that hearts are trumps and that Keats was not far out about the ore in the rift.

EAST COKER

F. R. Leavis

Sir, – Mr Eliot needs no defending, nor do I flatter myself that I am the defender he would choose if he needed one. But as a matter of decency there ought to be some protest against the review of "East Coker" that appears in your issue of yesterday, and I am writing in case no one whose protest would carry more weight has written and made my protest unnecessary.

If your reviewer had pronounced the technique of "East Coker" not altogether successful, or made limiting judgments of value in respect of the mood expressed in the poem, there would have been no call to do more than agree or disagree. What is not permissible in a serious critical journal is to write in contemptuous condescension of the greatest living English poet (what other poet have we now Yeats is gone?) and exhibit a complacent ignorance of the nature of his genius and of the nature of the technique in which that genius is manifested. If "East Coker" were an experiment on unprecedented lines your reviewer would have had some excuse. But the work of a decade and a half has led directly up to it, and it is some years since another critic thought it witty to express his

[Letter] [September 21, 1940]

contempt for "Ash-Wednesday" in a parody entitled "Cinder-Thursday." Your reviewer no doubt feels himself superior in sophistication to the parodist, but his commentary is not at a higher level.

As he himself observes, the cult of Mr Eliot has carried with it a great deal of snobbery. Now that fashion has shifted, some arbiters of taste of a kind familiar in Combination (or Common) Rooms – arbiters who know what poetry is and (as one of them has pronounced) believe that "a line scans when, without any straining of the words of melody, it can be sung to an easy and popular tune" – have found courage to expose themselves as your reviewer did and show that they have never been impressed by this unintelligible stuff. The present seems to me a peculiarly unhappy time for such an exhibition in *The Times Literary Supplement*: our riches of spirit are surely not so superabundant that we can countenance it.

F. R. LEAVIS

Downing College, Cambridge.

MR T. S. ELIOT'S
PROGRESS

Philip Tomlinson

[...] Mr Hayward's selections from the prose writings is no substitute for the body of Mr Eliot's critical work, but they do provide an excellent introduction, offering a glimpse of the whole pattern of his criticism, of his theory of poetry, of his orthodoxy, a rather idiosyncratic orthodoxy, in the affairs of literature, the State and the Church. And the reader is left asking what all this much-discussed iconoclasm amounts to. To read these extracts more or less chronologically, lifted from the particular drift of their arguments, is to find a sensitive man, discontented with his time (like Carlyle, Arnold, Newman), expressing the personal prejudices that have resulted from his experience of life and his wide reading. There is an aloof independence in the progression of Mr Eliot to the bosom of the Church from the fanfares, the

Points of View, by T. S. Eliot [November 8, 1941]

programmes, the intellectual yardsticks and the hair-splitting definitions of disciples. There is a consistent attitude to life and letters, but there is nothing, precisely nothing, to indicate that finality proclaimed by fervid admirers, that infallible, scientific, classic approach which settles the question of literary worth beyond appeal. And we are thankful for it. It is dogmatic enough, although disarmingly and artfully quiet, and is chiefly directed to persuading the reader to enjoy or dislike according to the taste of Mr Eliot. And its value is precisely in that Mr Eliot is a thinker with an interesting mind, who has brooded deeply over the burden of our times and has ranged the literatures of Europe. It is so much in the "tradition" that one wonders where the "revolutionaries" found it breaking new ground. Indeed, it is only in his later work, with the development of his general belief in discipline and his evolution into orthodoxy, that his attitude appears original compared with his contemporaries as he presses backward and they surge forward. [...]

MIDWINTER SPRING

Hugh I'Anson Fausset

[...] "Unless restored" – that is the burden of the poem. The ageing and the old must "become renewed, transfigured, in another pattern." All shall be well then, and Love, "the intolerable shirt of flame," which human power cannot remove, is the means.

> The only hope, or else despair
> Lies in the choice of pyre or pyre –
> To be redeemed from fire by fire.

Mr Eliot's expression of this theme is, at its best, impressive, because he realizes to the full how hard and costly the choice between the two fires is. But while this gives a tension to his utterance and a winter starkness to his imagery, which heightens the sense of a second spring breaking in the concluding lines, it also tends to reduce the music of poetry to the dry discourse of the moralist and the intellectual. His characteristic and recurrent use of

Little Gidding, by T. S. Eliot [December 19, 1942]

the paradox, too, is almost becoming a trick. Even when it defines
truly enough the intrinsic identity of opposites, as in the lines,

> What we call the beginning is often the end
> And to make an end is to make a beginning.

it is dangerously near to the trite. Mr Eliot has stood so long
between the two pyres, intellectually and morally aware of the
meaning of the redemption of one by the other, that we cannot help
wishing he could take, as a poet, an imaginative step forward. For,
to quote two lines of his poem.

> Last year's words belong to last year's language.
> And next year's words await another voice.

A GREAT MAN GONE

G. S. Fraser

A great writer and a great presence has gone from us. Mr T. S. Eliot
was full of years and honours and, in poetry, in drama, in social and
religious commentary, and in criticism had written what he wanted
to write. He might almost be said, with his friend and contemporary, Mr Ezra Pound, to have invented or created the "modern
movement" in Anglo-American poetry. He can be said, also, in a
few seminal essays to have laid the foundations of the view of the
English poetic tradition which has dominated university teaching
in England and the United States over the past thirty or forty years.
[...]
   Mr Eliot was both a shy and a proud man, and some critics have
thought that his insistence in early critical essays on the impersona-
lity of poetic art, on the irrelevance of the romantic ideal of the
poem as spiritual autobiography and self-revelation, on the sharp
distinction between the man who suffers and the artist who creates,
was partly a defensive manoeuvre, springing from an awareness of
how thoroughly, even in his earliest work, he had unlocked his
heart. From the same shyness may have sprung his dislike, up to
Ash Wednesday, of appearing in person as the "I" of one of his

[Article] [January 7, 1965]

poems. Certainly it is easy now to read the whole sequence of his serious and major non-dramatic poems as a kind of spiritual autobiography, the earliest poems presenting sometimes flippantly a mood of scepticism and malaise deepening into one of disgust and horror, *The Waste Land* and *The Hollow Men* marking a point of spiritual crisis, and *Ash Wednesday* and *Four Quartets* recording a process of acceptance of religious belief and slow and painful disciplining of the self. Yet the very painfulness of this process of self-revelation led Mr Eliot, in his later years, to the drama. His dramas still reveal him, but with an indirectness which was congenial to his temperament.

He was a great critic, but his greatness was perhaps flawed by a certain evasiveness. He did not himself either write or re-read his critical prose with pleasure and, though it is both packed and graceful, it is peculiarly elliptical or abrupt in the movement of its thought. Of two great Tory and Christian poets and critics whom he loved, Mr Eliot resembled Dryden in the apparently casual and informal movement of his thought rather than Dr Johnson in his orderly argumentation and combative briskness. He perhaps also resembled Dryden more as a person. Dryden, according to Congreve, had to be drawn out, and hated to appear to intrude; nobody could be kinder and more patient than Mr Eliot with young poets who wanted to consult him, but the courteous reserve of his manner had something faintly deterrent about it, and his close friendships were perhaps few. He lent himself generously to official social occasions, but had not the gift of easy and informal sociability. His conversation was slow, pondered, lapidary, a conversation of hints and implications. Some of these personal characteristics come out in his critical prose, where he always preferred the suggestive phrase or aphorism to the laboriously explicit argument; where Mr Eliot was laboriously explicit, usually, was in defining what he did *not* want to say. His earlier, but not so much his later, essays were enlivened by touches of pert and waspish wit; even in the later essays, written as lecture scripts where the earlier ones had been written mainly as review-articles, a certain demure mischievousness often lurks not very far under the grave surface. In his critical prose, as in his poetry, he appears as distinctly formidable by what he holds in reserve. [...]

One more thing should be said. It is sometimes forgotten how young he was, how new and raw to the complications of human experience, when he began to write great poems; no poet of our century means more to the young who are lucky enough to come on him in their late teens. He remained to the end exposed to the shocks of experience like a young man: "Old men should be explorers." For many readers Mr Eliot's death will be like the death of part of themselves, the death of the shock and exhilaration of one's first insight into the gulfs and heights, the bewildering threats and promises, of life; and it may be Mr Eliot's youngest and newest readers who will feel this most acutely.

INTENSE
TRANSPARENCIES

Christopher Ricks

Admirable in its wealth and in its continence, its tact and its tenacity, Dame Helen Gardner's book on *The Composition of "Four Quartets"* is simply and subtly the most inaugurative work of Eliot studies that we have – or are likely ever to have, since the only substantial manuscripts still unpublished are of work rejected by this most boldly discriminating of poets. Dame Helen is alive to, and equal to, the unique opportunities with which she was entrusted, and since her book breathes a sense (realistic, not belittling) of the great gulf between even the best of literary scholarship and the highest creativity upon which scholarship attends, it may be said without likelihood of misconstruction that she earns the words with which Eliot's loving collaborator John Hayward praised the draft of *Little Gidding* which Eliot sent to him: "the kind of work that consolidates one's faith in the continuity of thought and sensibility when heaven is falling and earth's foundations fail". Hayward's invocation of Housman was no flourish – from the embattled skies of the England of 1941, heaven was falling. [...]

Eliot submitted his work to others' searching as well as to his own, and because it was wartime and the circle was dispersed, there was created an unparalleled body of explicit, intimate, detailed

The Composition of "Four Quartets", by Helen Gardner [September 15, 1978]

epistolary consideration of a poetic masterpiece. As Dame Helen says, it is rare or even unique to find such discussion committed to paper. Eliot had a circle of remarkably acute friends and colleagues, sympathetic and un-kowtowing, of whom Hayward is only (though not merely) the most variously imaginative. It is to Hayward – or rather to the grounded trust between Hayward and Eliot – that the world owes Eliot's "And that, to be restored, our *sickness* must grow worse" (rather than *malady or ailment*); and "*To set a crown upon* your lifetime's effort" (Hayward's "crowning/finis coronat opus", rather than "*The final prizes of* . . ." or "*That put a period to* . . ."): and "*the laceration*/Of laughter at what ceases to amuse"; and "precise *but not pedantic*" itself beautifully apt to all of Hayward's suggestions. It is the hauntingly felicitous "waning dusk" which is at the heart of perhaps the most intractable of all Eliot's wrestlings with words. He tossed and turned: *at dawn . . . the first faint light . . . after lantern-end . . . lantern-out . . . lantern-down . . . lantern-time . . . the antelucan dusk . . . the antelucan hour . . . the antelucan dark*. And what was inspired about Hayward's suggestion of "waning dusk", astonishingly, is that it rightly defied Eliot's clear wish to make it clear that this was morning dusk and not evening dusk. For *waning* cannot but suggest the diminution of light, even while (even though) if the dark-sounding dusk wanes, the light must wax. It was a genially cooperative subconscious which moved Eliot, after all those efforts to find words with which to express this matter, and after he had accepted "waning dusk", to write to Hayward: "I cannot find words to express a proper manifestation of my gratitude for your invaluable assistance".

Yet Eliot thrived not only upon Hayward's poetic imagination, but also upon Geoffrey Faber's imaginative prosaicness, his implacably courteous shrewdness. Faber's comments were particularly apt and humorous whenever Eliot deviated into what Faber called "lecture-stigmata" ("I have suggested also . . .", or "Now, the point is . . ."). Faber was therefore quick to spot the dangerous moments when Eliot's utterances, by being lugubriously total, betokened a failure of sincerity or of humility. "The hint unguessed, the gift not understood, is Incarnation". Faber: "Isn't this in want of *some* qualification? You must guess and understand, or you couldn't say it; and you wouldn't claim to be the only percipient, would you?" Whereupon, pricked by Faber's percipience, Eliot doubled the truthful force of his asseveration by halving it: "The hint half guessed, the gift half understood, is Incarnation." That Eliot understood the truth of others' guesses about such things is itself part of his genius. His is an art which acknowledges the inevitability of some wincing when the truthtelling of others indicts one's failure to tell the truth, yet it is an art which manages not to wince away. One of the few occasions when Eliot silently refuses to acknowledge such a truth (the rarity of such refusals brings home his exceptional openness as a creator, his large disinterestedness) is à propos of the crack at Freud in *The Dry Salvages*: "To explore the womb, or tomb, or dreams." Faber made what Dame Helen drily calls a "dry comment" against Eliot's words "all these are usual . . . and always will be": "It's perhaps an unfair comment to say that psycho-analysis is a very *new* addition to the list."

The MS material is of remarkable and diverse interest, and it is deployed with great lucidity and handsomeness. (The printers, the University Press, Oxford, and the publishers, Faber and Faber, must share in the congratulations.) Eliot was right to decide that even his redemptive powers with language could not restore the word subservience to a proper praising: every word doing its part "In subservience to the phrase". But Dame Helen's work upon Eliot's words does evince a principled subservience. And, as I wished to make clear in the opening sentence of this review, hers is a book of remarkable continence. The temptation to remark upon her own discoveries, upon the significance and the imaginative force of Eliot's changes, must at every point have been almost irresistible. But to have yielded to it would not only have blurred the genre of this work of critical scholarship but would also have made for gigantism, arbitrariness, or paralysis. Since almost every one of Eliot's minutest changes of punctuation, capitalization, and rhythm, is of true significance, how could the scholar-guide ever fare forward except by a continual effort of "Ardour and selflessness and self-surrender"?

By the same token it is a difficult book to review, not just because there is so much on each page which reasonably beseeches comment, but also because it may sound as if the reviewer is handsomely drawing the author's attention to something inadvertently left unremarked.

Still, as an instance of the revelatory power of the MSS, revealing not something other than the poem (some sort of secret) but rather how it was that the poem perfected its manifest art, we might take the opening of the Dantesque section of *Little Gidding*, the greatest – because the most humanly substantial and passionately chastened – passage Eliot ever wrote. (This section, of seventy-two lines, occupies twenty-six pages of this book, and might occupy patient attention for years.) The first draft begins:

> At the uncertain hour before daybreak
> > Toward the ending of interminable night
> > At the incredible end of the unending
> After the dark dove with the flickering tongue
> > Had made his incomprehensible descension
> > While the dead leaves still rattled on like tin
> Over the asphalte where no other sound was
> > Between three angles whence the smoke arose
> > I met one walking, loitering and hurried
> As if blown towards me like the metal leaves
> > Before the urban dawn wind unresisting.

The final text is:

> In the uncertain hour before the morning
> > Near the ending of interminable night
> > At the recurrent end of the unending
> After the dark dove with the flickering tongue
> > Had passed below the horizon of his homing
> > While the dead leaves still rattled on like tin
> Over the asphalt where no other sound was
> > Between three districts whence the smoke arose
> > I met one walking, loitering and hurried
> As if blown towards me like the metal leaves
> > Before the urban dawn wind unresisting.

To be grateful for this book as magnificently fecundating is to acknowledge that it makes possible, as grounded critical speculation, a range of criticism which it was itself forced often to eschew. One of Eliot's root imaginative decisions here was metrical; as he himself later said (and as Dame Helen quietly pointed out in her book *The Art of T. S. Eliot* nearly thirty years ago), he created – as some kind of equivalent to Dante's terza rima – a simple alternation of masculine and feminine endings. Hence by an imaginative stroke of great simplicity and variability, the particular music of the

English heroic line is here a repeated flowing and then ebbing, a swell and a forebearance, such as is felt throughout the passage. The effect is felt by all responsive readers, and the means by which Eliot achieved it, the alternation of an unstressed final syllable with a stressed one, is recognised by many or most such readers – though even as recently as 1973 it was possible for someone to publish a book on Eliot which said, with self-contented imperceptiveness, "Eliot found that the English language did not adapt itself to the rhyming pattern of terza rima, and contented himself with an occasional and irregular chime of half-rhyme".

The interest of the MS is in its pressing upon us how it was that Eliot hoped to let the alternating rhythm be felt as pressing itself upon us. For the striking thing about the MS is that there only the third and the last line ended with what is our most common, the most naturally impinging, feminine ending: -*ing*. As with a great deal of great poetry, in part Eliot's achievement is to incorporate immediately an undidactic and tacit assistance as to how we should hear his poetry, and one crucial thing about the final text is the way, at once tactful and unignorable, by which the opening lines 1, 3 and 5 now all end in -*ing*. The art needs tact in order that it rise above the artful, and the tact is instinctive not only in Eliot's not letting all three of the endings be the easy participial -*ing*, but also in the way in which the even lines 2 and 4 have their -*ing* endings too, but not as endings ("ending" being not an ending but within the second line, and "flickering" being a flickering within the fourth). So it is not a mere assignment of -*ing* to the odd lines, but a plaiting, a moving in and out. And it is this weaving which returns at the end of this eerie sentence itself both "loitering and hurried", when that final word "unresisting" – "Before the urban dawn wind unresisting." – gives us exactly the right sense of rounding out, and rounding up, the sentence.

Nowhere is Eliot's sense of rhythm more assured – and a good thing too, since here rhythm must be in the front of our consciousness – than when he comes to use the word "rhythm" itself. Hence the lovely rhythmical change early in *The Dry Salvages*, when we arrive – after argumentative elongations – at the clearing: "His rhythm was present in the nursery dooryard ...". Or here:

> When the train starts, and the passengers are settled
> To fruit, periodicals and business letters

(And those who saw them off have left the platform)
Their faces relax from grief into relief,
To the sleepy rhythm of a hundred hours.

The word *relief* is a surprising contraction of *relax from grief*, as if it
were describing not a relaxing but a contracting, and the last line is
an inspired revision from "To the monotone of a hundred hours".
Not only does "sleepy rhythm" do its somnolent work while
awakening us to its own rhythm (as we are, for all our sleepiness,
very conscious of the rhythm when in a train), it also supports the
rhythmical felicity of *hours*, a word the sleepy rhythm of which here
is in its being neither one syllable nor two, and so opening the end
of the line out into something relaxed, relieved, a drowsy
insouciant uncertainty such as here attends the very saying of the
word. Tennyson said of *tired* in his lines –

> Music that gentlier on the spirit lies,
> Than tired eyelids upon tired eyes –

"making the word neither monosyllabic nor disyllabic, but a
dreamy child of the two". Eliot created a different, a darker
uncertainty within his word *hour* (this time pinioned within the
line, instead of free at its end), in the rhythm which opens the
Dantesque section: "In the uncertain hour before the morning
…". […]

THE COMPREHENSIVE
IDEAL

John Casey

Lucretius and Dante each wrote a poetic masterpiece that also
expressed a system of philosophy. The achievement is as rare as the
ambition is common. Wordsworth never wrote his philosophical
poem; and Johnson said of Pope's *Essay on Man* that "never was
penury of knowledge and vulgarity of sentiment so happily

T. S. Eliot's Intellectual and Poetic Development, 1909-1922, by Piers Gray
[September 10, 1982]

disguised". The *professional* philosopher who is also a great poet is one of the rarest of beings.

T. S. Eliot was a professional philosopher in the modern, academic sense of the term. His thesis on F. H. Bradley, several philosophical articles, a Harvard seminar paper, "The interpretation of primitive ritual" (much of which is published for the first time in Piers Gray's book), strongly suggest that he could have had a distinguished career as an academic philosopher, had he not chosen a better course.

The pioneer work on Eliot's philosophy and its pervasive presence in his poetry was done by Hugh Kenner in *The Invisible Poet* and there is not a very great deal of importance to be added. What Dr Gray has done, with skill and delicacy, is to show in much more detail how the poetry and criticism in the period up to and including *The Waste Land* reflects Eliot's philosophical ideas, and how Eliot's critical language is redolent of the concepts of philosophical Idealism.

There are dangers in extracting a set of propositions from a poet's work and presenting them as his "beliefs". This is partly because the doctrines a poet entertains in his poetry need not be ones he actually holds. (We can fully appreciate the "Ode on Intimations of Immortality" without attributing to Wordsworth an actual belief in Platonism.) But also beliefs may have a different existence in poetry from the one they have in philosophy or religion. Certainly Eliot was himself profoundly sceptical about the relations between thought and belief in poetry, and thought and belief outside it. He said that poetry offered not thought but its "emotional equivalent", that it was Shakespeare's business "to express the greatest emotional intensity of his time based on whatever his time happened to think", and that "neither Shakespeare nor Dante did any real thinking". Yet he confessed that his dislike of Shelley's verse might arise from a dislike of Shelley's beliefs. He also once suggested that literary criticism would need to be completed by criticism from a definite ethical and religious position. Apart from some glancing blows at Lawrence, he never attempted this "completion", and *After Strange Gods* was never reprinted.

Eliot's uncertainty about belief and poetry probably stems from the very philosophical tradition in which he was educated. It is the common doctrine of Idealism that the possibilities of thought determine the possibilities of experience. "Facts" are interpretations of experience from particular "points of view". Hence it will be natural for an Idealist philosopher to hold that the coherence and objectivity of the world as human beings construct and interpret it will be guaranteed only by the cooperative endeavour of a human community which unites all "points of view" into a comprehensive whole. Another characteristic Idealist doctrine – that truth is a matter of "coherence" among propositions rather than of "correspondence" between particular propositions and particular states of affairs – will go with this. The completest truth will be the completest coherence, the largest comprehensiveness of points of view. This comprehensiveness will seek also to relate the present to the past. The human cooperative endeavour to produce a coherent world, and to relate past to present, might result in a "tradition". The idea of tradition – a live and practical sense of the relation of our lives to those of our ancestors – will become pivotal in our understanding of human society and human knowledge. It was F. H. Bradley – Eliot's philosophical Master – who defined history as the expression of the "human tradition".

Eliot's most famous essay is "Tradition and the Individual Talent". In that essay he sets out an ideal of order and comprehensiveness expressed in extravagant terms:

> No poet, no artist of any sort, has his complete meaning alone.... The existing monuments form an ideal order among themselves, which is modified by the introduction of the new ... work of art among them ... the whole existing order must, if ever so slightly, be altered.

It is often not appreciated how unconservative, indeed how subversive Eliot's idea of tradition is. The *whole* existing order is altered by the really new work of art. The present alters the past just as the past influences the present. Eliot's idea of tradition is wholly anti-historical. We create the past from a sense of what can be done in the present. Eliot wishes to see the whole of European literature as part of a timeless present. In this he is very close to Ezra Pound who wrote, in *The Spirit of Romance*, of a literature "where the real time is independent of the apparent, and where many dead men are our grandchildren's contemporaries, while many of our contemporaries have already been gathered into Abraham's bosom, or some more fitting receptacle". Eliot's claim for tradition is that it enables a critic to have a "perception of relation that involves an organized view of the whole course of European poetry from Homer". And if one takes that claim seriously it will be very natural to derive it from a philosophical standpoint – in this case what F. H. Bradley says in his influential essay "The Presuppositions of Critical History":

> every man's present standpoint ought to determine his belief in respect to *all* past events: but to no man do I dictate what his present standpoint ought to be. *Consistency* is the word that I have emphasized.

The trouble is that neither Eliot nor Pound really attempted, as critics, to combine their sense of what it was possible for the individual talent to make new with that ideal completeness that would make it possible for a poet to write with the whole of literature from Homer in his bones. The past they give us is extremely selective, even fragmentary: Eliot's relative lack of interest in the Romantics, in Pope, in Milton, and, for that matter, in Shakespeare – all suggests a sense of the past that is guided less by an ideal of comprehensiveness, and much more by his central creative interests. Matthew Arnold who, with his "touchstones", produced a comparably "timeless" notion of literary tradition, and who attempted to place the English Romantics within a classical tradition of "high seriousness" – to see them *as* modern classics – produced a picture of the past and its existence in the present that is much more acceptable to the conventional literary historian.

Piers Gray relates Eliot's idea of criticism to his poetry, and sets both against the ideal of "comprehensiveness" implied by the Idealist tradition. He moves rather directly from the poetry to the philosophy – for instance reading *The Waste Land* as expressing a search for "an absolute degree of comprehensiveness". The trouble with looking for such a direct relation is that it leads one to read the poem as simply ironical: what we are shown is a gap between the actual experience of modern man and a postulated ideal of comprehensiveness. And it is true that the poem opens with an allusion to Chaucer's *Prologue*, as well as to the late Latin poem *Pervigilium Veneris* – poems which enact an awareness of "the mind of Europe and of our own country": ("April is the cruellest month, breeding/Lilacs out of the dead land".) It is true also that the "mind of Europe" rapidly degenerates into the mind of *Mittel Europa*, helpless individuals helplessly reliving their personal memories: ("And when we were children, staying at the arch-duke's,/My cousin's, he took me out on a sled,/And I was frightened.") But the contrast between fragmentary modern experience and a postulated ideal unity does not produce simply a painful irony. The contrast between horrible or painful scenes in the present – the neurasthenic Cleopatra, the seduced typist – and eloquent versions of them from Shakespeare or Sappho *dramatizes* the present and gives it an intense vitality. Eliot is doing what he learned from the French Symbolists – finding the greatest possible intensity in the imagery of modern life. The gap between the fragmentary and the comprehensive in the *poetry* has a quite different character – is much more complex than – an analogous gap between incomplete and complete experience as this is understood by philosophy. That is to say, poetry can be ambivalent about such a disparity, whereas Idealist philosophy is governed by a much simpler notion of "comprehensiveness". In philosophy the fully comprehensive is the fully real; whereas in *The Waste Land* the vitality of the fragmentary is itself fully real.

THE MODERNIST
MALGRÉ LUI

Donald Davie

It would not be particularly spiteful to wonder if the flood of books about Eliot, a river that has been in full spate for as long as any of us can remember, doesn't have its source in the commonplaceness of this poet's personality. Being commonplace, Eliot's personality is one that almost anyone can sympathize with. If we add, "except of course that he was very intelligent", the exception will seem to some to qualify the assertion to the point where it has no force. But this doesn't follow: the exceptional intelligence moved along tracks, and within categories (for the most part binary and

T. S. Eliot, by Peter Ackroyd. *T. S. Eliot: A Study in Character and Style*, by Ronald Bush [September 21, 1984]

opposed), that were indeed commonplace, not just in the United States but also in Britain, through the years – 1884 to 1914 – when Eliot was growing up. Indeed, more lamentably, the radical *either/ or* (in one gross formulation, impulsive yearning versus civic order) is what young and energetic minds still, in 1984, experience as the choice before them – which explains why Eliot's arcane and fastidious poetry has become, as it did even in his lifetime, a talismanic sacred deposit which hardly anyone is brave enough to question. Perhaps because Peter Ackroyd comes to Eliot after a study of Pound, he is brave enough to raise the question; and though he does so only suavely and by implication, it is this that makes his biography necessary and important.

Recently, other wary champions of Eliot, recognizing the vulnerable commonplaceness of his ideas and of the antinomies which he dredged from among them, have claimed for him, over and above his intelligence in the ordinary sense (sharp and probing), another intelligence, more fluctuant and fed from deeper sources, which they call – not without some prompting from the poet's own later lectures and essays – "musical". Ackroyd makes this claim. But the truth is surely that Eliot had at best a scrupulous ear for *vers libéré* – itself, so some would argue, an inherently coarse and compromised medium; in strict metre Hardy, and in true *vers libre* Pound, went far beyond him. And after all to say of Eliot that he was commonplace is only a rude way of saying that he was representative. It is entertaining therefore to see one commentator after another insist on the specialness of Eliot's tormented pasage through life. In fact what they see in that mirror is only their own torments (real ones, we need not doubt) writ large and writ special. [...]

The commonplaceness, of the sensibility, and of the lived witness; that we are forced back to. Bush at sometimes wearisome length establishes how the overtly "modernist" Eliot gave way, step by step in the years after *The Waste Land*, to the incantatory poet whose first and perhaps last hero was Edgar Allan Poe. The seemingly modernist poet of *The Waste Land* and *Poems, 1920* appears in the perspective as an artfully provisional and temporary persona – not fabricated, as some have thought, at the behest of Ezra Pound, but rather a product of that intelligence, Eliot's which showed itself at this as at all times predominantly an intelligence for manoeuvre, for polemical and rhetorical strategies. There is no question of betrayal, of "selling out"; on this showing Eliot's was throughout a late-Romantic sensibility, which adroitly cornered the market for a time by pretending to be otherwise, which then (the market once cornered) threw off the wraps and re-appeared in its true colours. And after all we hardly need Bush's close arguments to prove this; for how else can we explain how the author of *The Waste Land* should have become, as a middle-aged publisher, the patron of Edwin Muir? [...]

Ackroyd's touch deserts him lamentably, I think, when he proceeds to his peroration:

> Both as a writer and as a man, his genius lay in his ability to resist the subversive tendencies of his personality by fashioning them into something larger than himself. His work represents the brilliant efflorescence of a dying culture: he pushed that culture together by an act of will, giving it a shape and context which sprang out of his own obsessions, and the certainties which he established were rhetorical certainties. In so doing he became a symbol of the age, and his poetry became its echoing music – with its brooding grandeur as well as its bleakness, its plangency as well as its ellipses, its rhythmical strength as well as its theatrical equivocations.

This is distinguised writing; yet surely this dying fall should be resisted. For what is this culture that is declared to be "dying"? English? Anglo-American? European? And what does it mean in any case to say of a culture that it is dead or dying? Surely we may think that a culture dies only through a failure of nerve on the part of those who should sustain it, and purvey its values; by a willingness on their part to assist in its premature obsequies. It would be more modest and more plausible to say that Eliot's poetry witnesses, not to the death of a culture, but only to the end of an era. What happens surely, at the time of such an end, is that the ruling élite and the governing class (there is normally much overlap between them) prove themselves incapable of exercising the role that history has delegated to them. In Eliot's lifetime the high bourgeoisie of England – so it might be argued – proved itself a class or a caste from which in this way virtue had departed. Eliot, who as an American did not have to ally himself with this caste, in fact chose to do so. (This is the meaning of his Bloomsbury connections.) The era of their dominance is decisively over, though the veneration accorded not unjustly to Eliot's handling of language has the effect of concealing the sterility and frivolity of those for whom he chose to act as spokesman. What will survive the dissolution of this hegemony, and its suppression by some other, is that part or aspect of Eliot's writing which makes it part of the by no means dying culture of Christendom.

T. S. ELIOT

Gabriel Josipovici

Sir, – Why is everyone so keen to bury Eliot? Donald Davie (September 21) quotes Peter Ackroyd as saying, at the end of his new biography of the poet, that "his work represents the brilliant efflorescence of a dying culture", and himself opines that "It would be more modest and more plausible to say that Eliot's poetry witnesses, not to the death of a culture, but only to the end of an era". Yet from the moment I came to England at the age of fifteen and first read *The Waste Land*, I have felt that Eliot's poetry – all of it, from "Prufrock" to "Little Gidding" – was the most living and vital body of work in English, speaking to us as no more recent writer in English has been able to do of the pain and – yes – the exhilaration of exile and displacement. It might seem odd, in the light of Eliot's later prose writings, to see him as the spokesman for such experiences, but then the relation of any writer's best work to his theories is a good deal more complex than many critics of Eliot have made out. Why does a painter like R. B. Kitaj, who could hardly be accused of belonging to a gentlemanly, bygone era, find inspiration in Eliot as well as in Kafka and Walter Benjamin? It could be because Eliot, like Kafka, speaks not just of his own present but of ours, and does not only speak *of* it, but – much more important – speaks it. By this I mean that Eliot's style and content are of course one; he is exciting because he does not simply depict failure, fragmentation, the loss of community, but his style and language live that loss and so make it bearable. And it is not just the early Eliot I am talking about. It is merely bad reading to see "Ash

[Letter] [September 28, 1984]

Wednesday" and *Four Quartets* as purely religious poems in a style utterly different from that of the early poems. So many philosophical and theoretical debates going on at present – about intertextuality, about the relation of speaker to speech, of past to present – are gradually feeling their way towards the formulations not just of Wittgenstein (who is now seen as much less English than an earlier generation of philosophers tried to make out), but also of the Eliot of the *Quartets*. My own impression is that he is a figure not of the past but of the future – that we have yet to catch up with him. Why English literary (as opposed to artistic and musical) culture should be so keen to bury him is of course itself an interesting sociological and historical question.

GABRIEL JOSIPOVICI

A SCIENTIFIC
EXPERIMENT

Arthur Clutton-Brock

If Dostoevsky had believed nothing, on principle; if he had rejected all values from a disgust of false values and yet had pursued the same method, what would his books have been like? The answer, we think, is to be found in this book. Mr Wyndham Lewis pursues the method of Dostoevsky; he relates, not a story made by external events, but the, seemingly causeless, events of the mind – events often rather unconscious than conscious. Like Dostoevsky, and like Chinese poets, he does not try to rationalize those events. He does not give his own explanation, or the characters' explanation, of what happens to them. He relates what happens in, rather than to, their minds. Like Dostoevsky, he has unthought determinism. Each one is a fount of causation in himself; but for him, as not for Dostoevsky, the result, at present, is chaos. He proves that by his method, and with his deliberate refusal of principles, dogmas and values, you cannot produce a work of art, though you can produce a very interesting document. His people, artists living in Paris, have all themselves refused principles,

Tarr, by P. Wyndham Lewis [July 11, 1918]

dogmas and values. Either, like Tarr, an Englishman, they spend their time watching what happens in their minds, or like Kreisler, a German and the real subject of the book, they function quite blindly, function themselves to death. Now real people have principles, dogmas, and values, whatever be the origin of them. Mr Wyndham Lewis has left them out in a scientific rather than an artistic experiment. He himself seems to have taken a disgust against all the lies people tell themselves, against all the delusive play of the consciousness. He will deal with what lies below it. For him consciousness seems to have no reality at all, no connexion with what lies below it. His people are, not machines, but living creatures utterly disconnected from each other, or connected only by appetites which, themselves, are as much illusion as consciousness. [...]

THE WILD BODY

A. S. McDowall

Mr Wyndham Lewis's originality of vein, as well as that controlled violence of his which is given its own way now and then, are very deliberately employed in his new book of stories, THE WILD BODY (Chatto and Windus, 7s. 6d. net). They are used to construct a comic world, in which he shows us, with a characteristic frankness, not merely his puppets but the strings that pull them. Theories about laughter and the comic spirit, ingenious and seldom conclusive, are usually to be found in whimsical essays or in volumes more solemn than their subject. Mr Wyndham Lewis states his attitude in the course of a book of stories. This might expose the tales themselves to some risk, but on the whole we are glad he has taken it; for, while the main traits are visible enough, the two little essays which he has slipped in illuminate their motive. Human beings, then, are comic in his view in so far as they are things, or physical bodies, behaving as persons. This sounds like the inversion of Bergson's idea that we laugh whenever we find a person behaving like a thing; and Mr Lewis's scheme is a comedy of matter as well as of mechanism. [...]

The Wild Body, by Wyndham Lewis [December 8, 1927]

We may ask why we should have to accept Mr Lewis's emphasis on the body. But if we do accept it, playing the game according to its rules, a stimulus will repay us. It is the satisfaction to be got from a world that is true to its own queer laws and also to the idiosyncrasy of its author. The writing has an astonishingly vigorous precision. Mr Lewis's originality reflects a quality of mind alert, subtle, and powerful; and a mental force of this kind is precisely what is rare in fiction.

THE CHILDERMASS

Alan Clutton-Brock

Until the two remaining sections of Mr Wyndham Lewis's THE CHILDERMASS (Chatto and Windus, 8s. 6d. net) have been published, it would be unwise to say much about the opinions here offered, which take up a great part of this romantic *conte philosophique*. It will be sufficient to say that Mr Lewis here continues with his opinions about the mob, its hatred of great men, of the intellect and of art, and that he also deals with the desire of the average man to be a child, and with homosexuality. When the average man dies he becomes, according to Mr Lewis, more markedly and more horribly what Mr Lewis finds him on earth; and there are, we are told, special provisions that this may occur, while heaven itself is a heaven for children. [...]

Mr Lewis writes in that difficult variety of styles which is often employed nowadays to express the mood and temper of the characters as they are described or made to speak. We cannot say that there is any beauty in Mr Lewis's prose, but that it is extravagantly expressive there can be no doubt. Mr Lewis's fertility and invention are extraordinary. Whether there should be so much expression in what is after all primarily a *conte philosophique* is a doubtful question. Hitherto the exquisite lucidity of *Candide* has had no bad effect. But Mr Lewis's invention is certainly happily employed on the topography of the other world where the souls wait before entering their horrible heaven – for horrible it is, as the

The Childermass, by Wyndham Lewis [July 19, 1928]

Hyperideans point out, though we have not yet much description of it. [...]

THE APES OF GOD*

Orlo Williams

[...] Mr Wyndham Lewis's intention, so far as we can gather it, has been to express indignation in a long, coarsely-worded and rumbustious satire of certain elements in modern society which he considers deleterious. Unfortunately, the excess of his indignation is disproportionate to the importance of its objects and has blinded him to the fact that the imitation of triviality and tomfoolery is not in itself comic. This criticism applies particularly to the immensely long section on Lord Osmund's Lenten party, which is a kind of interminable harlequinade that taxes the reader's patience to the utmost limit. Naturally, the author's talent being what it is, one finds throughout the book pages of harsh and boisterous satirical description which are notable in themselves. [...]

Unless there is more meaning in it than meets the eye, this is one of the steppes or tundras of modern literature, only to be attempted by the hardy or the insatiably curious.

HITLER AND HIS
MOVEMENT†

Harold Stannard

[...] Mr Lewis gets on to firmer ground and adopts a more critical tone when he expounds the real character of Hitlerite anti-Semitism. In England the vulgarity which disfigures modern life is attributed to America; in Germany, and not only by Hitlerites, it is set to the discredit of the Jews. In this connexion it must be remembered that the vulgar Jew of the British caricaturist is largely

*The Apes of God, by Wyndham Lewis [July 3, 1930]
†Hitler, by Wyndham Lewis [April 16, 1931]

a reality in Central Europe. Still Mr Lewis believes that even in Germany the Jew is something of a scapegoat, and that Hitler himself, if he attained to power, would treat Einstein with proper honour. [...]

RED MEN IN LONDON

Geoffrey West

The first and the final parts of Mr Lewis's novel are set in contemporary Spain, and it is in these that he shows both most agreeably and most powerfully his capacity as a writer of fiction. There is a suggestion of the pictorial quality of Conrad in the account of the attempted escape of the English Communist organiser, Percy Hardcaster, from the Spanish prison; and the concluding motor-car dash of the duped artist, Victor Stamp, and his wife Margot to get across the frontier into France owes its thrillingness to much the same brilliant, concrete abilities.

The sections between – the greater part of the book – are more commonplace in their Bloomsbury setting, and also less palatable in their concentration upon almost entirely unlikeable types, the Red Men of arty, bohemian London as seen by Mr Lewis's satirical eye. [...]

Many readers will feel the book to be slightly over-tinctured with Mr Lewis's own anti-Communist outlook, and to turn at times too easily to mere satirical guying. It is, moreover, by intention more destructive than creative in purpose, trampling on weeds rather than cultivating blossoms. Nevertheless it remains electrically alive.

The Revenge for Love, by Wyndham Lewis [May 22, 1937]

THE PRICE OF
SINGULARITY

Julian Symons

The publication of a new edition of Mr Wyndham Lewis's first novel, *Tarr*, together with Mr Geoffrey Grigson's explanatory and introductory pamphlet, provides an opportunity for reconsidering Mr Lewis's talent specifically as a writer of fiction, and the reasons why during the past decade and a half this talent has been so markedly ignored. It was not – comparatively youthful readers may need to be reminded – it was not always so. Time was when Mr Eliot applauded the author of *Tarr* as a fascinating personality, a modern magician with the energy of a caveman, when W. B. Yeats found parts of *The Childermass* as powerful as *Gulliver's Travels*, when even Mr Cyril Connolly wrote of the "aggressive intellectual vitality" and the fine sensibility of a writer whom he found later to be driven merely by the spur of envious animosity. *Tarr* seemed to many critics, upon its publication in 1918, a signpost for English literature, a truly revolutionary work in style and feeling, that rejected the broad well-metalled road of Edwardian achievement in favour of a rocky but more interesting track. To-day it should be acknowledged that if *Tarr* heralded a revolution, it was a revolution that failed. The young novelists of the twenties and thirties turned away from the Edwardians, certainly: but they did not turn in the direction of Mr Lewis. Scores of contemporary writers have been influenced, at fifth or second-hand, by the thick verbal flux of James Joyce, or the thinner fluidities of Virginia Woolf; few have taken for their model the manner or the attitude developed in *Tarr*.

Manner and attitude are in fact inseparable. Mr Lewis's style is already, in this first novel, the hardest, sharpest and most distinctive in modern literature: a style expressive of a personal asceticism far more interested in ideas about the future of life and art than in the subtleties of human relationships as they preoccupied, say, Henry James or Joseph Conrad. "Deadness is

Tarr, by Wyndham Lewis. *A Master of our Time*, by Geoffrey Grigson [July 13, 1951]

the first condition for art," says Tarr, who may in these words be identified with his creator. "The second is the absence of soul, in the human and sentimental sense . . . good art must have no inside." The characters in this novel – Tarr himself and his mistress Bertha, the German Kreisler with his passion for destruction, and the fringe of artistic hangers-on – are delineated with an utter unconcern for their souls. With an eye for fantastic and significant outer detail unequalled by any English writer since Dickens, Mr Lewis conveys the feebleness of the hanger-on Hobson by describing his large, athletic but neglected body, with its appropriate trappings of dejected jacket and pendant trouser-seat; Tarr's' gauche puritanism is expressed by his white collar shining in the sun, his bowler hat striking out clean lines in space. Such an external approach, perhaps at this time only half-consciously chosen, is remarkable in its effect upon the page. The course of English literature had moved unvaryingly away from such external description and in the direction of internal analysis from the time when, in her three great novels, *The Mill on the Floss, Middlemarch* and *Daniel Deronda*, George Eliot began a fictional inquiry into the springs of human conduct from a psychological, rather than a strictly ethical, point of view.

That inquiry, elaborated by succeeding novelists as various as George Moore and Anthony Trollope, may be thought to have reached its peak of subtlety and interest in Henry James, and to show in later writers, however talented, the iridescence of a fictional convention in decay. Nevertheless, the still further elaboration of this convention by many notable prose writers of the twenties, such considerable figures as James Joyce and D. H. Lawrence among them, was a prime reason for the neglect of Mr Lewis's example. As Mr Grigson puts it, a little too simply:

> In the one camp Joyce, or Lawrence, or Virginia Woolf, flux which is captured; in the other Lewis and that which is made and made stiff. Obviously Lewis was going to be in isolation.

It would be inappropriate to analyse here the particular social pressures that forced fine artists along this path: but as a result of them the author of *Tarr*, so far from leading a revolutionary movement, certainly found himself in isolation. Isolation has its pleasures, and its very evident dangers. In Mr Lewis's case it gave the opportunity for a wide and brilliant analysis of modern society in such metaphysical and sociological excursions as *The Art of Being Ruled, Time and Western Man* and *Paleface*; it led to his half-humorous and half-serious, but upon the whole unfortunate, assumption of the role of "The Enemy"; and it provoked him to ignore rather often what Mr Grigson calls "the supine civility of author to author." The first section of an unfinished but masterly work, *The Childermass* (1928), and *The Apes of God* (1930), show their author at a height of literary power: but both books are marked by an insistence upon the influence of sexual inversion in contemporary life which appears as a personal obsession more than an effective criticism, and *The Apes of God* by personal portraits which are upon the whole weakening to this novel as a work of art.

Both *The Childermass* and *The Apes of God* are works of great imaginative power, containing scenes and images unrivalled in modern literature. *The Childermass* is set outside Heaven, where the unadmitted bicker, speculate, and argue about the nature of art and society with a cynical Bailiff who dispenses unheavenly justice from his Punch-and-Judy-shaped court. The sultry scene of rocks and sand, with swarthy peons moving over the desert, and the threatening hosts of Beelzebub murmuring heavily in the distance, is wonderfully well suggested. Even in its fragmentary state this extravaganza is full of riotous or gawky comedy; and its characters, lacking soul "in the human and sentimental sense," have their physical appearances stamped as if in metal. Typical of several portraits, alike in power and clarity, is the epicene but dryly schoolmasterish figure of Pullman waiting outside Heaven:

> At the ferry-station there is a frail figure planted on the discoloured stones facing the stream. . . . Sandy-grey hair in dejected spandrils strays in rusty wisps; a thin rank moustache is pressed by the wind, bearing first from one direction then another, back against the small self-possessed mouth. Shoulders high and studious, the right arm hugs, as a paradoxical ally, a humble limb of nature, an oaken sapling Wicklow-bred. The suit of nondescript dark grey for ordinary day-wear, well cut and a little shabby, is coquettishly tight and small, on the trunk and limbs of a child. Reaching up with a girlish hand to the stick cuddled

under the miniature oxter, with the other hand the glasses are shaded against the light, as the eyes follow the flight of a wild duck along the City walls northward, the knee slightly flexed to allow the body to move gracefully from the slender hips.

The Apes of God, again, offers dozens of such exact and memorable portraits from Lord Osmund, with "his blond pencilled pap rising straight from his sloping forehead: galb-like wings to his nostrils – the goat-like profile of Edward the Peace-maker," to the decaying gossip-column beauty Lady Fredigonde with her head only left alive and movable "upon the ruined clockwork of her trunk." The sexual and social antics of these galvanized puppets are shown largely by means of dialogue which, through a highly original device of style, enlarges mercilessly the inanities, *clichés* and small acidities of common conversation. The book ends with the General Strike, and the offence felt by the wrigglingly feminine hero Dan at offers of lifts from strangers; in moronic ignorance of what is going on, he thinks that he is being accosted. Such an incident is an appropriate end to the book; for the activities of these apes of godhead are meant to represent, in their creator's words, a society groping back to its childhood "beneath the shadow of a revolutionary situation."

The neglect of Mr Lewis as a literary artist is owed partly to his awareness of his shadow. Deeply concerned by the problem of power, he accepted in the twenties the inevitability of a cata-strophic, not a gradual, solution to the problems of modern society. He had come to the conclusion in 1928 that so much disturbed unhappy, serious-minded intellectuals five or ten years later:

> It is not even, then, that I have no beliefs that could be described as " political," but that no single individual can, as things are, effectively, *be* anything, politically, at all, except quite simply a "capitalist" or a "communist." Politically, if you do not thrill at the thought of the modern Capitalist State, and all that it entails, then you must be a communist ... Your "politics" are settled for you, then, once and for all. Physical forces of such magnitude wither those delicate playful illusions that, each in his way, the

Shelleys and Shaws have enjoyed and got so much innocent amusement out of.

It is one thing to understand: it is another, for a man aware of the wide range of his own talents as writer and thinker, to accept the implication of powerlessness. Mr Lewis attempted to evade his own conclusions, and to transform himself at least partially into a political pamphleteer. He wrote some ephemeral journalistic works, he carried on a Right-wing political flirtation which had an unfortunate effect upon his reputation and gained him some unwanted friends. The political excursions of artists rarely end happily. To the credit side, this preoccupation with the problem of power is the root of *The Revenge for Love*, his finest, and also his most neglected, novel.

Snooty Baronet, published in 1932, shows certain significant modifications in Mr Lewis's attitude towards fiction. The style is still wholly individual, but it no longer demands attention for its own sake; the narrative is put down in the first person, and an effort has been made to give it the conventional form and order firmly disregarded in all the earlier fiction. Ideas, however, are still Mr Lewis's chief interest: the hero's actions, which culminate in a murder committed irresponsibly as a kind of joke, are in a sense an elaborate parody of the doctrine of behaviourism.

The Revenge for Love appeared five years after *Snooty Baronet*, in the early months of the Spanish Civil War, when sympathy for the Popular Front was at its height. This fact is of some importance, for it contributed to the book's virtual suppression. The principal character, Percy Hardcaster, is a cynical and weatherbeaten Communist returned from Spain, who appears in a falsely rosy idealist light to the admiring group of Left-wing dons and artistic ladies and gentlemen that surrounds him. Through Hardcaster a comic but scarifying attack is made upon a variety of Leftish figures, innocent or knowing: and, through Hardcaster also, an amiable tenth-rate artist named Victor Stamp and his girl Margot are caught up in a plan to smuggle arms that ends in their betrayal and death. The plot is intricately woven and highly ingenious, and many passages of the book are richly and bitterly comic. Of these, one may be singled out for special mention: that in which the upper-class Communist Gillian is deeply shocked by Percy's incautious revelation that his story about ill-treatment by nuns in a

Spanish hospital was mere propaganda, and that his wooden leg was the result not of heroism but of simple stupidity. This revelation is the prelude to a lecture read by Percy to Gillian about realism in political conduct, and there follows a savage physical attack upon the crippled Percy by a brutish friend of Gillian's which alarms her because she feels that she may be accused of having taken part in an attack on a martyr of the Left. The incident ends with Gillian's departure from her flat to seek consolation from a Communist girl-friend, "full of class-hatred of the class it was her hard lot to have to save."

What particularly distinguishes *The Revenge for Love* from this writer's other fictional works, however, is that behind all the savage and outrageous comedy lies a deep sympathy for the hapless Victor and Margot, caught in the strong toils of those whose lives are ordered by devotion to an idea rather than respect for human beings. At the end of the book when Hardcaster, again in prison, reads of Victor's and Margot's death, his face freezes into a deeply offended yet wholly detached expression: but behind this mask even Percy Hardcaster is not immune from human sympathy. He hears a voice, "denouncing him out of the past . . . singling him out as a man who led people into mortal danger, people who were dear beyond all expression to the possessor of the passionate, the artificial, the unreal, yet penetrating, voice": and down the front of Percy's mask there rolls a single tear.

With the exception of one minor and unsatisfactory work, *The Revenge for Love* is Mr Lewis's most recent novel. Mr Grigson refers to the book's suppression, "not in fact, but by silence and opprobrium from the outraged": and it is possible that its unfriendly reception played a part in silencing Mr Lewis as a novelist. In a recent autobiographical volume, *Rude Assignment*, he wrote that *The Revenge for Love* would not be reprinted in his lifetime. Since then, however, Messrs. Methuen have arranged to issue it in the series of reprints of which *Tarr* is the first.

The considerable merit of Mr Grigson's pamphlet is that it provides a short, clear and comprehensive outline of Mr Lewis's ideas which cannot be found elsewhere: its defect is a tendency, common to Mr Lewis's supporters, to dogmatic assumption rather than reasoned persuasion. When he writes, for instance, that any page of one of Mr Lewis's more important book is "in its texture . . . more than a normal piece of professional writing such as you might find, shall I say, in a book by Mr Evelyn Waugh or the late George Orwell," the statement appears confused. There is perhaps no recent work in which style is more perfectly fused with subject-matter than *Animal Farm*: and Mr Lewis's style, sparklingly forcible and pungent, presents difficulties which are not always necessary, like the equally explosive and informed colloquial styles of Meredith and Carlyle. One of the most notable things about *The Revenge for Love* is that, with very little sacrifice of power, the style has become much less obtrusive.

But although Mr Grigson's form of expression may provoke occasional disagreement even among Mr Lewis's admirers, there should be no disagreement about the truth of his title: *Master of Our Time*. The reasons for the undoubted fact that this mastery has not been fully recognized rest in the spirit of our time itself. An artist with so rich and various a genius as Mr Lewis flourishes in a period when values are settled, and there is an accepted tradition in which he can work. It has been this artist's misfortune to be born into a society manifestly changing, in which no moral or artistic value remains unquestioned. The "shadow of a revolutionary situation," under which most of his artistic life has been spent, has led Mr Lewis into various extra-artistic activities, inevitable perhaps for one with his interests and preoccupations, but still to be regretted so far as they took him away from directly creative work. He has been at times tactless, at other times provocative; he has been deceived by unworthy causes: but behind all errors and confusions, behind an occasional rigidity of form and harshness of texture, there is plainly visible a figure whose talents are profoundly original, and have been manifested upon a heroic scale.

THE DEFEAT OF
OPTIMISM

Julian Symons

[...] The writer with whom Mr Lewis has most kinship, it has often been said, is Swift. If his work is of a lesser order than Swift's it is

The Human Age: Monstre Gai and *Malign Fiesta*, by Wyndham Lewis
[December 16, 1955]

partly because, on the simplest level, he is not so good a writer. His prose style is unique in modern literature but it is not, as Swift's was, under perfect control. Magnificent in paragraphs, his creative writing is overweighted with Carlylean ejaculations; his formations are often careless; as Carlyle said of Richter, his work is "interlaced with epigrammatic breaks, vehement bursts, or sardonic turns, interjections, quips, puns, and even oaths!" One does not mention this in the spirit of those "critics of the grammarian species" to whom such a style is "an unpardonable, often an insuperable rock of offence," but to point his difference from Swift. Mr Lewis's characteristic satiric effects are obtained by comic over-emphasis, Swift's by deadly literalness. Mr Lewis's style sometimes gets in the way of his satire, there is so much style that one can see nothing else. With Swift this is never so.

Yet *The Human Age* is manifestly one of the great prose works of our time, and in dealing with it – as in dealing with Swift – one comes back in the end to the view of the world literally conveyed in it. All sorts of symbolic meanings may be attached to the book; Pullman's progress may be conceived as a continuous intellectual treason, the beautiful but stupid angels may represent the natural powers that man has imperfectly harnessed. There are other possibilities. One canvasses them with interest, but are they really any more important than the key to *The Dunciad* or the symbolism of *Gulliver's Travels*? A work like *The Human Age* is judged at last on the literal plane: and on this plane what emerges most clearly is its creator's anguish and despair. Mr Lewis has plainly endured in the past quarter of a century the defeat of that optimism about man and society which in 1919 allowed him to look forward cheerfully to the complete rebuilding of cities by vorticist architects, and even in 1937 to proclaim himself "a pure revolutionary ... a man of the *tabula rasa*." Mr Michael Ayrton's illustrations catch perfectly the tone of the story.

The feeling that Mr Lewis seems to be expressing in this book, distinct, as far as it can be, from his conscious satiric aims, is that man is inherently stupid, violent and self-destructive; that all rulers are dishonest, all intellectuals betray themselves and others, and that below rulers and intellectuals is only a great faceless moronic mass. It is as an expression of the anguish and disillusionment suffered by a man of genius that Books Two and Three of *The Human Age* have an enduring value.

FIGURES OF ALLEGORY*

Julian Symons

[...] *Childermass* is a book about ideas, and so are the two volumes that succeeded it: but they are not the same ideas. Immense, disconcerting changes have taken place in the characters and their alignment. The "intellectual" Hyperideans are no longer "the only persons who are not blindfolded in all this gigantic bluffing," a group trying "to wrench off the blinkers from this doomed herd": but simply Fascists. The Bailiff himself is much diminished in scope and character. Dark Romance, simple-minded Revolution, and the apotheosis of the child have been forgotten. The greatest change of all, however, is that in the character of Pullman. Viewed in *Childermass* with an insistently satiric eye as a pedantic, fastidious, Bloomsburyish, homosexual figure, he has become in the later books, it seems, a representative of mankind's highest intellectual aspirations. The targets at which Mr Lewis aimed in the 1920s are no longer visible, or they no longer interest him; changes in the human situation over a quarter of a century have dictated the altered style and attitude of *The Human Age*'s later books.

Yet, although *Childermass* is dangerously tied to the fashionable ideas and illusions of its decade (even by way of exposing them), it is in a deeper sense a visionary work, the product of an extraordinary imagination which here, more perhaps than in any other book, found its perfectly suitable style.

THE ENCHANTMENT OF
A MIRROR†

A. S. McDowall

[...] It is an amusingly clear and yet enchanted glass which she holds up to things; that is her quality. This stream of incidents,

The Human Age: Childermass, by Wyndham Lewis [January 11, 1957]
†*Jacob's Room*, by Virginia Woolf [October 26, 1922]

persons, and their momentary thoughts and feelings, which would be intolerable if it were just allowed to flow, is arrested and decanted, as it were, into little phials of crystal vividness. Mrs Woolf has the art of dividing the continuous and yet making one feel that the stream flows remorselessly. The definite Mrs Durrant, the romantic little light-of-love Florinda, shy and charming Clara, the people in the streets, the moors and the sea, London and Athens – they all rise into delicious moments of reality and light before they melt back into the shadow. And each of those moments has caught a gleam of wit from the surface of the mirror, or a musing thought from the reflective depths in it. Ought we to complain, then, because Mrs Woolf can make beauty and significance out of what we generally find insignificant, or because her own musings tinge those of her personages sometimes? We know the stream of life at first-hand already; what this novel adds, with the lightest strokes, and all the coolness of restraint, is a knowledge of the vision of the author.

And it is much to be taken as far as we are here into that subtle, slyly mocking, and yet poignant vision; for Mrs Woolf has seldom expressed it more beguilingly than she does in this novel. It will even make us forget to treat the novel as a story. If, however, we come back to that, we should have to say that it does not create persons and characters as we secretly desire to know them. We do not know Jacob as an individual, though we promptly seize his type; perhaps we do not know anyone in the book otherwise than as a really intuitive person knows his acquaintances, filling in the blanks, if he is imaginative, by his imagination. And that, Mrs Woolf might say, is all we can know in life, or need to know in a book, if we forgo the psychology which she spares us. But it might still be questioned whether her beings, while they intersect, really act upon each other, or whether her method does not condemn them to be external. [...]

A NOVELIST'S
EXPERIMENT*

A. S. McDowall

All Mrs Woolf's fiction shows such an instinct for experiment that we may have to show cause why this new book should be called peculiarly experimental. "Jacob's Room," too, was an adventure. But there is one obvious difference between that novel and "Mrs Dalloway." While the other, however innovating in its method, observed the usual time-span of a novel, this one describes the passage of a single day. The idea, though new enough to be called an experiment, may not be unique in modern fiction. There was a precedent in "Ulysses." But Mrs Woolf's vision escapes disaster and produces something of her own. People and events here have a peculiar, almost ethereal transparency, as though bathed in a medium where one thing permeates another. Undoubtedly our world is less solid than it was, and our novels may have to shake themselves a little free of matter. Here, Mrs Woolf seems to say, is the stream of life, but reflected always in a mental vision. [...]

MRS WOOLF'S NEW
NOVEL†

A. S. McDowall

[...] Such are the bare bones of the framework; but one feels they are no more like the whole story than the skeleton carved in a medieval tomb is to the robed and comely effigy above it. For the book has its own motion: a soft stir and light of perceptions, meeting or crossing, of the gestures and attitudes, the feelings and thoughts of people: of instants in which these are radiant or absurd,

Mrs Dalloway, by Virginia Woolf [May 21, 1925]
†*To the Lighthouse*, by Virginia Woolf [May 5, 1927]

have the burden of sadness or of the inexplicable. It is a reflective book, with an ironical or wistful questioning of life and book, with an ironical or wistful questioning of life and reality. Somehow this steals into the pages, whether there is a sunny peace in the garden, or Mrs Ramsay is interrupted in a fairy-tale, or a couple is late for dinner, so that one is inclined to say that this question of the meaning of things, however masked, is not only the essence but the real protagonist in the story. [...]

VIRGINIA WOOLF*

We announce with regret that the death of Mrs Virginia Woolf, the novelist and essayist, must be presumed. Missing from her home since Friday, March 28, she is believed to have been drowned in the Ouse, near her home at Rodmell, in Sussex. A study of her work will appear in our next week's issue.

EPITAPH ON VIRGINIA WOOLF†

Orlo Williams

Between one great war and another the work of Virginia Woolf has been begun and ended. We cannot look back on it yet, for it is part of us and of our day – of our tormented day, for no moment of which, since 1914, has there been any comforting sense of stability. Every position has been shown to rest on sand, every rock proved to be a congeries of darting particles, nothing that we perceive but is inexorably conditioned by motion and time. Being a poet, with a peculiar sensitivity, Virginia Woolf saw this before we were aware of it. A few printed pages, bound in blue paper, could be sent in 1916 by an author in Alexandria to a critic at G.H.Q., as something new and entertaining with which to forget for a moment the boredom of military duties. The booklet contained some curious

*[Obituary announcement] [April 5, 1941]
†[Article] [April 12, 1941]

reflections prompted by the sight of a mark on a wall, and it seemed to the critic odd: his mind was still haunted by notions of stability. Yet out of that little brochure came "The Voyage Out," "Night and Day," "Jacob's Room," "Mrs Dalloway," "Orlando," "The Waves" and "The Years," all of which are variations upon one theme. Whether they will have long life depends upon the common reader, whose judgment Virginia Woolf, like Dr Johnson, respected; his tastes cannot be foretold from one generation to another. All that is certain is that, whenever the English narrative prose of the early twentieth century is brought up for critical judgment, the name of this writer will be mentioned with high honour.

It may well be that the common reader of our own day has not sufficiently appreciated her work, that he found it difficult, confusing, "above his head," some might even have called it weird. For this one must blame, among other things, a want of patience and even of intelligence. Virginia Woolf's statement of her theme was sometimes rhapsodical, and she never tired of showing how hazy were the outlines of what we call life: but in her own mental processes there was nothing hazy, as can easily be seen, not only from those admirable talks on books and writers collected in "The Common Reader," but in the two brilliant pamphlets which she wrote for the furtherance of women's influence – which she considered all too small – in the affairs of the world. "A Room of One's Own" dwells on the independence of women, its necessity, its laws and its duties; "Three Guineas" was an effort, forlorn but powerful, to enlist women in a "Society of Outsiders," rebels against the man-made world of conflicting loyalties and resultant war. Every sentence in those books is clear, every argument cogent, the wit like crystal, the passion like bare flame. And if the world was still too immature to be convinced, the failure was not due to any extravagance or weirdness on the pleader's side. It would be absurd to suppose that a mind so capable of lucid argument changed its nature when a novel was toward, wrapping itself in misty vapours or trotting out the whimsies of an overwrought nervous temperament. Virginia Woolf hated many things – cruelty, tyranny, materialism, acceptance of the second-best, smugness and vulgarity – but she hated whimsies also, simply because they are false things, while her quest was the ever-elusive truth.

THE "UNEXPRESSED"

Her view of literary truth and of the writer's problem was absolutely unclouded: and it is worth while to illustrate this fact from "The Common Reader," possibly in the hope of providing those who are still baffled by her novels with the clue they need. In "Notes on an Elizabethan Play," she compares the play in general with the novel; the one concentrated, the other richly accumulative, the former touching heights of which the latter is incapable; and she continues:–

> What, then, is the exclamation with which we close "War and Peace"? Not one of disappointment; we are not left lamenting the superficiality, upbraiding the triviality of the novelist's art. Rather we are made more than ever aware of the inexhaustible richness of human sensibility. Here, in the play, we recognize the general; here, in the novel, the particular. Here we gather all our energies into a bunch and spring. Here we extend and expand and let come slowly in from all quarters deliberate impressions, accumulated messages. The mind is so saturated with sensibility, language so inadequate to its experience, that, far from ruling off one form of literature or decreeing its inferiority to others, we complain that they are still unable to keep pace with the wealth of material, and wait impatiently for the creation of what may yet be devised to liberate us from the enormous burden of the unexpressed.

"The inexhaustible richness of the human sensibility," "the enormous burden of the unexpressed" – these are the two striking and revealing phrases. Some creative minds are not oppressed by the burden, but it overwhelmed Virginia Woolf. In the essay on "Modern Fiction" her complaint against the novels of Messrs Bennett, Wells and Galsworthy is that they are cut to a pattern which is not that of life. Is life like this? she asks.

> Look within and life, it seems, is very far from being "like this." Examine for a moment an ordinary mind on an ordinary day. The mind receives a myriad impressions – trivial, fantastic, evanescent, or engraved with the sharpness of steel. From all sides they come, an incessant shower of innumerable atoms; and as they fall, as they shape

themselves into the life of Monday or Tuesday, the accent falls differently from of old; the moment of importance came not here but there; so that, if a writer were a free man and not a slave, if he could write what he chose, not what he must, if he could base his work upon his own feeling and not upon convention, there would be no plot, no comedy, no tragedy, no love interest or catastrophe in the accepted style, and perhaps not a single button sewn on as the Bond Street tailors would have it. Life is not a series of gig lamps symmetrically arranged; life is a luminous halo, a semi-transparent envelope surrounding us from the beginning of consciousness to the end. Is it not the duty of the novelist to convey this varying, this unknown and uncircumscribed spirit, whatever aberration or complexity it may display, with as little mixture of the alien and external as possible?

THE SUSPENDED MOMENT

Could anything be clearer as a statement, or as a profession of faith? In these words Virginia Woolf expressed with exactness her view of life, her conception of form and her own procedure as a writer of novels. And if at that point one had asked her how, then, the novelist can ever select or grade, place the accent, or state the importance, she might have pointed to a passage in the essay on "Jane Austen" describing Miss Austen's particular gift of suddenly striking one note of her own, in perfect tune. She gives an instance:–

> Here is nothing out of the way; it is midday in Northamptonshire; a dull young man is talking to a rather weakly young woman on the stairs as they go up to dress for dinner, with housemaids passing. But, from triviality, from commonplace, their words become suddenly full of meaning, and the moment for both one of the most memorable in their lives. It fills itself; it shines; it glows; it hangs before us, deep, trembling, serene for a second; next, the housemaid passes, and this drop, in which all the happiness of life has collected, gently subsides again to become part of the ebb and flow of ordinary existence.

The suspended moment, in fine, the vision, the momentary illusion of beautiful permanence, and the subsidence into the ebb and flow – why, as we read these perfectly intelligible words, we are in the midst of "The Waves," reputed the most difficult of all her books simply because it carries out the notion that, if a writer were free to write as he sees, "there would be no plot, no comedy, no tragedy, no love interest or catastrophe in the accepted style"; the book in which Bernard the novelist, in the final section, elaborates the theory of life's atoms making up Monday or Tuesday as they go along at greater length and with richer fantasy, and in which the suspended moment, the vision that for an instant makes six lives one life, is twice described, once on the night in Hampton Court garden when the six characters experienced it, and again in Bernard's reflective retrospect. Here is Bernard's retrospect: let us read it, remembering the moment of Jane Austen:–

> We arose and walked together down the avenue. In the thin, the unreal twilight, fitfully like the echo of voices laughing down some alley, geniality returned to me and flesh. Against the gateway, against some cedar tree I saw blaze bright, Neville, Jinny, Rhoda, Louis, Susan and myself, our life, our identity. Still King William seemed an unreal monarch and his crown mere tinsel. But we – against the brick, against the branches, we six, out of how many million millions, for one moment out of what measureless abundance of past time and time to come, burnt there triumphant. The moment was all; the moment was enough. And then Neville, Jinny, Susan and I, as a wave breaks, burst asunder, surrendered – to the next leaf, to the precise bird, to a child with a hoop, to a prancing dog, to the warmth that is hoarded in the woods after a hot day, to the lights twisted like white ribbon on rippled waters.

LIFE STAND STILL!

Life went on, and what is the meaning of life? That is what, in "To the Lighthouse," Miss Lily Briscoe asks herself as she remembers Mrs Ramsay, her dead friend, sitting ten years before with her youngest child upon her knee in the very window that she is painting now:–

The great revelation perhaps never did come. Instead there were little daily miracles, illuminations, matches struck unexpectedly in the dark; here was one. This, that, and the other; herself and Charles Tansley and the breaking wave; Mrs Ramsay bringing them together; Mrs Ramsay saying, "Life stand still here"; Mrs Ramsay making of the moment something permanent (as in another sphere Lily herself tried to make of the moment something permanent) – this was of the nature of a revelation. In the midst of chaos there was shape; this eternal passing and flowing (she looked at the clouds going and the leaves shaking) was struck into stability. Life stand still here, Mrs Ramsay said.

That was the high aim of Virginia Woolf. She took reality as she found it – and it is fair to admit that her experience was limited to one class of society, to what are sometimes called the "ruling classes," which was a hindrance to universality – and tried to make life stand still at the significant moment. It is the aim of all great poets in every medium; and the tragedy is that, even for the greatest, the medium prevents the perfect realization. The clay and the marble, the paint and the canvas, the instrument, the singer, the metre and the very words, get in the way. If one could only create without material, or, as the elusive Rhoda exclaims in "The Waves": "If we could mount together, if we could perceive from a sufficient height, if we could remain untouched without any support," then the miracle might occur. Life would stand still, more perfectly than on Keats's Grecian Urn. But if that once happened, there would be no more death; the corruptible would have put on incorruptibility, man would be no more mortal, subject to time. Then the wave would never break again, and there would be no more novels; all would be contemplation, "calme, luxe et volupté." So the unequal struggle must be pursued, and life goes on; but in eternal renewal, thinks Bernard the novelist, there is a glory of its own. This is his final word:–

> And in me, too, the wave rises. It swells; it arches its back. I am aware once more of a new desire, something rising beneath me like a proud horse whose rider first spurs and then pulls him back. What enemy do we now perceive advancing against us, you whom I ride now, as we stand pawing this stretch of pavement? It is death. Death is the

enemy. It is death against whom I ride, with my spear couched and my hair flying back like a young man's, like Percival's when he galloped in India. I strike spurs into my horse. Against you I will fling myself, unvanquished and unyielding, O Death.

Let this be the epitaph of Virginia Woolf, a great artist, who pursued her vision with unswerving integrity.

FRAGMENTS OF TIME

Joan Bennett

Virginia Woolf's reputation began to decline with the contemporary critics after the publication of *The Waves*, just as George Eliot's reputation declined after the publication of *Middlemarch*. Attacks on Virginia Woolf's work came from divers quarters and with varying degrees of violence; Wyndham Lewis, Cyril Connolly, *Scrutiny* and Dr Joad are strange yoke-fellows in opposition to her. "Odd, these extravagant ups and downs of reputation ...," the diary comments. She felt every adverse criticism acutely; often she suffered a physical collapse when years of labour seemed to have ended in total failure. But her recovery took only a few days, because by the time one novel was finished or even before that there was the germ of another in her mind. "I will not be 'famous,' 'great.' I will go on adventuring, changing, opening my mind and eyes, refusing to be stamped and stereotyped." George Eliot had been praised for her English scenes, her sentiment, her humorous types; *Romola* had been forgiven, an aberration, a noble failure; the critics were ready to applaud if she would give them more Mrs Poysers and Dodson Aunts. But she continued to advance, her novels became more difficult, she changed the *genre*, she wrote – so the modern critics say, led by Virginia Woolf – the first novel for adults. And her reputation declined. That is part of the story.

Critics prefer to stereotype an author. More drastically and more obviously than George Eliot, Virginia Woolf changes the *genre* in

A Writer's Diary, by Virginia Woolf, ed. by Leonard Woolf [November 20, 1953]

each novel, seeking always to capture more of the truth as she sees it or to include some part of her vision that the last novel left out. And whether she concentrates solely on the impact of experience on the maturing mind, producing a pattern of monologues in *The Waves*, or whether she includes the external world of event and of comedy in *The Years*, or, more gaily and succinctly, in *Between the Acts*, the critics still demur; they had accepted *To the Lighthouse* and they wanted the mixture as before. There are, of course, other reasons for the decline of reputation. There is the tendency to iconoclasm, which accounts for the swing of the pendulum. Also Virginia Woolf's reputation suffered, and is still suffering, from the complex attack on "Bloomsbury" – complex in that it has so many sources, ranging from such petty impulses as envy (envy of an exclusive, cultivated, comfortably-off coterie) to such far-reaching disturbances as the loss of faith in man. Bloomsbury stood for the importance of human relations and for personal integrity, and for the open mind. Wars and revolutions are inimical to these values, which pervade Virginia Woolf's diary as they do her works: "More and more I come to loathe any dominion of one over another; any leadership, any imposition of the will," she writes in 1919, or, in 1932: "Why all this criticism of other people? Why not some system that includes the good . . . a system that does not shut out?" or, on September 6, 1939: "Any idea is more real than any amount of war and misery. And what one's made for. And the only contribution one can make – this little pitter-patter of ideas is my whiff of shot in the cause of freedom." The time has not yet come when Virginia Woolf's novels can be seen in a new perspective and can be judged for what they are, a series of experiments in the art of fiction, some superbly, some only partially, successful.

Are they novels? There was a moment when Virginia Woolf thought some other name would describe them better. "I have an idea I will invent a new name for my books to supplant 'novel.' A new – by Virginia Woolf. But what? Elegy?" Life and death is her theme; life in relation to death. The effect of her novels is akin to the effect of a poem in so far as they evoke feeling (what it feels like to be alive), where other novels describe people and events. And it is elegiac because her emphasis is on the fleetingness of time. Vividly she evokes the moments of intense experience, "spots of time" as Wordsworth called them; but also the stream of time, its continuity from birth to death with the odd discovery of growing old. And, besides the spots and the span of time in the individual life, she evokes a sense of historic time, the current within which those lives take shape; she tries to suggest this in the fantasy of *Orlando*, in the expanded canvas of *The Years* or, by means of the pageant and of Mrs Swithin's imaginings of prehistory, in *Between the Acts*. She evokes the sense of continuity in individual memory, and also a sense of the continuity of the human race. One impulse behind her experiments with forms or modes of presentation is the effort to find a medium which will render, as vividly as possible, the different experiences of time. The first of the experimental novels, *Jacob's Room*, established her position as a distinguished original novelist. But, though the "spots of time" are vividly given and the reader is keenly aware of impressions Jacob receives and impressions he makes as he grows from boyhood to manhood, yet the effect is fragmentary. She is pleased with the praise the book receives, but, "I don't want to be totting up compliments," the diary comments: "I want to think out *Mrs Dalloway*. I want to foresee this book better than the others and get the utmost out of it. I expect I could have screwed up Jacob tighter, if I had foreseen, but I had to make my path as I went." So it was each time; she was never satisfied; if there were laurels, she never rested on them.

The diary shows an acute sensitiveness to criticism, but it shows even more clearly that only self-criticism mattered to her in the long run. As the long agony of composition and revision draws to an end there is first elation, then despair and finally – after the relief because some praise the book, the dismay because many vilify it – there is her own lucid assessment of where the finished work falls short of the idea. Sometimes she refreshes herself by writing criticism, fantasies (*Orlando* or *Flush*) or by strenuous but different labour (*Roger Fry: A Biography*). But the seed of a new work of fiction has usually sown itself before the last is complete. During the revision of *To the Lighthouse*, for instance, the embryo of *The Waves* is in her mind: "I am now and then haunted by some semi-mystic, very profound life of a woman, which shall all be told on one occasion; and time shall be utterly obliterated; future shall somehow blossom out of past . . ." *Orlando* was to be written before serious work on *The Waves* began: "For the truth is I feel the need of an escapade after these serious poetic experimental books whose form is always so closely considered. I want to kick up my heels and be off." Again, after the intense inwardness of *The Waves*:

I find myself infinitely delighting in facts for a change, and in possession of quantities beyond counting: though I feel now and then the tug of vision, but resist it. This is the true line, I am sure, after *The Waves* – *The Pargiters* – this is what leads naturally to the next stage – the essay novel.

Slowly, and with immense labour and even more than her usual agony, work on *The Pargiters* (subsequently *The Years*) progressed. Reading the diary, one recalls how good the scenes are in that novel and yet how it falls apart, lacking, as it does, the discipline of poetic form. It seems, now that one looks back over the whole output, that symbolism was essential for her; her vision is dissipated unless it is held together by compelling symbols. Lily Briscoe's picture, Clarissa Dalloway's party, the day waxing and waning over the sea, Miss la Trobe's pageant – from these central symbols others radiate and the four finest novels are prose poems, each of them "a new elegy by Virginia Woolf." She writes of *The Years*: "Here I am breaking the mould made by *The Waves*." She broke that mould, but she needed to make another; in *Between the Acts* she achieved what in *The Years* she partly failed to accomplish, "to make a transition from the colloquial to the lyrical, from the particular to the general." [...]

INVITATIONS TO BLISS

P. N. Furbank

It gives one a jolt to find Virginia Woolf, as late as 1909, speaking as if literature were a more or less timeless and settled question, in contrast to the bursting innovativeness of music. "A critic of writing is hardly to be taken by surprise, for he can compare almost every literary form with some earlier form and can measure the achievement by some familiar standard. But who in music has tried to do what Strauss is doing, or Debussy?" Actually, given some insulation against French writing, one sees how it might then still have been possible to view matters in this light, though what gives it piquancy is that Woolf had already begun the novel that was to become *The Voyage Out*.

The Essays of Virginia Woolf [December 12, 1986]

She was writing those remarks for *The Times* (in some "Impressions at Bayreuth"), and one reflects that this, at least, is how *The Times*, and more relevantly *The Times Literary Supplement*, would certainly have wished to regard literature. But further, one may speculate that the very defects of the "gentlemanly" outlook on literature, the good-mannerliness and imperviousness to ideas which drove Ezra Pound wild, may in an unexpected way have been of solid benefit to Woolf. There are those who regard her *Common Reader* essays, a large proportion of which were written for the TLS, as her most enduring achievement; and, whether or not one agrees with this, one can confidently say that, in a life in which literary creation mainly represented agony, this was the part that she really enjoyed. Commissions to disembowel sauntering, scholarly biographies and fat volumes of memoirs, intelligent or silly, were an invitation to bliss. "It makes me rock with delight – thinking what a number of wonderful things I shall dig out of it in my article", she wrote to Violet Dickinson, apropos a book on Lady Hester Stanhope. "One gradually sees shapes and thinks oneself in the middle of a world."

It provides much of the pattern, not to say the pathos, of Virginia Woolf's life that she could not freely allow herself to do the things she most valued, and the kind of excitement that most promised ecstasy to her was also the most perilous. It was not only unfettered experiment in fiction that could plunge her into nervous distress; her diary-writing, also, involved her in dangerous emotions – in particular in that savagery and uncharitableness which for the reader can sometimes seem quite chilling and alarming. This may be one reason why this magnificently sharp-eyed observer of humanity (for it is what her diaries continually show her to be) was ready to content herself in her novels with rather insubstantial and conventionalized human material. It was not that human beings did not interest her, for they did so profoundly; it was that she found them oppressive – burr-like, vampirish and a threat to her being.

In not one but several ways, then, TLS essay-writing came to her as a salvation. Here at least she could be calmly judicious about character and conduct, as she was well fitted to be; for the dead do not have power to oppress us. Here, furthermore, she could tell herself she was writing in a tradition; never mind if it was a stuffy one, for she could always gently mock it if she felt inclined, and probably no one would notice. The beauty of a tradition was that it was something she could lean her back against; and on a superficial view there is nothing in the prose of these essays that you might not find in Bagehot, if you combined him with Walter Pater. Her own dragonfly skimmings consorted perfectly well with sententious quarterly-reviewer's wit and aspiring art-for-art's sake flights of eloquence. Even the unreceptiveness to ideas acquires a special value from her purposes; for a flight from "ideas" – and one can hardly remember a single reference to *theory*, whether philosophical or political or psychoanalytical, in these essays of hers – was actually a facet of her aesthetic modernism and the most radical gesture she had to offer against Victorianism in the shape of Buckle or Leslie Stephen.

She well knew all this for herself. She would fulminate with relish to Violet Dickinson about the monstrous behaviour of literary journals, how they delighted to mangle and tame what she wrote; but it was all good "copy", and the pleasure of outwitting editors was, for her, a keen one. Later in life she conjectured that the ladylike manner acquired with her Victorian upbringing had infected her essays: "I lay the blame for their suavity, their politeness, their sidelong approach, to my tea-table training." But instantly there follows the rider that "On the other hand, this surface manner allows one to say a great many things which would be inaudible if one marched straight up and spoke out." [...]

POETRY AND DISINTEGRATION

Hugh I'Anson Fausset

A recent writer has remarked that poetry, as a result of modern mechanization, has become more and more removed from the external common life of men: that its material is found more in the inner life of the individual, and its interpretation depends increasingly upon the individual's private and personal knowledge. And [this book is an] extreme example of that withdrawal

Poems, by W. H. Auden [March 19, 1931]

from the objective into the subjective world. Many passages in it are baffling, if not unintelligible, because they lack that measure of normality which makes communication between one individual and another possible. For mental idiosyncrasies, if they are extravagantly indulged, isolate a writer as completely as if he spoke in an unknown tongue. Thus in the first of his poems Mr Auden invites us, so far as we understand him, to discover, amid the horrors and humiliations of a war-stricken world, the "neutralizing peace" of indifference. But the manner of his invitation is often so peculiar to himself and so eccentric in its terminology that, instead of communicating an experience of value to us, it merely sets our minds a problem in allusions to solve. For example:

> Will you wheel death anywhere
> In his invalid chair.
> With no affectionate instant
> But his attendant?
> For to be held for friend
> By an undeveloped mind
> To be joke for children is
> Death's happiness:
> Whose anecdotes betray
> His favourite colour as blue
> Colour of distant bells
> And boys' overalls.
> His tales of the bad lands
> Disturb the sewing hands;
> Hard to be superior
> On parting nausea;
> To accept the cushions from
> Women against martyrdom.
> Yet applauding the circuits
> Of racing cyclists.

To Mr Auden himself the meaning of these last three stanzas is doubtless as clear as day, because they fit the peculiar habit of his mind and his experience. But although we can sense his general meaning, it requires a kind of effort to discover the exact relevance of his allusions which, even when we are sure of having done so, destroys the possibility of real enrichment. Such poetry, indeed, completely contradicts Keats's axiom that "poetry should surprise by a fine excess and not by singularity": that it should "strike the reader as a wording of his own highest thoughts, and appear almost a remembrance"; and it fails to make a living contact with us because it is the fruit of a too specialized kind of concentration. For intellectual analysis of emotional states, however sharp its focus, is poetically as barren as emotional diffuseness. And although Mr Auden can write –

> Coming out of the living is always thinking,
> Thinking changing and changing living,

the thinking process in most of his poetry is either arbitrarily imposed upon the living or the living impulse, weakened by uncertainty and disillusion, begets a symbolism which is full of personal caprice. For a sense of chaos and defeat not only underlies but determines the very texture of his verse [...]

THE ORATORS

Alan Clutton-Brock

[...] In the main the work appears to be an ironical and satirical description of life in England to-day. But Mr Auden's approach is oblique, capricious, and, as it were, from a distance; he breaks the ordered world of usage into fragments which he employs both to make a singular pattern of images and conceits, and also, with a satirical intention, to display the malign absurdity of organized society. Incongruities and odd juxtapositions are both his artistic medium and the weapon of his irony. Some of his jokes are simple and high-spirited, but more often he moves in a tangle of allusions and images between which the natural connexions are omitted. He delights in modern slang and technical diction which is so new that it has not had a chance to acquire a literary flavour, finding as much pleasure in these difficult and prickly terms as most young poets take in the diction of the old masters. In fact, the words which he seems to like most are those calculated to knock a sonnet to pieces, not only the technical terms of wireless, aviation, or war, but even the hidden indecencies of vulgar speech, of which he uses a good

The Orators: An English Study, by W. H. Auden [June 9, 1932]

many. He is insolently but exhilaratingly new, both in his technique and in the matter of his writing. Unfortunately the usual resource of quotation is denied to us, for, to be frank, isolated specimens are apt to sound silly and the quality of his writing is only displayed in extracts too long for convenience.

For, it should be said at once, Mr Auden's composition is not at all silly. Although it is obvious that this disintegrated poetry, and still more this "surréaliste" satire, might be one of the easiest of all forms of writing, a mere dribble of disconnexions, and if it were so would certainly be one of the dullest, this work is neither of these things. On the lowest level it is very clever, and Mr Auden's mind works with a fascinating agility. Conceits, parodies, and allusions flow in an unceasing stream from his pen. But, what is more, none of these are in the least pertly sophisticated or embarrassing. He never attempts a callow epigram. It is important to recognize this at once, for this is the most common characteristic of such bright young works, and only a mind which is really sincere and an artistic conscience which is really scrupulous can avoid it. [. . .]

A DRAMATIC EXPERIMENT

G. Buchanan

[. . .] Richness of language, a teeming range of subject-matter and types (if no characters), and eminent diversion – to bring these things together into the theatre at a narrow period is the merit to be chiefly applauded. To bemoan defects now would be captious – when later plays will no doubt remedy them.

The Dog Beneath the Skin: or, Where is Francis?, by W. H. Auden and Christopher Isherwood [July 11, 1935]

PARNASSUS OR F6?*

G. Buchanan

[...] A phrase of A. E., the Irish poet, is pertinent: "There's no age in his thought." Mr Auden's talent in the theatre has been quick and fertile in expedients but slow in unfolding a true stature. Possibly at the next attempt his *dramatis personae* may give us a feeling that they come not from *a* world, but from *the* world.

MR AUDEN'S PROBLEMS IN POETRY†

Alex Glendinning

[...] Such difficulties as we find are still due to obscurity of image and symbol, to compressions and rapid transitions which are to some extent inevitable. As Mr Eliot has pointed out, the variety and complexity of our present civilization impose complexity and "difficulty" on poetry which is thoroughly alive to its environment; and Mr Auden's is such poetry. He has brought the texture and imagery of our immediate life within the compass of poetry without loss of poetic intensity – a large achievement – and his best work reveals a medium flexible enough to embrace all phases and problems of modern life. There are several fully articulate and finely balanced poems in this volume, among others which are – and it is understandable – imperfectly projected and fumbling. Here and there an attitude is summed up in a phrase or line – "The baroque frontiers, the surrealist police" – and a stanza on sleeping schoolboys in a dormitory epitomizes an aspect of the modern plight to which D. H. Lawrence gave many pages. [...]

The Ascent of F6, by W. H. Auden and Christopher Isherwood [November 7, 1936]
†*Look, Stranger!*, by W. H. Auden [November 28, 1936]

COOLING WATERS

B. S. Gates

Mr Auden is at the stage when one wonders with a lively expectation whether the next fork in his road will take him towards poetry or the drama, or whether he will now go ahead in his own right, rediscovering a track which makes the best of both these worlds. But he is full of surprises; and this time he disappears, with a new companion, round a bend which seems at first to be hairpin but turns out to have the virtue of an S. His new book begins with the first canto of a letter to Byron written in a form and spirit with which his correspondent would be dangerously familiar; it contains an extraordinary "Last Will and Testament" which may amuse everybody but its innumerable legatees; and it ends with statistical graphs showing the distribution of population, industry and foreign trade of Iceland.

No one will be more surprised at this than Mr Auden was. He went to Iceland with a contract to write a travel book and with no idea how this should be done. (Authorship as an exacting affair of dates and delivery is a modern development about which Byron might have been glad to receive a stanza or two.) However, he read Don Juan on the way out, and received a challenge of virtuosity. To accept was a different matter, but Housman is not the only poet who has been spurred up Parnassus by a minor ailment:–

> Indeed one hardly goes too far in stating
> That many a flawless lyric may be due,
> Not to a lover's broken heart, but 'flu.

Mr Auden, gloomily nursing a cold in an Icelandic bus, suddenly saw, streaming before him, Byron as his way out. He would chat to Byron about cabbages and kings, and to other more accessible correspondents about Iceland. Light verse, poor girl, practised as she is only by "Milne and persons of that kind" and confined "to the more bourgeois periodicals," is in a poor way: she will be all the better for some fresh air:–

Letters from Iceland, by W. H. Auden and Louis MacNeice [August 7, 1937]

And since she's on a holiday my Muse
Is out to please, find everything delightful
And only now and then be mildly spiteful.

So he takes her, keeping his promise fairly well, for five longish cantos. [...]

THIRD AVENUE
ECLOGUE

Alan Ross

[...] More than any of his contemporaries, Mr Auden, besides being in some degree the *enfant terrible*, was the acknowledged legislator. He was the essentially middle-class Englishman who made his contemporaries citizens of the world; he was the Oxford intellectual who, with a bagful of poetic squibs in his Norfolk jacket, could shame a generation into a political awareness, a personal guilt that made it regret ever having thought him shallow, insincere or unfeeling. On the two levels of being an entertainer and of giving his age ("A Golden Age, A Silver ... rather this, Massive and taciturn years, the Age of Ice") a political awareness, Mr Auden was able to fuse their two elements and illustrate them in terms of each other.

His *Poems* in 1930 set the style for all his best poetry. They were sharp, occasional, topical, with just that brilliant economy in hitting off a contemporary feeling which has never deserted him. Yet the urgency of their implications was unmistakable. Where J. Alfred Prufrock had gazed ruminatingly through the ruins of a London mist, the protagonist of Mr Auden's poetry knew the hard message of a breaking-down machine by its noise, as well as from the newspapers, the night-club and the lover's arms. *The Orators*, published in 1932, elaborated, though much more elliptically and privately, the same theme; the tone of voice was more a schoolmaster's, but of one who had looked out on the world from a mountain top on a holiday expedition.

It was *Look, Stranger!* (1936), however, which really showed for

The Age of Anxiety, by W. H. Auden [October 23, 1948]

the first time the range and self-assured mastery of Mr Auden as a poet. The mists had suddenly cleared from the summit; the private joke, the suggestion of academic facetiousness, the over-condensed telegraphic style, had blown away and left a natural brilliance of light, a strength and beauty of expression which no longer gave the impression of having been contrived: "O love, the interest itself in thoughtless Heaven, Make simpler daily the beating of man's heart ..." In *Look, Stranger!* the handling of the verse is everywhere firmer, the technical excellence less obtrusive but, for all that, much surer. The tenor of the poetry is calmer and less hurried. The river has turned a sharp bend and a wider, richer sweep opens to the view. There is a landscape for love – "Yes, we are out of sight and earshot here" – and August is "for the people and their favourite islands." Mr Auden achieves emotional authenticity in *Look, Stranger!* and a seriousness of tone in the handling of personal themes, but yet the nonchalant lightness of touch remains, capable always of wounding or hurting with an unforgettable word:

> Climbing with you was easy as a vow
> We reached the top not hungry in the least;
> But it was eyes we looked at, not the view;
> Saw nothing but ourselves, left-handed, lost;
> Returned to shore, the rich interior still
> Unknown. Love gave the power, but took the will.

In *Look, Stranger!* he began also the series of portraits, the condensing of biographical information to point a particular conjunction of circumstances, which became the most important feature of *Another Time* (1940). Besides a handful of cabaret lyrics and potted biographies, *Another Time* contained, as well as some of Mr Auden's most beautiful short poems like "Lay your sleeping head, my love," the superb longer memorial poems to W. B. Yeats, Ernst Toller and Sigmund Freud.

> Dear Ernst, lie shadowless at last among
> The other war-horses who existed till they'd done
> Something that was an example to the young.
> We are lived by powers we pretend to understand
> They arrange our loves; it is they who direct at the end
> The enemy bullet, the sickness, or even our hand.

Resignation, fatalism, the sense of the end of an era had fallen like an autumn on the gay squibs of the schoolmaster offering his pupils fireworks with moral mottoes.

Mr Auden had seen his decade out. He had given it a poetic name, a language, a feeling of adventure. He went to America in search of a poetry which had less to do with life, which was outside occasional events, which was beyond the European schoolroom with its babble, its noisy protest, its sudden unwillingness for the end of term. In *New Year Letter* (1941), a long poem and technically suave, Mr Auden justified his complex poetic position:

> Aloneness is man's real condition,
> That each must travel forth alone
> In search of the Essential Stone,
> The "Nowhere-without-No" that is
> The justice of societies.

Nonetheless, in spite of its apparently simple conclusions concealed in a cotton-wool wrapping of Kierkegaard and Pascal, *New Year Letter* was beautifully written. If the first-rate poet seemed in danger of becoming a second-hand philosopher with less feeling for human realities, his feeling for the form and immediacy of poetry remained. It remained, too, in the first part of *For the Time Being, The Sea and the Mirror*, a poetic commentary on *The Tempest*, which had dark but lovely passages, a sad and ironic truth:

> Evening, grave, immense, and clear
> Overlooks our ship whose wake
> Lingers undistorted on
> Sea and silence; I look back
> For the last time as the sun
> Sets behind that island where
> All our loves were altered: yes,
> My prediction came to pass,
> Yet I am not justified,
> And I weep but not with pride.
> Not in me the credit for
> Words I uttered long ago
> Whose glad meaning I betrayed.

Now *The Age of Anxiety* shows the shoring up of the spirit of participation which gave so much life to Mr Auden's early verse.

The poet-protagonist has become the philosopher-commentator on the beach, who, having diagnosed the causes of the struggle correctly and clear-sightedly in the first instance, now watches the battle being fought out at sea; and he has a part in the action no longer.

For it is impossible not to read into Mr Auden's American dialogues his own *déraciné*, nostalgic predicament; the subconscious need for explanation which has developed into a neurosis, his own abdication from the issues of the heart. His writing betrays it over and over again. In *The Age of Anxiety* three men and a woman discuss Life, first in a bar on Third Avenue, then in a West Side apartment in New York. The four characters speak not as characters, in character, but through the medium of Mr Auden's mind. The dialogue proceeds through a series of *recherché* platitudes, a number of vulgarized philosophical conclusions, to a climax where Emble, a naval officer, "passes out on" Rosetta, a successful but slightly *passée* department store buyer. She looks at him, half-sadly, half-relieved:

> Did you lose your nerve
> And cloud your conscience because I wasn't
> Your dish really? You danced so bravely
> Till I wished I were. Will you remain
> Such a pleasant prince? Probably not.
> But you're handsome, aren't you? even now
> A Kingly corpse. I'll coffin you up till
> You rule again.

So that is where the long journey has led. The philosopher's stone has turned into an empty rye bottle, where

> there is only the flash
> Of negative knowledge, the night, when, drunk, one
> Staggers to the bath room and stares in the glass
> To meet one's madness . . .

It might be a little disappointing, if one were not safely in possession of Mr Auden's earlier, more urgent volumes. The writing on the blackboard is still well above most of the rest of the class, the virtuosity of form is astonishing, there is an occasional rare flash of poetry, but alas! the class is no longer listening; this is only revision.

The reasons for this appearance of recapitulation are not easy to analyse because whatever the generalization one may make about Mr Auden he himself, in one or other passage, confounds them. There is a sudden humility in his writing just when the mask of intellectual assumption is becoming intolerable, a sudden dazzle of poetry just when one is resigned to yet another brillant transcription of traditional poetic patterns. For Mr Auden, as he is never afraid to do, has gone right back in his effort to give a new vitality to verse-forms. The whole of this new poem is evidence of his adaptation of Langland's alliterative method, and, indeed, of the basic poetic structure of *Piers Plowman* – specially in passages like

> When in wanhope I wandered away and alone,
> How brag were the birds, how buxom the sky,
> But sad were the sallows and slow were the brooks,
> And how dismal that day when I danced with my dear.

Yet somehow even the *panache* with which Mr Auden carries it out fails to convince. The reader is left admiring but unmoved, as though all the time he were watching a brilliant public exhibition which was intended as a display of versatility rather than the result of any deep-seated conviction. The inclusive faculty, the concern for the audience, is missing. Mr Auden's characters appear to be talking at, rather than to, each other and that is fatal. The reader is at once the neglected guest outside the circle.

The Age of Anxiety fails, then because it lacks a discriminating human sympathy. Its ideas are rarely above the commonplace; its movement is the movement of a robot, faintly parodying its former self. The machine still works, but it has begun to move out of sight into a no-man's land where conviction fails. The poetry has become verse, and in making it so Mr Auden has written his one dull book, his one failure. Perhaps it may turn out to be the most salutary thing that has yet happened in an astonishing career.

THE LAUREATE OF
AMBIGUITY

Peter Porter

One of the many quotations from other writers which Auden used to underpin works of his own – in this case affixed as epigraph to *New Year Letter* – comes from Montaigne: "We are, I know not how, double in ourselves, so that what we believe we disbelieve, and cannot rid ourselves of what we condemn." When I first read *New Year Letter* this seemed, like most of Auden's gatherings of other men's flowers, alert and relevant enough, but not an outstandingly pertinent insight. Now, after finishing Humphrey Carpenter's extraordinarily thorough exposition of Auden's life, I find it comes to mind with daunting force. On my pilgrimage through Mr Carpenter's book, everything about Auden has begun to seem double.

Carpenter, for example, distils a great sense of Auden's unhappiness, yet we know how much Auden hated wet-legs, how constantly he repeated his many litanies of his own good fortune. His prodigious taste for work and his powerful self-discipline ("I thought their Protestant Work-Ethic/ Both practical and sympathetic") existed alongside both the chaos of his daily life and that helplessness commented on by Hannah Arendt ("... I still found it difficult to understand fully what made him so miserable, so unable to do anything about circumstances that made everyday life so unbearable for him ..."). His leadership and dominance often subsided into dependence and disappointment, with rebuffs and rejections by those he had bullied for their own good – the dependence exemplified clearly by his relations with Chester Kallman and the disappointment by Benjamin Britten's later coolness towards him. The sincerity of his return to the Christian church could still permit him to be doctrinally carping and liturgically snobbish, and the ethics of his sexuality never precluded predatoriness: he loved Chester Kallman despite Kallman's many infidelities, yet he wrote one of the most unimaginative of rebukes to the bits of trade he made

W. H. Auden: A Biography, by Humphrey Carpenter [July 3, 1981]

use of – "In the Hungry Thirties/boys used to sell their bodies/ for a square meal./ In the Affluent Sixties/they still did:/ to meet Hire-Purchase Payments." The Leader and Saviour (Wyndham Lewis's "new guy who's got into the landscape") became "the minor Atlantic Goethe"; the Englishman an American memorialized in Westminster Abbey; the aphorist one of the few poets of this century who could handle extended forms; the marvellous celebrator of orthodoxy one of the most eccentric figures of the age.

Auden's doubleness is his triumph. He was, as Humphrey Carpenter gives us ample opportunity to witness, a fallible, indeed treasonable clerk, but he was also a creative genius who humanized inspiration. Looking around at the desolation produced by genius at its most egotistical (let me start with the names of Joyce, Yeats, Schönberg, Pound, Beckett – and then stop before I lose my courage), one rejoices in Auden's Old Adam, in his recognition that seriousness is a contract between the artist and his talent and not between the divine afflatus and the historically conditioned mob. There have been supreme artists this century whose seriousness is so olympian that it is unruffled by history or swank – Stravinsky and Wallace Stevens for example. But Auden's double vision, if it prevented his achieving what Stravinsky and Stevens did and kept him out of the ranks of the Modernists, fitted him to be the laureate of our age; one might adapt a title of his and call this The Age of Ambiguity.

Even his famous request that his friends burn his letters, and his well-known views on the biographies of artists ("Gossip-Columnists I can forgive for they make no pretences,/not Biographers who claim it's for scholarship's sake"), seem to have been wittingly double-edged. Tributes, memoirs and anecdotes have poured forth, and two major biographies have appeared in the eight years since his death. Somehow one feels he must have expected this and half-welcomed the prospect. Charles Osborne's biography, published early last year, certainly follows the gossip columnist's precepts more closely than it does the scholar's, but is no less enjoyable for that. It is more gracefully written than Humphrey Carpenter's new book. But it was clearly compiled too quickly, and Osborne did not have access to much of the material, chiefly those unburned letters, which has been made available to Carpenter. Carpenter's book amounts almost to an official biography: it is very thorough and, while sympathetic to Auden, does not gloss over his many peculiarities and occasional nastinesses. One of the most commonly repeated complaints about Osborne's book was its apparent lack of any sense of Auden as a great poet. If this means that Osborne failed to locate the heart of Auden's life in his poetry, then it is probably a justified complaint, and one which Carpenter cannot be accused of. However, Carpenter's book is not a work of literary criticism either – why should a biography be such a thing? – and readers wishing to gain enlightenment about Auden's work should read through the now deepening thickets of academic criticism devoted to him, starting with the most sensible and practical study of all – John Fuller's *Reader's Guide*.

Humphrey Carpenter takes as his key and his justification Auden's own view that while the life of an artist will not help explain his art, his works may, on the other hand, throw light upon his life. Accordingly, his point of departure throughout the book is what Auden was writing at any one time. Or, at least, that is ostensibly the case: in practice, Carpenter, like any sensible biographer, uses whatever sources he can locate. There is strong evidence that his guide has been Edward Mendelson, Auden's chief literary executor, and he has also enjoyed the cooperation of many of Auden's close friends, who have allowed him to quote from letters and personal documents and have given him reminiscences and explanations of Auden's conduct. Because they have trusted Carpenter, Auden's friends have conveyed an unofficial imprimatur to his book, and he is able to quote from Auden's own written-in annotations of his poems, identifying some of the people behind the vignettes, tableaux, pronouns and masks of those often cryptic works.

The faces sometimes fit as you would expect, sometimes not. I greeted with a homely nod, not a shock of recognition, Carpenter's identification of the character of Rosetta in *The Age of Anxiety* with Auden's surprising heterosexual lover Rhoda Jaffe. But I would never have thought that the villanelle "If I Could Tell You", with its refrain line "Time will say nothing but I told you so", might refer to Kallman; nor that the charming birthday poem "Many Happy Returns", with its immortal warning to "so many in the USA" not to "be ashamed of any suffering as vulgar", was directed at Kallman and that the dedication of this poem to John Rettger, sub-teen son of Auden's hosts at Ann Arbor, was a mask for a lecture to Chester as well as a thank-you for hospitality received. These are only the merest samples of the many identifications which Mr Carpenter makes in the course of his considerably extended parade of Auden's friends and acquaintances. He starts these initialled annotations very early on, in Auden's English period, and keeps them going to the end.

An inordinate amount of Mr Carpenter's space is devoted to Auden's love-life: never pruriently, never stupidly and never completely irrelevantly – but not without discounting the surrounding seriousness of his life and work either. Perhaps homosexuality is the misleading spirit here. Byron's lovers were legion, and many have been identified, and other poets who had only one or two lovers have forced their biographers to make the most of what was available. But the heterosexual hero has not been so subject to the biographer's sense that a name or a face made manifest nothing less than a mystery explained. Charles Osborne, in his account of Auden, was accused of gossiping. Humphrey Carpenter is likely to be applauded for honestly tracing those connections in Auden's life which emerged as salient shapes in his poetry. The truth seems more likely to be the moderate view that Carpenter has taken more trouble over his identifications than Osborne did and that he received more help from Auden's friends.

Humphrey Carpenter does not shrink from examining the once unmentionable subject – what Auden liked in bed. John Fuller has already discussed those actions Auden called "plain sewing" and "Princeton First-Year". Carpenter tells us that Auden was an oral man: fellatio was his number. Kallman was "an anal passive". Further, we are informed that Auden liked men who were "wellhung", perhaps because he considered his own penis to be undersized. None of this is shocking or untoward. But it tends to get solemnized in a biography and to be made to explain more than it should.

The basic trouble must lie with the art (or semi-art) of biography itself. A man of action – the Duke of Wellington or Barnum or even Goethe – can be described in terms of his undertakings, his associates and his opponents. A writer's bequest to posterity is his works, which always have an ambiguous relationship to his life. His life is likely to be unheroic, and its highpoints may well be concerned with sex. So the biography of a writer homes in on his lovers, since they are the palatable equivalents of the man of action's deeds. But there, away from all revelation, stand the works themselves – in Auden's case that beautiful gathering of poems which has given so much pleasure to people who have never heard the names of Gabriel Carritt or Orlan Fox or Hugerl of Vienna. It is partly Auden's own fault that one finishes Humphrey Carpenter's book impatient at all the exposure judged necessary after the previous reticence. Humphrey Carpenter has not escaped, perhaps, the accusation which Auden levelled at biographers – he has used the life (sex life expecially) as sauce to the real dish, the poems.

Yet Carpenter's book is also continuously interesting and sometimes highly illuminating. A measure of his success is that the better you know Auden's poetry the more interested you will be in the unfolding of his life as Carpenter presents it. He does justice to that series of conversions, reversions, convictions and contradictions which are the true course of Auden's intellectual development. He is also very good at explaining how many of Auden's pieces, not least the plays he wrote with Isherwood, are palimpsests, with bits taken over from all sorts of previous works. His outline of the plot of *The Enemies of a Bishop*, forerunner of *The Fronny* and so of *The Dog Beneath the Skin*, makes it sound the purest piece of Joe Orton *avant la lettre*. He quotes from a letter Auden's phrase "copotomy and sodulation", which is also among the aphorisms in the early Notebook owned by the British Museum. He describes in considerable detail the incomplete visionary poem *In the Year of My Youth* which Auden subsequently plundered for many other works, the best known of which is "The Witnesses", adapted from a song by Titt and Tool, two farcical characters in the earlier extravaganza. These lines from *In the Year of My Youth* are forerunners of Rosetta's speeches in *The Age of Anxiety*:

> From Puffin Conyers, place for peacocks.
> Came General Gorse of the white moustache,
> Beside him Betty his obedient wife,
> Christopher their son with the shishi walk,
> And Antonelli their Italian chauffeur,
> A family in fortune, rich in Rolls.
> Then driving dangerously in a blue Daimler
> Admiral Hotham with his breakwater chin
> From Honeypot Hall, haunt of doves,
> His wife Faun, frequent in embraces,
> And one-eyed Bert, his faithful A.B.

All this is more thoroughly and better done in *The Age of Anxiety*, but the tone is certainly a pre-echo. Carpenter also tells us that among student poems included in *The Badger*, magazine of The Downs School where Auden taught in the mid 1930s, is one which begins "Now the snow is falling fast/ Nurse's flowers will not last". The Downs's resident poet could spot a good thing when he saw it, and so we got Auden's "Autumn Song".

> Now the leaves are falling fast,
> Nurse's flowers will not last,
> Nurses to their graves are gone,
> But the prams go rolling on.

On the other hand, the fact that there are passages in the chorus from *The Dog* beginning "The Summer holds ..." which were taken from Anthony Collett's *The Changing Face of Europe* does not lessen their value or impact. A notion which is decorative or discursive in prose may be central and poetic in a well-shaped verse:

> Not only is the North Sea so shallow that if St Paul's was planted anywhere between the Dutch and English coasts the golden cross would shine above water ...   (Collett)

> Calm at this moment the Dutch sea so shallow
> That sunk St Paul's would ever show its golden cross
> And still the deep water that divides us still from Norway.
>   (Auden)

Throughout his life Auden was a snapper-up of both unconsidered and often-considered trifles. "It's later than you think", "a whole climate of opinion" – did Auden coin them or merely make them famous? It is his special genius, as it was for so many poets in the past and tends not to be among poets today, to use language proverbially. Carpenter is helpful in tracing or at least emphasizing the important cross-fertilization in Auden's work whereby passages conceived under one dispensation were transferred on instinct to another. Only prigs worry about this. It is, after all, well-known and seldom deplored in music: much of Berlioz's thematic material was conceived in his early years and worked over thereafter, and Handel borrowed prodigiously from both himself and others. Isherwood's famous remark that many of Auden's early poems were made up of lines assembled from unsuccessful works is probably an exaggeration, but it testifies to an important truth about Auden's mind. Add to this the trope of Valéry's which Auden loved to quote – "a poem is never finished but only abandoned" and you appreciate that his poetry was a whole landscape to him, every poem fitting into the not-yet-finished mosaic. Each was a feature, each turn of his enthusiasm and conviction another view of the whole of creation: the phrases, feelings and images nod across the years and styles which apparently separate them from each other. I have never understood the orthodoxy which asserts that early Auden and late Auden are miles apart. It isn't just that abandoned lead mines, beam engines and overshot waterwheels are common both to sagaland Auden and to the late lexically enriched Auden, nor even that he has an abiding fondness for aphorisms and neologisms, but rather something much more haunting: all of his work exhibits a tone of voice, social, oracular, sadly reasonable, frightened of extravagance yet welcoming the baroque to avoid hectoring plainspokenness, a deeply civilized cry from the heart of an uncivilizable species. This is what makes Auden an Old Master rather than a Modern Master.

Humphrey Carpenter does what he can to make the dubious perfection of Auden's life fit the closer perfection of his art, but inevitably one notices oddities and spicy facts more than the overall plan. His early pages are especially interesting since he quotes from juvenilia which none of us can have seen before – this chilling verse, for instance:

> Tommy did as mother told him
>   Till his soul had split;
> One half thought of angels
>   And the other half of shit.

Yet the "queer-making" power of mother is not the whole story. Auden had great respect for his father from whom he believed he inherited his intellect. "Mother wouldn't like it" may have been one of his constant forms of disapproval, but I know from many reminiscences of his friends that he would enquire avidly of people what their fathers did and what they felt for them.

Much of the unpublished verse which Carpenter prints is either poor or merely characteristic, but there are some unexpected gems.

Consider this from a poem called "California" (a village near Birmingham). It dates from Auden's fifteenth year:

> The twinkling lamps stream up the hill
> Past the farm and past the mill
> Right at the top of the road one sees
> A round moon like a Stilton cheese.
>
> A man could walk along that track
> Fetch the moon and bring it back
> Or gather stars up in his hand
> Like strawberries on English land.

Some of the lines edited out of *New Year Letter* are also thoroughly worth reading

> For maudlin stupid Mr Chips
> Owns several heavy battleships,
> Ridiculous young Lohengrin
> Has camps to put his audience in.
> Cher monsieur Prudhomme aime la gloire
> Et l'amour-propre et le pouvoir
> And the plain proletarian lie
> Is held up in position by
> Noble police and the ornate
> Grandezza of the Russian State.

But whatever the interest of such discoveries, most readers will rightly feel that the centre of Carpenter's book is its account of Auden's relationship with Chester Kallman. This "marriage" was the most serious thing which ever happened to Auden, just as John Donne's marriage was in his life. Carpenter treats it with insight and understanding, and if he shows how much suffering Kallman's unfaithfulness caused Auden, he doesn't underestimate the high price Kallman paid for living in tandem with Auden. Whatever Kallman's gifts might have amounted to ordinarily, there can be no doubt that he was perpetually eclipsed by Auden. Kallman's qualities are to be seen not just in passages from *The Rake's Progress* (viz the auction scene and graveyard scene in Act Three), but peep out in anecdote, recorded conversation and in such comments as this one from a letter about their Henze opera *The Bassarids*: Kallman explained that they didn't want to produce "any species of that Glucky Greekiness which permits itself to be staged by combining the Modern Dance with the side-views of a Grecian Urn".

The tumult of love-betrayed scared Auden and is probably the reason for his repetition of the unconvincing litany of his good fortune and happiness in later years. As Carpenter asserts, his most successful relationship was probably with his art. This did not maintain itself at its previous high level towards the end, but nor was it something he felt tempted to turn his back on. It is true that Auden was very tired and despairing just before he died, but even here the loyal reader has two texts to choose from and may guess which is the more relevant. The first comes from "Talking to Myself".

> Time, we both know, will decay You, and already
> I'm scared of our divorce: I've seen some horrid ones.
> Remember: when *Le Bon Dieu* says to You *Leave him!*,
> please, please, for His sake and mine, pay no attention
> to my piteous *Don'ts*, but bugger off quickly.

The second is from "Lullaby":

> now you fondle
> your almost feminine flesh
> with mettled satisfaction,
> imagining that you are
> sinless and all-sufficient
> snug in the den of yourself,
> *Madonna* and *Bambino*:
> *Sing, Big Baby, sing lullay.*

Auden was a double man right to the end, but there is nothing ambiguous about the love his readers feel for him.

ART OR LIFE?

Mme Mary Duclaux

The dominant note of our new age is sensibility – a sensibility extraordinarily rich and ample, and yet delicate, sensitive as the

A la Recherche du Temps Perdu: Du Côté de Chez Swann, by Marcel Proust
[December 4, 1913]

impressions of convalescence, fresh as the first images of childhood. And indeed the most characteristic of recent French novels have dealt with a sensitive child; and the student of human nature might range on his shelf, just below the great autobiographies, such stories as the early volumes of "Jean Christophe," or "Marie Claire," or M. René Boylesve's "Jeune fille bien elevée," or the "Charles Blanchard" of the regretted Charles-Louis Philippe, or M. Edmond Jaloux's "Le reste est silence," or especially, to cut short a list that might be alarmingly long, this extraordinary novel with its enigmatic title, "Du côté de chez Swann."

The book with which it is easiest to compare it is Mr Henry James's "A Small Boy," though that, indeed, is concise and simple compared to M. Marcel Proust's essay in reconstituting the fresh, vague, shimmering impressions of a child, the wonderment with which it regards places and people which, in our eyes, possess no vestige of magic or glamour. But, in the case of the novel before us, the vision of reality is complicated by a theme not infrequent in the fiction of the twentieth century – a theme inaugurated, we think, by Mr James some fifteen years ago in "What Maisie Knew": the impression made on a child by the mysterious iniquity of its elders. M. Proust's hero is a small boy living in the bosom of the most regular of families – one of those vast French families, closely knit, whose tissue unites grandparents, great-aunts, uncles, cousins in such quantity as to limit the possible supply of outside acquaintance; one most familiar friend, however, there is, the friend of the family, a "hereditary friend" as Homer would say, M. Swann. He is a man of the world, a member of the Jockey Club, a friend of the Prince of Wales and the Comte de Paris, a great collector; but for the small boy and his family he is especially "le fils Swann," the son of their old friend the member of the Stock Exchange ("qui a bien dû lui laisser quatre ou cinq millions") who has made a ridiculous marriage with a demi-mondaine – a case of all for love and the world well lost. And the world is lost the more completely that the impossible lady continues her adventures unabashed and unabated after matrimony. She therefore is not received, or indeed hardly mentioned, in the ample respectable home of the small boy; so that Swann and this unlikely love of Swann's, this beautiful wife of Swann's, and Swann's remote, intangible, but not invisible little girl, are the constant objects of his romantic curiosity.

There are two walks at Combray: you may set out in the direction of Guermantes or else go round by Swann's; and to the childish hero of the book these two walks gradually accumulate round them the material for two views of life – Swann standing for all that is brilliant, irregular, attractive, Guermantes representing an orderly and glorious tradition. This long novel, "A la recherche du temps perdu," sets out to recover, in three volumes, a child's first impressions in both sorts, but this instalment records (in 500 closely printed pages) the earliest images "du côté de chez Swann": images forgotten by the intellect, mysteriously resuscitated by the senses – by a tune sung in the street, or a whiff of thyme or mignonette, or (as in the case of our author) by the flavour of a fragment of sponge-cake dipped in tea; images in which matter and memory are subtly combined in a sudden warm flood of life revived, without the intervention of the understanding. In all this the influence of Bergson is evident. But can we imagine the twentieth century in France without Bergson? As well conceive the eighteenth century without Rousseau. Such a delicate excess of sensibility does not exist without disorder; such a need to fuse and unite the very depth of the soul with the ambient world – such a sense of the fluid moving flood of life – exceeds the strict limits of a perfect art. Evidently M. Proust's novel, by its faults as well as by its qualities, is admirably adequate to the spirit of our age. But let us own that, while we read with delight the delicate, long-winded masters of our times, we think sometimes with regret of a Turgeneff, no less subtle, who, even as they, wrote at tremendous length and recorded the minutest shades of feeling, but, having finished, went through his manuscript again, pen in hand, and reduced it to about one-third of its original length.

When we open, by chance, one of those old novels, still famous, long unread, which nourished the minds of our ancestors – "Clarissa Harlowe," "La Nouvelle Héloise," or "L'Astrée," or "Amadis," or any other of those immense untidy romances, vast bazaars or stores of their age, which provided several generations with every necessary of life – we are nearly always astonished to find them so interesting and so good. Our forefathers were no fools: what they loved in these books, which were for them a school of feeling, was not Art but Life. Nothing is more instructive in this connexion than to read a letter of Mme de Sévigné's on the interminable masterpiece of La Calprenède; the great lady, so delicate, so difficile, "blessée des méchants styles," can scarcely understand her own enthusiasm:

> Le style de La Calprenède est maudit en mille endroits; de grandes périodes de romans, de méchants mots je sens tout cela . . . et, cependant je ne laisse pas de m'y prendre comme à de la glu; la beauté des sentiments, la violence des passions, la grandeur, des évènements, tout cela m'entraîne comme une petite fille.

And even as Mme de Sévigné read "Cléopâtre" – even as we only yesterday were reading "Jean Christophe" – to-morrow a new public will be reading "Du côté de chez Swann." But for these last two novels, so representative of our own times, we fain would claim more than the influence of an hour. Will neither precept nor example persuade our authors to prune their genius? M. Proust's novel, in particular, is the more bewildering that it is conceived as it were on two planes: no sooner have we accustomed ourselves to the sun-pierced mist of early reminiscence than the light changes, we find ourselves in glaring noon; the recollection becomes a recital; the magic glory fades from M. Swann and the fair frail Odette de Crécy; we see them in their habit as they lived and among their acquaintance; we smile at the evocation of an artistic coterie under President Grévy, and suffer a sort of gnawing under our ribs as we realise the poignant jealousy of the unhappy Swann. And then the light shifts again; we are back in childhood; and Swann is again the mysterious idol of a dreamy, chivalrous little boy:–

> Il me semblait un être si extraordinaire que je trouvais merveilleux que des personnes que je fréquentais le connussent aussi et que dans les hasards d'une journée quelconque on pût être amené à le rencontrer. Et une fois ma mère, en train de nous raconter comme chaque soir, à dîner, les courses qu'elle avait faites dans l'après-midi, rien qu'en disant: "A ce propos, devinez qui j'ai rencontré aux Trois Quartiers, au rayon des parapluies: Swann," fit éclore au milieu de son récit, fort aride pour moi, une fleur mystérieuse. Quelle mélancolique volupté d'apprendre que cet après-midi-là, profilant dans la foule sa forme surnaturelle, Swann avait été acheter un parapluie.

Perhaps this brief and casual quotation, better than our criticism, will show the fresh and fine reality mysteriously recovered from the back of our consciousness (where it exists in a warm penumbra of its own) which is exhaled, as naturally as vapour from a new-ploughed autumn furrow, by some score of pages in this fascinating book.

THE EUROPEAN
TRADITION

Richard Aldington

M. Marcel Proust has collected in this volume certain miscellaneous writings. In spite of his inordinate (though not inexplicable) admiration for Ruskin, M. Proust is an author for whom one feels respect, whose books can be opened with the certainty that the time spent in reading them will be well employed. M. Proust has well-defined characteristics which might almost be called mannerisms, but he is never a victim to mere eccentricity, he has no "bee in his bonnet." If his admiration for Ruskin and the minuteness of his method lead him into enormities like a sentence seventy lines long, he atones for them by packing such sentences full of thought and meaning. He works on an ample scale, but the flood of his speech is never the divagation of an empty brain proferring nothing but words; it is the outpouring of a mind which is so stored with perceptions, so tranquil, so leisurely, that it can only find adequate expression in a rich voluminous prose. Even these "opuscules" bear the mark of a fine, well-equipped intelligence. [. . .]

Pastiches et Mélanges, by Marcel Proust [July 31, 1919]

THE DEVELOPMENT OF
M. PROUST*

Richard Aldington

[...] Again Mr Proust's observation seems at fault when he speaks of a certain monarch as highly delighted with a very intellectual *milieu* he was far too uncultivated to understand; and, once more, when he chooses a rich *American* woman as one "qui n'avait jamais possédé d'autre livre qu'un petit exemplaire ancien, et jamais ouvert, des poésies de Parny, posé parce qu'il était 'du temps' sur un meuble de petit salon." He is wrong, generally quaintly and miscellaneously, and not with judgment and intelligence. But the minuteness of these censures can only prove an anxiety that every possible fault shall be removed from so inspiring a work.

M. MARCEL PROUST
TRANSLATED†

Cyril Falls

It was right and proper that M. Proust, one of the most-talked-of writers of our time, should have had a first-class designer for his English dress. A hack translator would have made gibberish of him; an ordinary "workmanlike" translation would have lost all that mysterious essence, so precious to his admirers. This is better than workmanlike. Very close to the original, it is yet written in fastidious English; indeed, it lacks some of that placid dullness which many devotees roll upon their tongues and declare to be the only true flavour for really cultivated palates. And here we think that the translator has made one mistake, if he wished to preserve the quality of the original. He has cut up some of the interminable

A la Recherche du Temps Perdu: Sodome et Gomorrhe, by Marcel Proust [June 9, 1921]
†*Swann's Way*, by Marcel Proust, translated by C. K. Scott Moncrieff [September 21, 1922]

French paragraphs, with speeches buried in their middles, which are so characteristic of M. Proust. This certainly gives an air of greater lightness and clarity to the text, but neither of these *bourgeois* virtues is a mark of this aristocratic author. [...]

TRIBUTE TO
MARCEL PROUST

John Middleton Murry

To the January number of *La Nouvelle Revue Française*, which is entirely dedicated to the memory of Marcel Proust, the following letter has been sent by a few among the many readers of Proust in England: –

> Sir, – A few English lovers of literature and English men of letters very much wish to express their sympathy in the loss which France has recently sustained in the lamented and too-early death of M. Marcel Proust. While we in England always have been accustomed to look towards France for yet another of those masterpieces which France so abundantly bestows upon the world, it was with more than usual interest and excitement that we began to read the work of M. Proust. Here, we felt, was a new and great French writer, presenting us with a beautiful and new picture of that life in Paris and provincial France of which we can never read enough. But it seemed to us even more than that: in "La Recherche du Temps Perdu" M. Proust seemed to have found, not only his past, but our own past as well, to give us back ourselves, life as we too had known and felt it – our common and everyday experience, but enriched and made beautiful and important by the alchemy of art. We have followed with eagerness the progress of that great work; the news that its author's career is ended has come to us with a sense of personal grief, and we therefore wish to be allowed to associate ourselves in the homage which is being paid to the memory of this great

[Article] [January 4, 1923]

artist, and to express our share of sorrow in the loss which the world of the spirit has suffered in his death.

Lascelles Abercrombie,	Charles Scott Moncrieff,
Harley Granville-Barker,	J. Middleton Murry,
Clive Bell,	Logan Pearsall Smith,
Arnold Bennett,	J. C. Squire,
Joseph Conrad,	Lytton Strachey,
E. M. Forster,	R. C. Trevelyan,
Roger Fry,	Arthur Waley,
Edmund Gosse,	A. B. Walkley,
Aldous Huxley,	Virginia Woolf.
Desmond MacCarthy,	

PROUST AND
THE MODERN CONSCIOUSNESS

The tribute printed above bears witness to the high place which Proust held in the affections and admirations of his English contemporaries. Perhaps, at a time like the present, when the outward and political relations between England and France appear to have lost something of their former cordiality, this spontaneous expression of the sentiments of Englishmen towards a writer who is universally acknowledged to have been the chief of his generation in France may be more valuable evidence of the true feelings entertained by the one country for the other than the angry and embittered reproaches which are too often heard.

For Englishmen, indeed, Marcel Proust has already become one of the great figures of modern literature. The feeling is common to many of his readers that in some way his work marks an epoch. What kind of epoch it is harder to say. Is he an end, or a beginning? And, again, yet another question insinuates itself continually as we pass slowly through his long volumes. What precisely – if answers to such questions can be made precise – was his own intention as a writer? Not that it necessarily makes the least difference to his own importance whether he succeeded or failed, whether he was consistent or spasmodic in following out his own plan. But we, at least, should be the happier for some indication of the thread to follow. For there comes a time in the reading of a long novel – and "A la Recherche du Temps Perdu" is surely one of the longest –

when we feel the need to stand aside, to contemplate it as a whole, to grasp the pattern, to comprehend the general vision of life on which its essential individuality depends. Only thus, it seems, can we really make it our own.

In this respect Marcel Proust's book may be fairly said to bristle with difficulties. Its obvious theme, its surface intention, as we perceive it in the brilliant opening pages of "Du Côté de chez Swann," is the presentation by an adult man of his memories of childhood. We feel, though with peculiar qualifications to which we must return, that we are on the threshold of a spiritual autobiography; we are to be the enchanted witnesses of the unfolding and growth of a strangely sensitive consciousness. But no sooner are we attuned to the subtleties of this investigation and have accustomed ourselves to Proust's breathless, tip-toe following of the faint and evanescent threads of association: no sooner have we begun to take a deep and steady breath of rich fragrance of Aunt Léonie's house at Combray, and to imbibe the luxurious atmosphere of the old town, whose shifting colours are as opulent as the lights of the windows in the cathedral round which it clings: no sooner have we prepared ourselves to watch with an absorbed interest the process of growth of a mind nurtured in this almost intoxicating soil – than the thread is abruptly snapped. We do not complain at the moment, for the episode "Amour de Swann" is the highest sustained achievement of Proust as a prose-writer. Perhaps the devouring passion of love – "Venus toute entière à sa proie attachée" – the smouldering, torturing flame of unsatisfied passion, which by the law of its own nature can never be satisfied, has never been so subtly and so steadily anatomised before. Perhaps it has been more wonderfully presented, but never more wonderfully analyzed.

No wonder, then, that in the fascination of this intolerable and unwonted history, in which every psychological subtlety of the author is properly and beautifully dominated by the tragic theme, we forget that this is not at all the thing we went out to see. The boy whose history we have been following could not have known of Swann's discomfiture before he was a man. It has happened, indeed, before the narrative of "Du Côté de chez Swann" opens, before the bell of the garden-gate tinkles and Swann takes his place with the family on the verandah; but it can have no place in the story of the boy's development until he is old enough to understand it. In other words, the angle of presentation has abruptly changed. Into a narrative concerned, as we imagine, solely with what a boy knew and felt, and how he knew and felt it, is suddenly thrust an episode of which he could have known nothing at all.

These two sections of the book – composing the yellow-backed "Du Côté de chez Swann" with which Proust's early admirers had so long to remain content – were at once baffling and fascinating. Moreover, they do actually contain Proust's very finest work: he was never again to sustain himself on this level for so long. But, considered in themselves (and there were three or four years in which we had no choice but to consider them so), they could be made to yield a pattern. On the one side was the vague and heroic figure of Swann as he loomed on the extreme horizon of the boy's world, the mysterious visitant whose appearances in the household made an agony of his solitary going to bed; on the other was the Swann of reality, the reserved, silent, ineffably refined darling of the *beau monde*, who held his teeth clenched, like the Spartan, while the fox gnawed at his vitals. The contrast, the building up of the character of Swann, as it were, from two sides at once, was the quite sufficient motive of the book. But, so understood, it was Swann's book, not the boy's.

But the next volumes brought us back to the boy's history. As we read of his love affair with Albertine, his adoration of the Duchesse de Guermantes, his adventures in the rarefied atmosphere of the Faubourg St Germain, it became more and more evident that "Amour de Swann" was, in spite of its beauty and power, only an irrelevant interlude, after all. And in the narrative of the boy's stay in the hotel at Balbec came frequent hints that the key to the story as a whole might be found in the earlier emphasis upon the manner in which the author went in search of the past. At the beginning of "Du Côté de chez Swann" he had been at pains to give us not merely his results, but his method also. He was a grown man, suddenly waking from sleep, trying to locate himself once more in his room, and his room in the world; and something familiar in this strange sensation had reminded him of his sensations in his bedroom as a child. But "reminded" is altogether too coarse and summary a word for the delicate process on which his researches depended; rather it is that a familiarity in the strange sensation whispers to him that it holds a secret for him if he will only explore it. It conceals something that he must know. Again, it is the vague familiarity of the faint flavour of a *madeleine* dipped in tea, which the grown man is eating in his mother's company, which ultimately yields up the magnificently vivid picture of Combray and Aunt Léonie. These sensations, or presentiments of the past, come to the boy also. There is, for example, the beautiful account of his mysterious excitement at a sight of the spire and towers of Martinville Church when he is driving with his father. Again he has the sense of memories he cannot grasp, of a secret and mystical message that he cannot make his own; it is the occasion of his first attempt at writing. These premonitions become more frequent during his stay with his grandmother at the Balbec hotel. Then the sudden sight of a tiny clump of trees seen while he is driving with the Marquise de Villeparisis makes him feel that they are stretching out imploring arms towards him in a mute appeal. If he can divine what they have to tell him (they seem to say) he will touch the secret of "la vraie vie," of life indeed. And then the writer warns us that the story of his search to make this secret his own is to come, and that this premonition of a task to be accomplished was to haunt him throughout his life.

At this moment perhaps Marcel Proust came nearest, we believe, to revealing to the reader the hidden soul of his own book. There is room for different interpretations, of course, and it is admitted that in any case he was frequently distracted from whatever plan he had by his delight in a pure description of the human comedy from the angle most familiar to him. Neverthless, we are persuaded that Proust brought to the exact and intimate analysis of his own sensations something more than the self-consciousness of talent – some element, let us say, of an almost religious fervour. This modern of the moderns, this *raffiné* of *raffinés*, had a mystical strain in his composition. These hidden messages of a moment, these glimpses and intuitions of "la vraie vie" behind a veil, were of the utmost importance to him; he had some kind of immediate certainty of their validity. He confessed as much, and we are entitled to take a man so reticent at his word.

We may take him at his word also when he acknowledges that the effort to penetrate behind the veil of these momentary perceptions was the chief interest of his life. The first of these illuminations – the vision of Martinville spire – had taken shape in a piece of writing which he gives us. We suspect that the last did also, and that its visible expression is the whole series of volumes which, after all, do bear a significant title – "A la Recherche du Temps Perdu"; we suspect that the last page of the last volume would have brought us to the first page of the first, and that the long and winding narrative would finally have revealed itself as the history of its own conception. Then, we may imagine, all the long accounts of the Guermantes' parties and the extraordinary figure of M. de Charlus, would have fallen into their places in the scheme, as part of the surrounding circumstances whose pressure drove the youth and the man into the necessity of discovering a reality within himself. What he was to discover, when the demand that he should surrender himself to his moments of vision became urgent and finally irresistible, was the history of what he was. Proust – and amid the most labyrinthine of his complacent divagations into the *beau monde* a vague sense of this attends us – was much more than a sentimental autobiographer of genius; he was a man trying to maintain his soul alive. And thus, it may be, we have an explanation of the rather surprising fact that he began his work so late. The two volumes which went before "Du Côté de chez Swann" were not indeed negligible, but they were the work of a *dilettante*. The explanation, we believe, is that in spite of his great gifts Proust was a writer *malgré lui*; he composed against the grain. We mean that had it been only for the sake of the satisfactions of literary creation, he would probably not have written at all. It was only when writing presented itself to him as the only available means for getting down to the bedrock of his own personality, as the only instrument by which his *fin-de-siècle* soul – the epithet is, in his case, a true definition – could probe to something solid to live by, that he seriously took up the pen. It was the lance with which he rode after the Grail – "la vraie vie."

Proust at the first glance looks wholly different from a man who rides off on a desperate adventure. There seems to be no room for desperate adventures in the Faubourg St Germain. It is hardly congruous to some senses to ride through the Waste Land in a sixty horse-power limousine. Nevertheless, it can be done. The outward and visible sign is not for the first time different from the inward and spiritual grace.

So by a devious path we return to our first question. Proust marks an epoch. What kind of an epoch? Is it an end or a beginning? And the answer we have reached is the answer we might have expected in the case of a figure so obviously considerable. Proust is both an end and a beginning. More an end than a beginning, perhaps, if we have regard to the technique and texture of his work. In the art of literature itself he opens up no new way. And, in the deeper sense, he indicates a need more than he satisfies it. The modern mind, looking into the astonishing mirror which Proust holds up to it, will not see in it the gleam of something to live by; but it will see, if it knows how to look, an acknowledgment of that necessity and a burning desire to satisfy it. By so much Marcel Proust marks a beginning also. It is the flame of this desire which smoulders always through his book, and at times breaks out; it is this which makes it his own; and this which gives it, in the true sense, style.

PROUST'S LAST WORK

Cyril Falls

[...] One is impressed by the courage which shines through the concluding pages. He knew he was doomed; he felt his powers, bodily and mental, failing; he was racing against time. Perhaps he did not accomplish all that he had hoped for, yet he was able to write "The End" below his work only a short time before his death. The astonishment wherewith that work, quite unique in literature, was first received has now died down, and it must be left to fight its own battle with time. The more extravagant utterances of his disciples will probably cause posterity, if ever it encounters them, to smile, but it can confidently be said that the work itself will live. Whether, however, that life will be instilled by the breath of the general reading public, or merely by that of those intelligent enough to appreciate the greatness of the mind behind an effort possibly ranked as a failure, Time – let us give it Proust's capital and consider it for a moment with his veneration – Time must be left to decide.

Le Temps Retrouvé, by Marcel Proust [January 19, 1928]

PROUST BY
SAMUEL BECKETT*

Alex Glendinning

Mr Beckett's analysis of Proust is largely an analysis of the nature and effect in Proust's work of "that double-headed monster of damnation and salvation – Time," with its attributes "Memory and Habit." [...]

It is impossible here to do more than sketch the main outline of Mr Beckett's book; he contrives to pack a great deal of subtle analysis into seventy-two pages. His prose is compact, full of energy and rich in valuable metaphors. [...]

BECKETT ON PROUST†

Martin Turnell

[...] The essay was first published in 1931 and is reprinted without alteration or revision. No one has even bothered to correct the misstatement that Gilberte Swann became the Duchesse de Guermantes. It bears the stamp of its period. The frivolous though gifted 1920s were over: the solemn 1930s with their obsession with social realism had begun. Proust's reputation had reached an all-time low.

> Proust's style [said Mr Beckett] was generally resented in French literary circles. But now that he is no longer read, it is generously conceded that he might have written even worse prose than he did.

The young Mr Beckett himself found the style, now so greatly admired, a trifle tiring. [...]

Mr Beckett's own manner is lightly portentous, but his essay is illuminated by moments of genuine insight:

Proust, by Samuel Beckett [April 2, 1931]
†*Proust*, by Samuel Beckett [December 30, 1965]

Surely in the whole of literature there is no study of that desert of loneliness and recrimination that men call love posed and developed with such diabolical unscrupulousness. After this, *Adolphe* is a petulant dribbling, the mock epic of salivary hypersecretion.

The last sentence is a characteristic example of Mr Beckett's rather acid wit. He scores a palpable hit when he describes Proust the letter-writer as "the garrulous old dowager of the letters". And another when he remarks that "for the Baron [de Charlus] Musset's *infidèle* must be a buttons or a bus-conductor". Best of all is his comment on Proust's statement that Chateaubriand and Amiel were among his spiritual ancestors: "It is difficult to connect Proust with this pair of melancholy Pantheists dancing a fandango of death in the twilight."

CHRONICLER
OF THE DECADENCE

John Middleton Murry

[...] The world of Proust's experience is a humanly intolerable world. Some would say it is a perverted world for the simple and, in its own way, sufficient reason that sexual perversion plays so great a part in it. That, as we have seen, is more than accidental: it is not to be explained away by saying that it was in fact prevalent in the society he knew, and that as a faithful chronicler it was his duty to portray it. The sociological fact is certainly exaggerated; but the distorted emphasis is inherent in his theory or his experience of love. Object and subject correspond. As his world is intolerable to him, so is he intolerable to himself. If we are carried away by enthusiasm or very charitable, we shall say that he rediscovered, with a new patience of investigation, the truth enounced by Pascal: "le moi est toujours haïssable." It is so, indeed; but there are points in the texture of ordinary human experience where the "ego" passes into abeyance. The chief of these is love. By handing that

Introduction to Proust, his Life, his Circle and his Work by Derrick Leon
[December 21, 1940]

whole province over to the deathly tyranny of the "ego," Proust falsified human values and left himself no refuge save in a complete subjectivity. [...]

PICTURE OF A REGIME IN DECLINE

D. W. Brogan

[...] There is an egalitarian bias native to this age that must be overcome if Proust is to be approached in a proper spirit of willingness to listen, to be converted. His characters are, for the most part, rich and idle and vicious. The few we are allowed to admire without important reservations are either the narrator's own mother and grandmother, who were neither aristocratic nor idle, or female servants. The standards of French family virtues are represented by Françoise and she, in a far deeper sense than the Guermantes, represents the permanent glories of the France of 'Saint-André des Champs or the habits of mind and behaviour of the *chansons de geste*. The Faubourg Saint-Germain as depicted in Proust is a vast Drones' Club. Cut off from political activity, hiding the degree to which it is involved in modern business, dealing with M. Nissim Bernard only at a directors' meeting or with Marcel's father only on an official board, the Guermantes clan are as apparently divorced from the current life and achievement of France as so many court nobles of old Japan, playing their part in the ritual life of the divine emperor, while all real power, real activity was in the hands of the clan chiefs round the Shogun.

The comparison of Proust with the "Tale of Genji" of Lady Murasaki has occurred to many readers of the two books. But not only is the court world of Genji not quite so idle, not quite so divorced from political reality as it was to become and as the Faubourg was by 1890, the culture of the Mikado's Court was more genuine. The smattering of outdated learning, the obsolescent novelties of taste that make absurd the pride of the Guermantes

Remembrance of Things Past, by Marcel Proust, translated by C. K. Scott Moncrieff. (*Time Regained* translated by Stephen Hudson) [October 18, 1941]

circle in the *esprit* of the clan, were part of the unconscious comedy of the Faubourg. It was A. B. Walkley who noted as one of the most convincing examples of Proust's art as a chronicler of the best society, that the jokes of the Duchesse de Guermantes never quite come off. So it was with her taste in art. She bought Elstirs only because Swann told her to. She admired too soon – or, too late – and although these faults in taste were not confined to the Guermantes circle, though the beauty and grace of Oriane made her lapses more tolerable than the manner of young Madame de Cambremer did hers, the world of the Guermantes had now no more than an aesthetic justification. A Legrandin, like Madame de Cambremer, had links with the still living, growing, working world of the bourgeoisie that made her musical snobbery merely ludicrous, not a failure of functions.

The cruelty with which Proust exposes the intellectual nullity of the Guermantes circle is only one of the many proofs of his severity towards the aristocratic society to whose study he seemed, to some of his friends, to have narrowed his mind and given up gifts that might have been more generously, more fruitfully, spent. But whatever judgment is passed on Proust's choice of a way of life or of a literary theme, there is no flattery here of the old French aristocracy, none of Paul Bourget's reverence for the established social church. As Mr Raymond Mortimer has pointed out, Proust is not merely critical but unjust to his aristocratic models. There must have been to hand better Christian mothers than Madame de Marsantes, better husbands than Basin de Guermantes, better friends than Robert de Saint-Loup, less fatuous diplomats than M. de Norpois, less extravagantly contrasted combinations of virtue and vice than M de Charlus. The most hostile outside critic of the Faubourg Saint-Germain could not have done as much to reveal the emptiness of its claims to leadership as Proust has done. If these are the "notables," then the "fin des notables," the refusal of the French people to trust power to the old aristocracy, needs little explanation or justification. [...]

PROUST'S UNPUBLISHED NOVEL

Pamela Hansford Johnson

On October 20 the Prologue to Proust's unpublished novel, *Jean Santeuil*, appeared in *Le Figaro Littéraire*, which, in the two weeks following, contained respectively two fragments from the same work: the introductory section of "Un Amour de Jean Santeuil" and a study of "L'Affaire Dreyfus." *Jean Santeuil*, a work of 900 manuscript pages, is to be published by Gallimard next year.

It is a little hard to see why Proust's executors have held up this work for so long; but though it would be an exaggeration to praise them for their insight in so doing, there can be little doubt that it could scarcely appear at a better time than now: when it is hardly possible to ignore the fact that in France Proust's reputation is at last beginning to grow solid in the sense that a classic is solid – one may not admire it, but one can no longer asperse the integrity of those who do. The first instinct of the reader, on running hastily through the Prologue to *Jean Santeuil*, is to feel that the work is of no particular value except to the Proustian scholar. The immediate impression is that this, like the stories in *Les Plaisirs et les Jours*, is no more than a fumbling for the major work to come.

A second reading, however, followed by a more intensive study of the "novel within a novel," "Un Amour de Jean Santeuil," may make the reader feel that his first instinct has been no more exact than that which makes us uneasy in the presence of a stranger who happens to resemble physically someone with whom we are intimate. The fact is that this mysterious apparition, this unsure and half-despairing attempt at a work of genius, is, nevertheless, a work which could only have come from a man in whom genius existed. [...]

Jean Santeuil, by Marcel Proust [December 14, 1951]

THE AESTHETIC CITY

Martin Turnell

[...] Proust's life was no work of art, but it can with some justice be described as a destiny. Mr Painter is right to explode the myth of his lack of will power. Proust pursued his ambition to become a great writer with a ruthless, single-minded determination which can seldom have been equalled. Everything that happened to him conspired to help him write the masterpiece that he felt he had been born to write. His parents died at precisely the right time; his asthma was an alibi which kept him prisoner and saved him from the fate of his own Swann; his vices and his hatred of society provided him with his materials. Even his failure to finish *Jean Santeuil* seems to have been the result of the obscure workings of his destiny. For Mr Painter points out that if he had managed to finish it, it would not have been too far in advance of the novels of France and Barrès to be assimilated by the public, that it might have made his name and "rendered *A la Recherche* for ever impossible." He was ready to sacrifice everything – family, friends, life itself – to it. In the end it killed him, as *Bouvard et Pécuchet* is said to have killed Flaubert.

It is here that we find the true parallel between Proust's life and work. He speaks somewhere of "the malady that Swann's love had become." What he deals with in the novel are parasitic growths, excrescences, perversions which prey on the social and the emotional life and destroy both. One of the strangest of his exhibits is jealousy. It is the malignant growth which not only destroys the love that produces it, but survives it. So it was with the masterpiece which ended by devouring the life of its creator. [...]

Marcel Proust, by George D. Painter [November 13, 1959]

A CLEAR VIEW OF
COMBRAY

Robert M. Adams

[. . .] To review properly a new translation of a new edition would require a reviewer with total recall and limitless perspectives to read Proust through four times over, in the original and revised French texts, in the original and revised English translations. That's more than can be asked of flesh and blood – of *this* flesh and blood, anyway. But the practical implications of the situation are simply and quickly summarized. Henceforth, there's no reason for anyone to read Proust in an English translation other than the Moncrieff-Kilmartin version. For anyone already familiar with the original Scott Moncrieff translation, there are only marginal reasons – apart from the fundamental pleasures of rereading Proust – to study the new version. Unless you have a precise verbal memory and an extremely sharp ear for the details of prose rhythm, there are hundreds of pages where, without word-for-word comparison, you would be hard put to tell one version from the other. Some major variations are found in the later books; in the earlier ones, except for occasional nuances of tone (where frequently the translators, equally faithful, are faithful to different elements of the original), the versions are very close indeed. Irregularly spaced, of course, the modifications probably average about three to five per page.

Kilmartin sees as in need of correction his predecessor's fondness for the precious word and the purple patch, as well as his occasional failure to extricate himself completely from the coils of French syntax. The remedy of both blemishes is the same: greater simplicity and directness in the prose. A few details will illustrate. Scott Moncrieff attributes to the asparagus that Françoise is preparing a "rainbow-loveliness"; for Kilmartin, it is simple "iridescence". What Proust wrote was "ébauches d'arc-en-ciel"; so the honours are divided – there is no "loveliness" in Proust but

Remembrance of Things Past, by Marcel Proust, translated by C. K. Scott Moncrieff, Terence Kilmartin and Andreas Mayor [June 12, 1981]

there is a rainbow. Both translators miss the tentative quality of *ébauches*, but finding the proper light touch in English is perhaps impossible. Again, Proust writes, "Le passé n'est pas fugace, il reste sur place". Scott Moncrieff translates, "The past not merely is not fugitive, it remains present". Kilmartin reduces to, "The past is not fugitive, it stays put" – a clear improvement. Scott Moncrieff has a fondness for "albeit" which Kilmartin regularly reduces to "although" or "though". Scott Moncrieff uses, for Proust's expressive "muffle", variations on "caddish" or "like a cad". Kilmartin avoids the moral disdain and gains precision by translating "boorishly" or "rudely". [. . .]

Changes of this magnitude, it will be appreciated, amount to very little when considered individually; it's mainly in the later volumes that the new version, based on a new text, starts to present occasional units a paragraph or two in size that were not to be found in the older translation. (Among the Addenda to Volume II, there is a striking and extended passage in which the Baron de Charlus, infatuated with an ugly, coarse, and ignorant bus conductor, repeatedly rebuffs the overtures of the Princesse de Guermantes, with the result that she tries to poison herself. The passage is alluded to in the established text of the novel, but never found a place there.) And yet the cumulative effect of the detailed changes would alone justify the new edition. They give Proust a more crisp and energetic tonality, in keeping with modern standards of plain, uncluttered prose; they cut down on the soft Proust and bring out the hard Proust, who was there all along, no more the "real" Proust than his counterpart, but better adapted to modern tastes and, perhaps, to Proust's new position in literary history. Reflections on these matters are the inevitable fruit of a re-reading of the novel – which, if it isn't morally obligatory might well use the new version as a welcome pretext.

Nobody would be more alive than Proust himself to the ironies that spring from a repeated reading, under different circumstances, with different eyes and feelings, of the same text. To lapse for a moment into the personal – but with canonical authority: "In reality", says Proust, "every reader is, while he is reading, the reader of his own self" – my own reading of the novel goes back nearly if not altogether fifty years. About the time of that first reading, my family was in Europe for the year, and their roots being partly aristocratic, I could sense through their contacts something of the old world they had only half discarded. It was a flavour the more pronounced because it touched my senses so lightly, so briefly, from such an immense distance, I recall meeting, in the Hague, a severe, massively courteous old Swedish baron; there was brief talk of his younger brother, who had suffered an obscure and fatal misfortune – I only knew what it was, decades later, from the film *Elvira Madigan*. My mother, who took her genealogy only less seriously than the Duc de Guermantes, made contact with some of the sprawling and ancient family of De la Gardie, with whom her own family of Teutonic knights were somehow – in ways not really to be explained by the quarterings on the family crest – intricately allied. There was talk of visiting their seat, somewhere in Occitania, but I don't think anything ever came of it. In these and other ways, it was possible for someone born during the First World War, and in a culture as alien as New York City, to grow up with a sense of Proust's world as only a moment and a step away – to feel that Proust's nostalgia for an age of peace, plenty, and deference had somehow been extended to oneself, that in fact he was really a contemporary writer.

Another ambiguous and subtle bond with Proust was his Jewishness, an affinity all the more binding for not being explicit – one aspect of which was perhaps a secret sense of pride at having some access to "good" society but scorning to make use of it. One of my college contemporaries wrote some years ago of having been an "artificial Jew". It was a frequent experience of the 1930s; some of us, to adapt the words of the chronicler, became "more Jewish than the Jews themselves". To "pass" in the reverse direction was a matter of pride. I recall once being called away from a conversation with my best friend, son of the rabbi of Weehawken, because a fellow student wanted to invite me to pledge a Jewish fraternity, and didn't want to do so in the presence of "that gentile". And to this sense of a private and vital society of outcasts (private merely in the sense of dismissing external marks and official distinctions with the wry outsider's wit and cynical intelligence to which we at least aspired), Proust lent his example. (I don't think we were similarly impressed with his homosexuality, nor am I much impressed by it to this day. Proust seems to me a man addicted to love, not to any particular expression of it; the long essay on the "men of Sodom" at the beginning of *Sodome et*

Gomorrhe is one of the flattest and most extraneous passages of the book.)

Well, then, if one grew up taking Proust as an accomplice to one's own fantasies, the passage of fifty years must work remarkable changes in one's relation to the book; and so, of course, it has. As age brings out the basic structure of a well-known face, stripping off the soft contours to reveal that sparse, angular framework of bone which may have an energy of its own, so Proust with the years reveals himself more and more as a moralist in the severe, sententious vein of the seventeenth century. Beckett, with his special appetite for despair and futility, would reduce Proust's logic to a diagram of his own stark nihilism; but the mere dimensions of Proust's work are against him. We don't need to read a million and a half words to learn that all knowledge is vain and all affection futile. Proust is interested in law: he said so. "There is a feeling for generality which, in the future writer, itself picks out what is general and can for that reason one day enter into a work of art". He writes axioms, aphorisms for the memory. These axioms of Proust are mostly stoic in their tonality; like those of Montaigne, or for that matter Madame de Sévigné, they focus on the conduct and management of the affections. That is why there are so many of them; they grow out of, and never depart far from, the concrete business of life. But behind diversity they seek, and often discover, the inexorable working of natural law. One reason why there is so little morality in Proust is that there is so deep a sense of natural destiny. Thus it makes very little difference what specific society Proust chose to depict; the game of ins and outs played in all of them (sometimes in the name of "love", sometimes more frankly) is much the same everywhere. The novel seems to write itself incrementally by following its own logic; and now, by a slowed-down but continuing process of change, even after its publication, continues to exfoliate new meanings and absorb new feelings. It is a special privilege of the new version (but really of all "mere" translations) to be able to reflect and even forward this process, as not even a precious, unchanging original, which isn't exempt from the perils of familiarity, can do.

MINDS, GREAT AND SMALL

Malcolm Bowie

[...] The English selection of Proust's early letters has been produced by a distinguished triumvirate: Philip Kolb edits, John Cocking introduces and Ralph Manheim translates. The volume which results from their concerted labours will be of special interest to those who have already read Proust's novel in English and found themselves wanting to know more about the emotional and stylistic workshop from which this supremely complex artefact emerged. Many of the letters collected here are experiments in feeling: whether Proust is expressing filial adoration or homosexual ardour or concern for the health and glory of his favourite society tigresses, the tone often seeks not simply to discharge emotion but to discover how much of it there is and how best it can be manipulated. During these years Proust's letters are strenuously orchestrated even when anecdotal and try out an astonishing array of stylistic registers. The arts being tested are often the lesser ones of gossip, badinage, flirtation and flattery, but these very arts, perfected, transcendentalized, helped to give *A la recherche* its unique versatility of tone.

Proust writes to Reynaldo Hahn's sister, for example:

> My nerves are frayed from insomnia, but I am enjoying my visit here thanks to Reynaldo, and you are associated with all my impressions, oh, my sister Maria, confidante of my thoughts, beacon to errant sadness, protectress of the weak, helpmate of the sick, source of goodness, spice of wit, sparkling rose, courageous kindness, breeze upon the sea, song of happy oars, shuddering sea foam, glory of morning, perfume of friendship, soul of the nights which you dazzle with your brilliance ...

And so, exhaustively, it goes on. This letter, as Cocking remarks in his delightfully pointed introduction, "might have been written by

Marcel Proust: Selected Letters, ed. by Philip Kolb, translated by Ralph Manheim [February 17, 1984]

Legrandin in a moment of delirium". And exactly the delirium of
such utterances – the attempt to supersaturate experience with
words – was to become a major source of comedy in Proust's novel.
In training in these letters is the parodic imagination which was
eventually to produce the grandiose verbal aberrations of Legrandin, Norpois, Cottard and Brichot – those accomplished professional people who each have a manic appetite for redundancy in
speech. This range of character-portraits is based upon Proust's
sense of stupidity not as a native condition of certain minds but as a
localized mental lesion. In these cases, which are quite different
from those mainly studied by Hughes, fatuously bludgeoning
verbal performances are perfectly compatible with intellectual
adroitness and professional success. Off their guard, obedient to
the whims of salon society, preening themselves at parties, the
engineer, the ambassador, the doctor and the academic speak their
passions with visceral insistence and abandon.

In this extraordinarily revealing volume, Proust not only
provides a laboratory notebook towards that "physiology of
chatter" which so excited Walter Benjamin in *A la recherche*, but
explores, again in an improvised preliminary fashion, the subject
which, above all others in the novel, was to show the viscera of the
professional class dangerously astir: the Dreyfus case. The
energetic satire of contemporary antisemitic discourse which we
eventually find in the novel begins modestly enough in these
letters. Antisemitism is a pervasive force in the society Proust
chooses to frequent and the paths that it follows in everyday
conversation are traced by him with saddened vigilance. Writing to
Hahn about dinner at the Daudets, for example, he is prepared,
perhaps over-generously, to allow Alphonse Daudet his talent and
his charm, yet finds the suspicion of Jews and the explanations by
"race" which permeate the household an affront to the very powers
of mind that Daudet in other respects emblematizes. Daudet is at
once "a pure and brilliant intellect" and "simplistic in his
intelligence". Having studied such mental hybrids and moral
amphibians over countless dinner-tables, and having lightly
sketched them for friends, Proust went on, in *A la recherche*, to
produce a weighty critique of the society which fostered them. [. . .]

THE MAGIC MOUNTAIN

Orlo Williams

Mr H. T. Lowe-Porter is entitled to our congratulations on his translation of Thomas Mann's novel, "The Magic Mountain." Here and there it is a little stilted and wanting in freedom, but, considering the difficulty of the task and the immense field of thought and special knowledge traversed by the book, the whole performance must be considered very good. It is a portentous book, not one to which lovers of light literature are asked to sit down, and a contrast indeed to the dashing, confused and cynical spirit which inspires so many novels of our day. Here is no breaking up of life and consciousness into bright-coloured fragments, but, on the contrary, a laborious, exhaustive, and *gründlich* putting of them together. This, indeed, is the fundamental purpose of the book, patiently and inexorably philosophical. Hans Castorp, the hero, a mediocre, good-hearted, upright, rather lazy and self-indulgent young German of Hamburg, before entering the shipbuilding business to which he is destined, is ordered a holiday in the mountains. He goes to visit his cousin Joachim, a military officer-to-be, who is undergoing a cure for tuberculosis in the International Sanatorium Berghof at Davos. Hans arrives on a three weeks' visit: he stays seven years. He comes a raw, ignorant, inexperienced youth: he leaves for "the flat land," to fight for his country, a tried and instructed soul, with a trained mind, a full experience and a deep vision into the mysteries of time, life and death.

At first sight the choice of scene for this long story of enlightenment seems strange; to bring a youth into the artificial existence of an Alpine sanatorium for the purpose of teaching him what life means seems a contradiction; and the copious details of hygienic routine, of huge meals spaced out by rests, of medical details and corruptions of the flesh, at first repel the reader. Yet, like the personality of the impressive Dutchman, Mynheer Peeperkorn, who appears in the second volume, the book imposes

The Magic Mountain, by Thomas Mann, translated by H. T. Lowe-Porter [July 7, 1927]

itself by its very stature, the largeness of its design and its exhaustiveness; and one comes to see how, in a rarefied atmosphere and in the midst of a mixed cosmopolitan company, all idle and all feverish, the spiritual foundations of such a soul as Hans Castorp's might be truly laid better than amidst the distracting preoccupations of life "down below." [...]

A MODERN FAUSTUS

Dr W. von Einsiedel

[...] This is the crucial question: whether or no a creative artist can play the role of Faustus. In contrast to the artist Faustus is scarcely driven from within, scarcely conditioned from without; he is not predetermined, not obsessed by singleness of purpose. His will is free to choose, his realm is that of potentialities and possibilities, not of necessities. It is hard to see, furthermore, how the life of any artist, necessarily personifying a single individuality and recognizable by its fruits alone, can symbolize the fate of a nation or of a society, both more free in decision and more dependent on the impersonal chances of history, more harmless in desire, more dangerous in uncontrolled action. Adrian Leverkühn's conflicts are those of the genuine artist in modern society (though strangely enough in his human relationships he seems to lack passion); his achievements and faults are purely artistic ones, and hardly concern the world at large. Even his fame is of an esoteric nature, savagely attacked by his vulgar compatriots. What, then, has he gained, what betrayed, by selling himself to the Devil? What evil has he wrought comparable to the evil his compatriots have perpetrated? His final succumbing to madness is a relief from unbearable tension rather than a disaster comparable to the fall of Germany. As an artist he is scarcely typical of his race. And his background, consisting almost solely of academic lecture halls, idyllic farmhouses or literary salons, cannot be said to resume the German society of his time, even if some of Dr Mann's ideological discussions reflect the process of disintegration among the German middle classes.

Doctor Faustus, by Thomas Mann [February 14, 1948]

It is easy to admire, however, the bold grandeur of Dr Mann's attempt and, at the same time, enjoy the countless felicities of phrase, the flashes of insight (some dazzling, but some illuminating), the highly entertaining digressions of a story which gathers the memories and thoughts of a lifetime into the loosely woven net of an ironically glittering prose.

GERMAN ABSTRACTIONS*

Anthony Powell

[. . .] *Doctor Faustus* reminds us of the old rhyme:

> The Germans in Greek
> Are sadly to seek –
> Not five in five-score
> But ninety-five more
> All, save only Hermann:
> And Hermann's a German.

In novel-writing there would be a temptation to estimate the German percentage even lower than this; and – although Dr Mann's gifts are undeniable – he is, like Hermann, German of the Germans. Zeitblom is pictured as a bore of the first water, and, in entrusting the narrative to his hands, the author condemns the reader to long-winded dissertations and a point of view of artificial naivety that puts on him an almost intolerable strain in following the story. [. . .]

THE ARTIST AND THE
REAL WORLD†

Erich Heller

[. . .] Some of the profoundest aesthetic speculations to be found in modern thought, from Schopenhauer and Nietzsche to Rilke,

Doctor Faustus, by Thomas Mann [May 6, 1949]
†*Meine Zeit*, by Thomas Mann [January 5, 1951]

Valéry, Dr Mann and Mr T. S. Eliot, are based on an apparently irreconcilable dualism between empirical reality and a sphere of pure vision, between what the artist is as a real person and what he produces as a mere medium of impersonal forces. There is a direct line which, in spite of their obvious differences, connects Schopenhauer's aesthetic philosophy with Mr Eliot's essay on "Tradition and the Individual Talent," a line which is marked by Nietzsche's *Birth of Tragedy*, Rilke's "Elegy to a Young Poet," Valéry's M. Teste and, above all, by Thomas Mann's numerous works dealing with the problematic relationship of the artist to reality. The common experience linking the ideas of these men is the increasing sense of a tremendous devaluation of the real world, or, rather, of what is spontaneously accepted as real in the modern world.

There is no doubt that the creation of a work of art is something qualitatively different from the "artistic" expression of subjective feelings and experiences; no doubt whatever that the vision of the artist must reach beyond the field hemmed in by the wilful purposes of the self, and that genius consists in the gift – rare at all times – of surrendering freely to a command issuing from a truth beyond appearances. But only a complete reversal of the order and hierarchy of reality, as embodied in the religious tradition of Europe, could lead philosophers to speak of unreality and nothingness where reality is comprehended more fully; and what the great teachers within our spiritual inheritance have taught about the nature of a person had to be forgotten or perverted before artists could feel that they cease to be persons precisely at the point where the real person begins: in the act of submitting to an objective vision of the world. It is hardly thinkable that the builders of Greek temples, or medieval cathedrals, were haunted by a sense of unreality, or that Homer, or Aeschylus, or Dante felt that his poetic pursuits entailed a loss of personality. It could more truly be said that a loss of the spiritual significance of life within the consciousness of the age has raised art in modern aesthetic theory to a status beyond "reality," and manoeuvred the artist into an isolation from the real world where the denial of his life as a person is exacted as the price for significant creation.

This spiritual devaluation of life – the very essence of Schopenhauer's philosophy – has roused the passionate indignation of his greatest disciple, Nietzsche; and between Schopenhauer's indictment of life and Nietzsche's advocacy of it lies the source of much of Thomas Mann's irony. While many other modern writers and artists accepted the gulf between the spheres of empirical living and artistic vision as unavoidable, Thomas Mann, with as much experience and knowledge of it as others, found in this situation a cause for great moral uneasiness.

The deep personal experience of the dissolution of an established form of civilized life (the theme of *Buddenbrooks*), opposed by the moral determination to maintain the traditional values of European society; the suspicion, furthermore, that many of the impulses behind artistic pursuits come from dubious sources, such as a "perversion" of life, a vital insufficiency, the inability to live; a suspicion held in check by the writer's resolution to justify morally his existence as an artist – this situation is reflected in most of the books which Thomas Mann has written. Thus he could not become one of the great innovators (or reducers to absurdity?) of the modern novel. He has maintained and refined the form of realistic narrative, his insistence on the traditional form being the outcome of a moral decision. There may be something of the comic-heroic futility of a Don Quixote or of the pathos of a Sisyphus in Thomas Mann's persistent effort to express the very disintegration of consciousness and sensibility by means of most highly organized artistic forms. [...]

THE STORY
OF AN ARTIST

Erich Heller

[...] The central and most serious concern of Thomas Mann has undoubtedly been the problem of art itself, or of the artist-writer. "*Felix Krull* is in essence the story of an artist," he said at a time when only the fragment existed. It is also the comedy of the aesthetic sensibility, or the farce of inauthentic living, or the parody of civilization, just as *Death in Venice* and *Doctor Faustus*

Confessions of Felix Krull, Confidence Man, by Thomas Mann, translated by Denver Lindley [November 11, 1955]

realized the pity of it all. As early as *Tonio Kröger* (1903) Thomas Mann was fascinated by the idea of the artist-criminal, the personified alliance between artistic creativeness and moral derangement. In that story the anecdote of the fraudulent banker who, while serving a prison sentence, becomes a writer, is the bizarre foil to the moral scruples of the young artist: "One might be rash enough to conclude that a man has to be at home in some kind of jail in order to become a poet." And again, when Tonio, through a misunderstanding, is molested by inquisitive policemen, he feels reluctant to insist on his law-abiding innocence: "For after all, were not these guardians of civic order slightly justified in their suspicion? In a sense he quite agreed with them."

In *Felix Krull* the agreement expresses itself in comic abandon. On one occasion this self-confessed charlatan comments on his gift of lyrically exalted speech: "Poetry came easily to me by virtue of the delicately balanced unreality of my existence." It is the unreality of the poetic existence, this most persistent and most personal of all the themes of Thomas Mann, that is at the same time humourously realized and outrageously parodied in *Felix Krull*. This book, therefore, is made of the stuff of which the world's great comic creations are made: a grave affliction of the soul resolved in laughter, a laughter which reverberates with many echoes of the writer's anxious passage through a melancholy age, and as the anxiety was not only his own, but the sadness of our fragile civilization itself, Felix Krull stands a good chance of becoming a literary archetype. [...]

MANN AND
HIS BRETHREN

Michael Hamburger

[...] An open-minded reader may be struck by the recognition that both *Tonio Kröger* and *Death in Venice* would be just as valid and effective if their respective heroes were not writers or artists at all; that it was only Thomas Mann's preoccupation with his personal

The Ironic German, by Erich Heller [October 3, 1958]

problems that caused him to formulate the basic antinomy in terms of art and life, artist and citizen – and to send whole generations of students and critics vainly scurrying along the same track. Tonio could be any social misfit of his class with aesthetic leanings; and it is an error of Mann's and his critics to treat "artist" and "aesthete" as synonyms. Some of the most extreme aesthetes are wholly uncreative, and many creative artists are curiously indifferent to beauty as such. Aschenbach could be a professor, a politician, a managing director or any professional man accustomed to a regular routine and to minding his ps and qs. The basic conflict is not between life and art but between conscious will and unconscious impulse. The "vicious circle" which Professor Heller discovers in comparing the two works is no vicious circle at all. The bourgeois world to which Tonio is drawn is not "artless," as Professor Heller calls it, but a product of art; nor is it life that defeats Aschenbach, but the attraction of death for those whose unconscious impulses have been suppressed beyond hope of release. That is one reason why these stories have a much wider appeal than their "problem" would seem to warrant.

How far Thomas Mann himself was misled by his false categories is all too clear in his writings on politics and literature. His reference to "Brother Hitler," mentioned by Professor Heller, is a case in point. Mann was so obsessed with his equation of art with illness that he forgot the two most relevant considerations: that Hitler was never an artist, only a neurotic with an "artistic temperament," and that some of the best artists have been rather healthier and less neurotic than the next man. The antithesis between "life" and *Geist* – rather recklessly rendered throughout as "spirit" by Professor Heller – was the worst offender of all; if Mann knew what he meant by either word at any one moment, his reader can only guess. "Life" could denote the civilized bourgeois at peace with his environment, or nature; *Geist* the intellect, the intelligentsia or intellectual life of the country, plain intelligence or the numinously spiritual.

These confusions, unfortunately, did enter into the imaginative works, but only into that stratum of them which was deliberate and willed. It is easy enough to allow for the element of pure play that characterizes Mann's treatment of ideas; and to take them less literally than Mann was apt to do when he translated inner tensions into verbal concepts. We can appreciate a character like Peeperkorn without knowing or caring whether he stands for art or life; Gerhart Hauptmann, of whom Peeperkorn was a caricature, stood for both, as it happens. We can enjoy the adventures of Krull without knowing that Mann described this novel as "in essence the story of an artist" – simply because Krull is amoral, a confidence man and an imposter – or that the novel is the most intimate of all Mann's confessions. In fact it is hard to avoid the conclusion that the less we know about Mann's intentions, the better for him and for us. [...]

MANN IN HIS TIME

J. P. Stern

[...] Of the critical selfconsciousness of Thomas Mann's heroes three things can be said: it is timely, it is complex but not absolute, and its condition is solitude.

It is timely: by this I mean that Mann's heroes live up to their historical moment, that they are not the naive and spontaneously acting personages of earlier literary conventions. The young Nietzsche – the author of *The Birth of Tragedy*, and even the not-so-young author of *Beyond Good and Evil* – saw the cultural impasse of his age in its loss of unreflective spontaneity; and he hoped, for a time at least, to find this spontaneity in Wagner's musical dramas. Thomas Mann does not indulge in these thoughts, which were soon to become to fashionable, not to say notorious. He creates no clodhopping peasants, gamekeepers who have only one thing on their minds, or Stakhanovite workers intent only on fulfilling their norm. Thomas Buddenbrook, Tonio Kröger, Prince Klaus Heinrich (the hero of *Royal Highness*), Gustav Aschenbach, Hans Castorp, the old Goethe, Joseph (the hero of Mann's biblical tetralogy), Adrian Leverkühn, and Felix Krull – they all display an acute, though often only momentary, awareness of their own identity, which includes an awareness of what it is that threatens or enhances the psychic integrity of their persons. They are by no means necessarily intellectuals, but they are always reflective, and

[Article] [June 6, 1975]

their reflectiveness invariably includes some awareness of their age and their place in its history.

By saying that their self-consciousness is complex and relative, I have in mind a strange game which Thomas Mann plays with them, a game of leapfrog. For no sooner do they understand what the author has in store for them, and how he wishes them and their lives to be understood, than he moves on, confounding or cancelling out their understanding, or superseding it by a new and further interpretation which they in turn will have to catch up with, or which will not be made available to them any more. The author has usually the last word, but not always; sometimes the hero catches up with the author's final comment, consciousness exceeds the events of the story and is carried to the point of tedium.

And the condition of their knowledge is solitude. Like Prince Hamlet – or rather like the Prince Hamlet of Freud's interpretation – their knowledge is a burden, or perhaps a sort of caul, that separates them from other people, especially from those who are closest to them and whose uninformed affection seeks to penetrate their solitude. [...]

RAINER MARIA RILKE

T. W. Rolleston

If there is anything in Mr George Moore's theory of the determining influence of the names of authors, then it is obvious that Rainer Maria Rilke could not possibly help being a poet, and it is also tolerably clear what sort of poet he would be. One thinks of a genius melodious, feminine and melancholy, remote and mystic, drawing, in a few clear but subdued colours, things whose hidden meaning must be delicately wooed to come forth if they come at all – into the light of intelligence. And this is really very much what his work is like. [...]

Neue Gedichte, by Rainer Maria Rilke [February 26, 1920]

RAINER MARIA RILKE

Alec Randall

Rainer Maria Rilke was born in Prague on December 4, 1875; he died at Montreux on December 29 last. One need not go so far as Herr Musil, in his commemoration address, where he declares the dead poet to have been the finest German lyric-poet since the Middle Ages; this enthusiasm was the reaction – a justifiable reaction, one may add – against the understatement of several of the German obituary notices. Among critics of literature as a body it would be generally acknowledged that the lyric poetry of Europe, which was made the richer by his life, was left the poorer by his death at an age when he had, most probably, not yet wrought to its finest the thread of his imagination.

Fine, it is true, that thread had become, and in the bad as well as the good sense of the word. The poet's personality had been so drawn out that it had become, sometimes, almost too attenuated for comprehension. Yet no one could doubt that the personality was genuine, that the verse to which it gave utterance sprang from a union between emotion and reality. [...]

A little before his death he had been "taken up" by the *Nouvelle Revue française*, and an early criticism against him by a German writer, that he was altogether "un-German," was revived, even after his death. The remark is shallow. Off the main road of German national poetry his work certainly is. The shadow of the East fell early across his mind, and in the darkness he groped, as no German before him, except Hölderlin, for reality. He is saved from ineffectiveness by his sense of the beauty of words and images, by his command of form, above all in his odes and elegies. This artistic passion gave life and illumination to his thought; where argument might well have proved unavailing, it compels us to follow him into the innermost recesses of his mind. And there, at least, is restfulness, peace, not from completeness, not from a satisfaction in achievement, but in patient contemplation of mystery. [...]

Rede zur Rilke-Feier, by Robert Musil [July 28, 1927]

RILKE – THE LAST PHASE

Alec Randall

[...] Rilke's view of life rested on an intuition. Even the composition of the Sonnets, which were written, with the other poems mentioned, in three concentrated weeks of creation, Rilke describes as having been achieved under dictation, though their form obviously reveals technical gifts of a high order. The immediate occasion of this "enigmatic" inspiration was the death of a friend's innocent, intensely vital, young daughter; this unstopped the channels of expression, and round the symbolical figure of Orpheus, mediator between life and death, torn in pieces but alive again in the beauty of creation, Rilke wove the rich pattern of his contemplation. To describe this as aesthetic pantheism might be to use too cold a formula, but it would not be misleading if understood in the sense of Shelley's "Adonais." Rilke's own words are apt:–

> We, local and ephemeral as we are, are not for one moment contented in the world of time nor confined within it; we keep on crossing over to our predecessors, to our descent, and to those who apparently come after us.

The whole long passage from which this is taken is given by Mr Leishman and is a valuable clue to those who – and Rilke did not discourage their search – ask for a "meaning." There is, however, more in the Sonnets than this. There is a pondering on, a visionary grasping of problems that are very close to Rilke's time and our own. Machine versus Man – it is unforgettingly summed up in one short lyric; the individual and the community, the questionings of modern psychology, Rilke embraced these. Apparently – and it seems to be the chief point open to criticism in Mr Leishman's excellent interpretation – it failed of perfection by not embracing Socialism as Mr Leishman understands it. In other words, Mr Leishman is anxious that Rilke should not be a poet but a prophet as well, if not a member of the Labour Party. There is also a curious footnote implying that Rilke is in some way an emotional

Sonnets to Orpheus, by Rainer Maria Rilke [October 31, 1936]

complement to a process said to be worked out socially in Soviet Russia, "putting the individual in his place." It may be asked, what place, and is it the right place? In the same week as this edition of Rilke's Sonnets was published Herr Hitler was reported as having said, "I will preserve with ruthless determination the highest interests of the nation against the madness and egotism of the individual." This is merely mentioned to show the irrelevance – it is, we repeat, the only really questionable part of Mr Leishman's work – of associating Rilke with current controversy. Rather should we associate his optimism with the great mystics (and our own Mother Julian of Norwich might profitably have been mentioned), his humility and simplicity with St Francis of Assisi, and his individualism with Blake. [. . .]

RAINER MARIA RILKE, UNIVERSAL POET WITH A GERMAN TONGUE

Alec Randall

[. . .] Rilke was born in Prague of German parents, but in all probability with Slav forebears. It would be unwise to ascribe much significance to this question of race; but Rilke's place of birth and upbringing, between the Slav and Germanic worlds, and where, too, there was an appreciation for contemporary French literature, undoubtedly had a lasting influence on this intensely nervous, highly receptive mind, tortured by the five years he had to spend at the military academy and seeking, against much discouragement, to set up a barrier of imagination between himself and the harsh material career for which his father had destined him. Rilke was enabled to escape this, and the quantity of his early works bore witness to the fertility of his invention and the quick reaction of his imagination to many varying stimuli: among writers, Czech folk-song, Heine, Maeterlinck, Hauptmann, the Danish novelist

Rainer Maria Rilke, by E. M. Butler [April 26, 1941]

Jacobsen; among personalities, Lou Andreas-Salome, friend of Nietzsche, his passion for whom led to a lifelong friendship of crucial importance for his life and art; among places, Venice and Florence and Viareggio, at the last of which he had what Professor Butler believes to have been that vision or hallucination which, while it went to the writing of the early play, *The White Princess*, made also a permanent mark on Rilke's mind.

This versatility of emotion, this wide scope of influences to which Rilke was open, was a constant feature of his life. Persons, books, places, things, but always places and persons rather than Nature in the Wordsworthian sense, formed his mind and gave direction to his impulses. Sometimes Rilke was mistaken, and after him his readers and critics equally so, in estimating the significance of particular influences. His visits to Russia, for example, used to be commonly set down as having awakened that inborn sense of mystery, that kinship with the poor and ignorant which the devotees singled out as one of Rilke's chief messages to his generation but which, in slightly cynical but exceptionally well-informed pages, Professor Butler shows to have been based on a highly individualist and idealist reading of Russia and, in any event, due primarily to Italian experiences, above all the frescoes of Fra Angelico. The truth is that while some of Rilke's experiences, such as his acquaintance with Rodin and discovery of Cézanne, his aversion from and then irresistible attraction to Paris, had a tangible influence on his mind and work, there were other instances in which the same part was played not by material reality but by what Rilke imagined to be reality. It would be wrong to decry this; we need hardly be disturbed by the fact that "The Notebooks of Malte Laurids Brigge" were inspired by Rilke's erroneous belief, perhaps instilled in him by his much-maligned mother, that he was the last scion of a noble race. All we need note is that like Keats – whose letters may profitably be read in this connexion – Rilke craved sensation rather than thought, and that, at his highest moments, what his imagination seized as beauty became truth indeed, independent of the make-believe, the romantic fallacies and the occasional meretricious accompaniments which Professor Butler describes. It is true that, as Professor Butler argues, Rilke deluded himself that his passion for solitude concealed a love for the bustle of cities, his restless travelling from country to country a deep longing for bourgeois stability, his invocation of death as a triumphant reality inseparable from life an instinctive shrinking from disease and bodily dissolution, his hymning of love a fear of sex. But when analysis has completed this destructive interpretation what exactly has it shown? No more, surely, than that Rilke was neither saint, seer nor mystic in the true sense of the words, and that his best work had only that religious validity which is inherent in all great art.

It is a real merit of Professor Butler's book that, with some brutality, it helps us to disengage the poet from the would-be prophet. We can thus start afresh, reading with the interest it deserves, but not necessarily accepting as the ultimate truth, such a document as the poet's long explanation of his "Duinese Elegies," noting, but not necessarily agreeing with, his later depreciation of some of his early work because it did not conform to the philosophical mission he had assumed for himself. The rhapsodies of the disciples, the learned exegeses of the philosophers, from the phenomenologists and the anthroposophists, anxious to claim him as their own, to the post-Nazi Revolution writers, hoping to demonstrate that Rilke's ostentatious withdrawal from the immediate problems of his age was more than balanced by a self-identification with the deepest instincts of his race – these things fall away as irrelevant, as no more required for our appreciation of his poetry than an acceptance of Godwin is to the value we put upon Shelley's "Hellas," or "The Origin of Species" upon "In Memoriam." Useful these things are to the critical understanding, but they are not essential to enjoyment, to the heightening of emotion and the sharpening of vision which we receive.

The first thing to note about Rilke, the artist, is that he had no roots in his race or nation. After the juvenilia he yielded himself to influences in almost all parts of Europe except Germany – and, we must add, England, which he curiously neglected, not reading *Hamlet* even until the latter part of his life. Not that Rilke was always indifferent to Germany; his five war-hymns were a remarkable interlude, and he lamented that Germany, after 1918, had not followed the idealistic path. But the tower within which he chose to withdraw himself was built of varied European materials – not including, however, the Christian tradition, a fact obscured by his highly personal and ambiguous use of Christian terms. Rilke was a European poet, not only in the non-aesthetic sense that he had no exclusive patriotism, but also in that he gathered in rays from all four corners of the Continent, passed them through the prism of his own personality and projected a light coloured by nothing German except the accident of language. Apart from the original word-formations and innovations of rhyme and rhythm, which only German could have permitted, much of Rilke's work could quite well have been written in French, and it was in this language that he wrote poems towards the end – a subject on which Professor Butler has an interesting chapter, pointing out that the symbols which had been delicate and subtle enough in German, in French "flutter melodiously towards invisibility," so that "nothing is left but a small overturned scent-bottle whose fragrance is perfuming the air." It was the poet's farewell.

A European poet he was, then, and his like has not been seen since and may not be seen again. [...]

A MAN OUT OF TIME AND PLACE

Michael Hofmann

Rilke may well be the apotheosis of the German language: the poet in whom its persuasions, abstracts and music are most triumphantly effective. The best exponent of its inflections, genders, moods, word-order and latencies; who writes in "the language of word-kernels" for which it is so particularly well-suited. To an extraordinary degree, the miracles of Rilke are the common features of German: the image-fostering capitalization of nouns; the suppleness of word-order and the strictness of declension and conjugation; the permissible drift of a word from one part of speech to another; the way a word can be assembled, disassembled, reassembled, dissembled; and, throughout, the utter transparency and naturalness of it all. When he wrote – and there were times when he couldn't – he wrote cleanly, fluently and rapidly. He wrote fair copy. He tore up the page where his pen had slipped. It was, as

The Selected Poetry of Rainer Maria Rilke, translated and ed. by Stephen Mitchell. *Rainer Maria Rilke: Selected Letters, 1902–1926*, translated by R. F. C. Hull [July 22, 1988]

he said, describing the way the first lines of the first Elegy came to him on the wind at Duino, like taking dictation. German underwrote him. Stefan Zweig was surely right in saying translation could produce no more than a colourless shadow of Rilke. In custom-driven English, his translators have tried to hide in the extraordinary, the stilted, the obscure, the calculatedly dazzling – all enemies of Rilke.

Since his death in 1926, every decade has had its translators of Rilke: Sidney Keyes, Leishman and Spender, C. F. MacIntyre, Randall Jarrell, W. D. Snodgrass, Robert Bly. Now, the American translator Stephen Mitchell has put forward the first consistently readable versions of Rilke that I have seen; the first that can be read on their own, without requiring toning up or down by others; the first not to depend on mirrors, pulleys and trust. An English reader can now see something of Rilke for the first time. This is not to say, of course, that Mitchell's solutions are in every instance to be preferred to those of his predecessors: Leishman and Spender score some fine magniloquent hits in the *Elegies*. But a compilation of Rilke translations would be half made up of Mitchell's, if not more.

To begin with, he passes the negative tests: he writes English, he is accurate, clear and seemly. He avoids poetizing, the writing of ten deadly lines in the attempt to write a deathless one. His watchwords are sense and tautness, though he is not afraid to expand a phrase or clause that is too compact. "For there is no place where we can remain", he says, for "Denn Bleiben ist nirgends". (Leishman and Spender have "For staying is nowhere.") The result is that the sound of Rilke's thinking becomes audible for the first time; that he is heard pleading, reasoning, improvising even, a man to men, scooping up arguments and instances wherever he can; and there is an end to the pompous darkness that had previously appeared to be an essential adjunct to Rilke in English, and there is an end too to the whole misprision of Rilke as a weaver of unfathomable opacities round a few untranslatable concepts. The conscientious infelicities of earlier translations stand revealed as quite groundless as well, as Mitchell is mostly more accurate into the bargain.

The Rilke he is most comfortable with – and whom he is most generous in representing – is the late Rilke of the *Elegies*, the *Sonnets*, and the elusive flotsam stuff that washed up afterwards. Half this selection is devoted to work published after 1923 (and

Mitchell has gone on to translate, in a volume so far only available in the United States, all the *Sonnets to Orpheus*, complete with those Rilke decided were surplus to requirements). Against that, his choices from the *Neue Gedichte* of 1907 and 1908, while sound – "The Panther", "Portrait of My Father as a Young Man", "Self-Portrait, 1906", "Orpheus. Eurydice. Hermes" and "The Flamingos" are all included – are a little mean. As he was about to embark on them, in 1903, Rilke wrote: "Mir ist, als hätte ich immer so geschaffen: das Gesicht im Anschauen ferner Dinge, die Hände allein." ("It seems to me that I have always written in this way: my regard fixed on some faraway object, my hands by themselves.") Over the next twenty years, the emphasis shifted from the hands to the mysteries contemplated; or, to use another distinction from the programmatic poem "Wendung" ("Turning-Point") also included by Mitchell, from "work of the eyes" to "heart-work". My own preference, or that of my time in life, is still for the work of the hands (and eyes): the *Neue Gedichte*, "exercise-poems", tasks devised in emulation of the continual labour of Rilke's "Master" Rodin; not deep, but effortlessly well-made poems, rhymed and musical iambics with a keen, almost metallic presence:

> Auf einmal kreischt ein Neid durch die Volière;
> sie aber haben sich erstaunt gestreckt
> und schreiten einzeln ins Imaginäre.

> A shriek of envy shakes the parrot cage;
> but *they* stretch out, astonished, and one by one
> stride into their imaginary world.

Compared to that, how quiet (*kleinlaut*), how lacking in majesty, how marginal almost, is the ending of the *Duino Elegies*:

> Und wir, die an ein *steigendes* Glück
> denken, empfänden die Rührung,
> die uns beinah bestürzt,
> wenn ein Glückliches *fällt*.

> And we, who have always thought
> of happiness as *rising*, would feel
> the emotion that almost overwhelms us
> whenever a happy thing *falls*.

Even in the *Elegies*, though, Rilke may often be seen writing with his hands as well as his heart. His use of similes, for instance, is surprisingly practical, even humdrum: the loss of self "wie die Hitze von einem / Heißen Gericht" (even more so in Mitchell: "like steam from a dish / of hot food"); consolation "clean and disenchanted and shut as a post office on Sunday". How much strength Rilke draws from these, with his parabolist's intentness on *meaning*. And there is the wonderful intelligence of his sudden reversals of cause and effect, of chronology: "that man with the broken nose, unforgettable as a suddenly raised fist"; a scene with the Rodins, at which Madame "began to push all the things about on the table, so that it looked as though the meal were already over". There is a sublime economy and functionality about such writing, and Rilke never lost it. It corroborates the most startling, sympathetic and provocative witness in Donald Prater's recent biography of the poet: "The painter and writer Hermann Burte, who met him now for the first time, recalled how much more down-to-earth, rational and orderly a person he was than he has often been depicted." [...]

Selected Letters 1902–1926 is a pretty supine piece of publishing, being a straight reprint of a book that first appeared over forty years ago. [...]

One thing that Quartet have run to is the commissioning of a briskly centrifugal introduction by John Bayley, in which he tries to make a case for Rilke as "a great European genius, probably the last of the breed". I think Bayley could not be more wrong. Practically any genius alive at the time of the First World War – and any Austrian genius in particular – would have a stronger claim. To have been born in Prague and died in Switzerland, to have written in German and lived in Paris, and to have been called, by turns, Rainer or René, does not make one a European; to have visited Spain and Scandinavia, and to have thought of oneself for many years as a Russian *manqué*, doesn't either – and, in fact, it puts up the first counter-argument: namely, that Rilke was simply too wide-ranging in his travels, that he had neither a particular place nor a particular direction in which to go from it.

For even the designation "European" implies constraints as well as freedom. Rilke was too set on invulnerability, too fearful of extending himself, to be a European. When his hosts' dog died, he complained; ideally, he would have forbidden it. He was without either loyalty or acceptance. He lived in Paris to be alone. The stars by which he sailed were randomness and self-interest: the chance invitations of patrons and the ruthlessness of Number One. The best image of Rilke I have seen is in one of his own letters – not selected, as it happens – where the poet has strayed into the *Oktoberfest* (Horváth country!), and walks around carrying a peacock feather; while the crowds around him use similar feathers to tickle and tease one another, the poet feels his own is far too proud to be used in such a way, and instead he just looks at it. It is a quite internal image of pride and alienation. Rilke felt qualmed and doubtful about using the plural (in *Malte*). How could he be a European? He was a man out of time and a man out of place. Who could claim Rilke as a fellow-citizen or a contemporary? Was there an Age of Rilke, and if so, where should it be located? His own plans for further study specifically excluded "the history of art or any other histories". Confusing early and late paintings, he spoke instead of the expression of the Mona Lisa "on that particular day". On a particular day in August, he sought out part of a garden that seemed to him less like summer: autumn was his favourite season. What price Rilke as part of something bigger, deregulated, *sans frontières?* He noted, in 1914, "the excellent news from the Russian front". Would you buy a spindly beard and peasant blouse from René Osipovitch?

Nor was he any more constant in his personal attachments. His letters to his discontinued wife – and that means even those passed for publication in the saintly 1930s – are often quite reptilian: crass, devious and wounding ("a sobering experience for his wife Clara", Bayley concedes). He writes to *her* of how he spoke to the womanizing Rodin "of Northern people, of women who do not want to hold the man fast, of possibilities of loving without deception". I think it was this kind of thing, and not anything to do with "the spirit of that [prewar] civilization" that led John Berryman to call him a "jerk", or, strictly speaking, a "*jerk*". Even his gallantries have something unpleasantly indirect about them: "And then (if I were rich) I should give you my favourite dog so that he might look at you and be near you." And then, quickly, as if even that were too much: "But I am poor." Rilke cannot be called European because he never committed himself to anything beyond himself and his poetry. [...]

SOME GERMAN NOVELS

Alec Randall

Franz Kafka, the author of the first two novels in this varied collection, has been called "the most original of contemporary German writers." He has also been labelled – since his death, which occurred in June, 1926 – a "sur-réaliste." And certainly these two posthumous works from his pen reveal an unusual talent, strike a new and, we are inclined to think, abiding note in modern German fiction. The shortest way of describing his method would be to say that he writes a novel which, for the most part, might be taken as ordinary realist narrative, except for occasional doubts, which become more and more frequent as we proceed, and at length grow so insistent that we become aware of the underlying symbolist intention. At the end we want to begin again, and on the second reading it is the mystical interpretation which we seem to perceive all the time. Especially is this true of the novel "Das Schloss." [. . .]

"Amerika" is less easy to follow in the inner meaning because its outward meaning is so evident. After a short reading of "Das Schloss" we feel sure that it is not meant to be a mere realistic narrative, nothing but a satire on bureaucratic circumlocution and obstruction; but "Amerika" might well be an attempt to portray the rough and tumble, the lack of settled culture, the undisciplined emotions which the writer imagined as characteristic of American civilization. [. . .] Those critics who have condemned the novel on the ground that it misrepresents American conditions may well be right; Kafka, a petty official in Austria, was probably never in the United States. But to set up realistic standards like this seems to be rather beside the point. The book should be read for the sudden and, because sudden, sometimes grotesque and irritating flash-lights it throws on character and human destiny.

Das Schloss, by Franz Kafka. *Amerika*, by Franz Kafka [November 29, 1928]

A SOUL ACCUSED

R. D. Charques

"The Castle," an earlier novel by Franz Kafka, who died soon after the end of the War, appeared here some years ago. "The Trial" is similar in spirit and in manner. It is a fable, a parable, an allegory – none of these descriptions quite hits off the character of the book – whose subject might variously be defined as the soul, the search for self-knowledge, the life spiritual. The difficulty in trying to put the work into a recognized category is not due to any vagueness of intention on the author's part, but rather to the individual fashion in which he seeks to imprison in the stuff of commonplace experience rare and fastidious metaphysical essences. The story he has to tell, though its symbolism is immediately apparent, is concerned with what appear to be insignificant details of domestic routine – getting up, going to work, eating an apple, going to bed – and rigorously avoids conventional excitements of any sort. It is told, moreover, in a remarkably elaborate and flowing style, whose twists and bends leave one in doubt all through as to the direction that is being taken. [...]

There are moments in the story when the author seems to call on fantasy for fantasy's sake. But the symbol is never obscured for long, the hidden meaning never far off. The mere ingenuity with which the quest for "spiritual wholeness," as Kafka's motive is described by his friend Max Brod, is conveyed in the imagery of a dull and colourless routine, without resort to a word of intellectual protestation or argument, is sufficiently striking; but the ingenuity is plainly derived from a rare passion in these matters. The book is not likely to be everybody's taste; its serpentine flow, though doubtless suited to the theme, tends to weary the reader, who feels he might have been allowed to reach the prison chaplain's profound little story by less devious ways. Still, "The Trial" is a notable book.

The Trial, by Franz Kafka, translated by Willa and Edwin Muir [July 3, 1937]

FATHER AND SON:
KAFKA'S CONFLICT

Edwin Muir

This is the first biography of Kafka which has yet appeared, and it is extremely interesting in itself, as well as for the light it throws on Kafka's work. Dr Brod was Kafka's most intimate friend; for a number of years they saw each other almost daily. The portrait has the sympathetic understanding and candour which spring naturally from such a relation; and as Dr Brod has waited for over ten years to draw it – for Kafka died in 1924 – it has a certain authority as well. We feel we know Kafka now, after knowing less about him than about any other modern writer of the same rank.

Everyone who has read "The Castle" and "The Trial" must have felt that in these two books Kafka was dealing with his own life. The hero of the first is K. and of the second Joseph K.; and in the preliminary draft of "The Trial" Kafka actually used the first person. In both stories the chief figure is at odds with a semipaternal authority which refuses to accept him at his own valuation. "The Trial" describes that authority as arbitrary, incomprehensible, and yet inescapable; the hero rebels against it and is finally destroyed by it. In "The Castle," while still finding it arbitrary and incomprehensible, he tries to penetrate to it and be accepted by it; he trusts it, but it refuses to trust him until, quite worn out, he is lying on his deathbed. "The Castle" came after "The Trial," but neither book was ever finished; they represent stages in a personal conflict which began long before them and continued for some time after them, indeed till shortly before Kafka's death: the conclusion of "The Castle" was therefore prophetic of his own experience.

The conflict described in these two stories was, by the evidence of this biography, the conflict between Kafka and his father. His father was a man of enormous strength, imposing presence and dogmatic opinions, who had begun in extreme poverty and who ended as the owner of a flourishing business in Prague. Franz took

Franz Kafka, by Max Brod [April 9, 1938]

after his mother, who came of a family of scholars, dreamers and eccentrics. He was a sickly child, shrinking but obstinate, but he felt very early that his father was disappointed in him. This relation never changed essentially until the last two years of Kafka's life, when he at last broke away from his family and went to Berlin to live with Dora Dymant, a young girl belonging to a Jewish Chassid family. Before this, when he was thirty-seven, he had written a long letter to his father in which he analysed with extraordinary penetration and objectivity their relation from the beginning; whole passages in it could easily belong to the two great novels. In this letter he explains that he had always wanted to trust his father, but could never win his trust; it is the theme of "The Castle." At one point he says:—

> All I have written has been about you, I only poured out in it what I could not pour out on your breast. It was a deliberately prolonged farewell to you, a farewell imposed by you, though I determined its course.

In this extraordinary letter he both implicates and exonerates his father; one is reminded again of "The Castle," where the castle authorities are both accused and justified.

Kafka's whole conception of life, his ideas of divine justice and divine grace, his theory of salvation, were coloured by this relation. The pitiless judges in "The Trial," the benevolent but inaccessible authorities in "The Castle," are images of his father. And when he began to study Kierkegaard, what moved him most deeply was Kierkegaard's interpretation of the story of Abraham and Isaac, in which divine justice ordains an act wrong by human standards, the sacrifice of a son by a father, and yet remains in the right and must be obeyed. The problem returns again and again in his stories. In "The Metamorphosis" the faithful, obedient, hardworking son is turned into a loathsome insect, yet even then is worried by nothing but the fact that the change will prevent him from following his occupation and supporting his father and mother. And in the third of the great novels, "America," the opening sentence relates how the hero, a boy of sixteen, had been "packed off to America by his parents because a servant girl had seduced him and got a child by him" -- a characteristically ironical statement of the mystery of paternal justice and injustice.

Kafka's conflict with his father sometimes became so critical that it drove him to thoughts of suicide. After working all day, he set himself for a time to write all night, but had to give it up. Once or twice he confessed that he had been tempted to jump out of the window and end everything. Outwardly he was cheerful and loved all sorts of amusements, swimming in particular; but how much he suffered from the constraint put upon him may be seen from his diary:–

> What a terrific world I have in my head. But how can I set myself free and set it free without going to pieces? And a thousand times better go to pieces than hold it back or bury it within me. For this is what I am here for; that is quite clear.

There are flashes of humour in this book which remind one of the stories. Once, for instance, when Kafka was visiting Herr Brod, he had to pass through a room where Herr Brod's father was sleeping on a couch. The father wakened, and Kafka said in a soothing voice as he went past: "Do please look on me as a dream." A very strong impression comes through of his charm, his goodness, his inflexible honesty, his complete lack of affectation, and the great powers which he was incapable either of parading or concealing.

HARD-LUCK STORY

Anthony Powell

[...] The novel recalls in many ways German and Central European films of the twenties with their crude and cruel – though often effective – humour and sense of ill-omen, and it must be admitted that the tyrannous and inexplicable rule suggested by the atmosphere of the earlier novels was to become only too familiar in the totalitarian States.

In *America* this sense of doom is less apparent, and here the author undoubtedly made an effort to write of more tangible things. Its world, however, remains one read of in books and not experienced at first-hand, not merely on account of lack of all

America, by Franz Kafka [October 7, 1949]

resemblance to the United States – in itself perhaps unimportant – but in a more general way, because Kafka as a writer has little if any grasp of individual human associations – except in so much as these had reference to a father-son relationship. How small was this grasp can be seen if we compare the unforgettable lift-boy of *A la Recherche du Temps Perdu* with poor Karl, the lift-boy of Kafka's imagination. Dr Max Brod supplies a postscript.

PARABLES FROM NO MAN'S LAND

Roy Pascal

[...] His social and religious attitudes seem increasingly to issue from his very personal situation, his illness. Though by no means a recluse, and kept in touch with modern movements in art by friends like the busy Brod, he felt more and more apart from – alienated from – the world, living, as he said, "in a borderland between loneliness and community" and at home in neither. Faith, he once wrote, is identical with "to be", and one might say that his whole effort was devoted to discovering the secret of confidence, of trust in life, a state of mind he marvels at in one of his earliest manuscripts. Here the boy, half asleep, hears his mother calling down to a neighbour in the garden: "What are you doing, love? What a heat!" And the answer comes up in an expression of utter heart's content: "Ich jause so im Grünen" (I'm enjoying myself [and refreshment] in the green). The inaccessibility of such matter-of-fact security and contentment also determines many of Kafka's definitions of his artistic purpose. His writing, he says, is his only refuge, the only weapon with which he can "take up the struggle with the monstrous [uncanny] world". His dreams, sleeping and waking, come to be his chief resource, and he defines his literary purpose as "the representation of my dream-like inner life". "Bewitchment and logic" are his instruments, not the phenomena of common experience.

The strange thing is that the evidence of a pathological element

[Article] [June 7, 1974]

in Kafka's temperament and of the exceptionally subjective sources of his images has in no way diminished the recognition that his works express a general condition of his times, present, as he once said was his aim, a general experience reduced to its simplest principles. Even the Marxist Georg Lukács could in *Wider den missverstandenen Realismus* (1958) discern in Kafka's distorted images the true image of a distorted world, and acknowledge the intensity and integrity of the experience communicated in his works, criticizing him only for succumbing to "a blind and panic Angst before reality", for refusing to believe in the possibility of changing the world. The peculiarly subjective nature of his inspiration only makes his representativeness the more miraculous. [...]

AN INFINITY OF FRUSTRATION

R. J. Hollingdale

You are expecting to receive tomorrow a letter the contents of which may determine the course of your life, though again they may not. You go to sleep thinking about this letter, and you wake up the following morning thinking about it. You open the curtains and see that outside it is snowing hard. You say to yourself: "The postman will be late this morning because the snow will delay him." The thought is about to make you nervous and irritable – for you want to get the letter into your hands as soon as possible – when it occurs to you that it may have just the opposite effect: the snow may cause the postman to walk faster than usual so as to finish his round as quickly as he can and return to the warmth of the sorting office. Under the influence of this idea you go out into the hallway to see whether the post has perhaps not already arrived. But it has not. After all, it is still a quarter of an hour earlier than the time at which it usually arrives, and the postman is not likely to have been able to increase the speed of his round to this extent, especially since he is hampered by the snow. And even if he does

The World of Franz Kafka, ed. by J. P. Stern [March 6, 1981]

intend to complete his round more quickly than usual, it may be his intention will be frustrated: for the snow is now falling more thickly than ever and the pavement is piled high with it.

No, there is really no question of an early delivery: a delivery at the usual time would be almost a miracle, and the most likely thing is that the post will be late or perhaps not arrive at all. You resolve to accommodate yourself to this possibility, though you also find yourself listening intently for a sound that might suggest the tumbling of letters on to a mat. A quarter of an hour passes in this way: then, at precisely the time the post usually arrives you hear the clack of the flap of the letterbox. You retrieve the post from the floor and search through it for the letter you are waiting for but cannot discover it. The letter has not arrived. "In that case", you say to yourself, "it will arrive tomorrow. Unless it has been misaddressed and has already arrived somewhere else." You then notice that the letters you are holding in your hand are not intended for you at all but have been delivered to you in error. You open the door in the hope of being able to call back the postman: but the postman, overcome by the intensity of the cold and the crushing weight of his mailbag, is lying dead in the snow.

None of the events, mental or physical, in this anecdote is in any way impossible in the real world: what is, however, very improbable is that they would all take place on the same occasion. You might be awaiting a vitally important letter, but probably it would not be snowing. Letters intended for another address might be mistakenly delivered to you, but probably you would not at that moment be expecting a vitally important letter. A postman might collapse and die, but probably he would not have just delivered to you letters intended for a different address. It is not the events themselves but their juxtaposition which makes the total event seem unreal.

Here is a recollection of Kafka reported in J. P. Stern's introduction to *The World of Franz Kafka*:

> On a rainy day in Marienbad Kafka watches a famous rabbi with his solemn entourage in search of medicinal waters after the springs have all been shut for the day, the bottle brought for the purpose meanwhile filling with rainwater – a Marx Brothers scenario which Kafka ends with a comment on one of the rabbi's followers who "tries to find

or thinks he finds a deeper meaning in all this: I think the deeper meaning is that there is none, and in my opinion that is enough".

Two events – a group of people trying to find a place open and a bottle filling with rainwater – which taken by themselves possess no "meaning" that goes beyond their plain and apparent meaning seem when they are juxtaposed to acquire some hard-to-grasp, "transcendental" meaning: the total event seems to be "saying something". Kafka, however, denies that it is saying anything at all, and asserts that that is the "deeper meaning" of the event. A step further would be to imagine a series of incidents between which there is no logical connection whatever (e.g., awaiting a vital letter and finding a postman dead) and seeing whether some other kind of connection could not be interpreted into it.

The extent to which the two procedures suggested here are a valid description of Kafka's method must depend on how calculating an artist you think he was. But there is a third procedure, if I can continue to use that word, which was certainly in no way calculated, and in *The World of Franz Kafka* we can see very clearly why.

I entered *The World of Franz Kafka* expecting to find little but praise for him and I was not disappointed: as far as I can see, the only serious adverse criticism is that contained in an extract from Günther Anders's *Kafka: Pro and Contra*, which originally appeared as long ago as 1946. For the most part, Kafka is treated as being self-evidently a "great writer" – and yet his private life is frequently examined and employed in a manner that implies that you cannot understand his writings unless you possess more information than their author has himself supplied.

There are, for instance, repeated allusions to his two engage-ments to Felice Bauer and to the crises he experienced in connection with them; so much, indeed, has been published on this topic that it could threaten to replace his work as the main source of interest in him: but if the implication is that you cannot understand "The Metamorphosis", *The Trial* or *The Castle* unless you have a fairly detailed knowledge of Kafka's private life, it is either one that has to be denied or constitutes a concealed admission that he was not after all a very successful writer – that his private life is not *aufgehoben* into his work, but on the contrary his work is only an aspect of his private life.

The same consideration applies to the much-advertised difficulty Kafka experienced in his relations with his father, to which there is likewise repeated reference in *The World of Franz Kafka*: if it is implied that "The Judgment" is fully understandable only when its text is supplemented with facts from his biography, this must carry the further implication that "The Judgment" is a literary failure.

We do not need Kafka's biography, we need only his texts themselves, to be aware of the "view of life" he wants to transmit: the depressing view that living in the world is such a difficult thing to do that it is almost impossible to do it. But where the biographical essays of the present book can help us is in seeing how directly this literary effect corresponds with Kafka's own experience of life.

The view and feeling of life he transmits to the reader is life as it presented itself to him. His troubles with his father and with Felice Bauer are evidence of that. So is his famous "perfectionism": his compulsive rewriting of a piece again and again and again, often employing almost the same words, only in the end to find the provisionally final version still inadequate; and while doing this to declare himself the very embodiment of "literature", the man in whom "the literary life" had become flesh and blood. His actual vocation, to which he devotes himself with such single-mindedness, presented him with inordinate difficulty.

There is an illuminating contradiction here: for if "literature" were as difficult as Kafka found it there would be very little of it, and the public art practised with some degree of success by Balzac, Dickens and Tolstoy, and in Kafka's own time by Proust and Joyce, would barely exist.

It seems to me that this incapacity to find anything simple and easy, to do and have done with it, did not merely enter into Kafka's fictional world but actually created it: it is the bodying forth of his own unconquerable inhibition.

In its typical and characteristic manifestations, Kafka's fictional world is a place where every act is a repetition, more or less disguised, of a previous act: a world the inhabitants of which do only one thing over and over again. The effect can be comic and parodistic, as in the case of the bureaucrats of *The Trial* and *The*

Castle, who do nothing, day or night, but produce heaps of official documents which they are too busy adding to ever to read and no particular one of which can ever be found when it is needed: in this and comparable instances the "character" is nothing but his function, which he continues to perform so as to continue to exist. But this parodistic effect is peripheral: the central effect, produced by much more subtle and varied means but essentially the same, is of all life, and in particular the life of the central figure, as a compelled repetition of the same act. Kafka's inventiveness is never greater than when he is fashioning images of frustration: no one who has read it, for instance, is likely to forget "An Imperial Message", with its messenger vainly trying to get out of the imperial palace:

> still he is only making his way through the chambers of the innermost palace; never will he get out of them; and if he succeeded in that nothing would be gained; he must fight his way next down the stairs; and if he succeeded in that nothing would be gained; the courts would still have to be crossed; and after the courts the second outer palace; and once more stairs and courts; and once more another palace; and so on for thousands of years; and if at last he should burst through the outermost gate – but never, never can that happen – the imperial capital would lie before him, the centre of the world, crammed to bursting with its own refuse. Nobody could fight his way through here ...

In this parable, the central figure cannot get out of the castle; in *The Castle* the central figure cannot get into it: the reason for their frustration is the same in each case – the distance to be traversed is in practice infinite, so that a step forward is in practice the equivalent of standing still.

Now, I cannot be persuaded to think this way of experiencing life anything but idiosyncratic – for it goes without saying, I hope, that the distance from the centre to the perimeter, or from the perimeter to the centre, is infinite only if you think so: but it was this idiosyncrasy which produced the "Kafkaesque" world which everyone has come to recognize.

On the following morning you wake up wondering whether the letter will arrive that day. Outside the sun is shining brightly: but will the new postman not perhaps have difficulty in finding his way? Certainly he will be slower than the old postman, who had been doing the same round for years. Probably the post will not be on time. *Und so weiter*. Subsequently you will try to see the head sorter in an effort to discover the whereabouts of the letter (but will see only his assistant, who will be so busy sorting letters he can hardly spare the time to listen to you); you will visit the house whose number is the number of your house reversed, in case the letter has been delivered there by mistake, and the occupant, Fräulein B, will act strangely though perhaps not so strangely as all that, you will know what she has in mind, but she will say she hasn't seen your letter; you will do a (potentially) infinite number of things which are all, however, the same thing: pursuit of your vitally important letter. Needless to say, you will never get your hands on it – even assuming it exists, for which there is no evidence whatever – since if you did you would have to start doing something other than look for it. But never, never can that happen.

This, in a rendered down, "schematic" form is the "world" of Franz Kafka. I have tried to understand the literary technique which produced it: what cannot be conveyed secondhand, however, is the downbeat quality of the affects which inform it. There is an emotional dreariness about Kafka's novels and stories which makes it almost unbelievable that his interpreters have seen in them valid images of the real human world. The one affect which is gratified at all adequately is cruelty: Kafka is the only imaginative writer I can think of more elevated than a writer of pornography who invents characters in order that they shall be punished and then sides with their punishers. That he probably identifies himself with the victims as well does not improve the picture – quite the contrary.

That he is a very fine writer is perfectly clear and I do not doubt that his style will save him from oblivion: time, which pardons Paul Claudel for writing well, will do the same for Kafka. But I think the claim implicit in the present volume that he is a great modern master – a status which appears to be accorded him quite generally – needs scrutiny.

His obsession with "literature", to the demands of which he subordinated everything else in his life has to be adjudged in the light of the fact that he published only a very small part of what he wrote and failed to put his chief works into publishable form. Publication, however, is a precondition of a "literary life". A dimension which has to be present in any "great artist" is missing in Kafka: outgoingness, the urge to imprint yourself on other people's minds and hearts, at the very least a desire for fame. Kafka wrote almost exclusively for himself: the mere urge to communicate seems to be lacking.

Everyone knows that he left his manuscripts to Max Brod with instructions to destroy them but that Brod says that he had previously told Kafka that if he ever received any such instructions from him he would not carry them out. If this story is accurate in every part, and if Kafka remembered his conversation with Brod, its meaning must be that at the moment of his death Kafka wanted not to know whether or not his life's work would survive him. Leave aside the weirdness of this frame of mind: have you ever heard of any other writer who on the edge of extinction played such tricks with himself? To communicate by writing, not to communicate by keeping hidden what has been written: his indecision was, to the end, final. It is an attitude which, whatever else it may make of a man, does not really make of him a master of the great public art of literature. [...]

II

INTERNATIONAL FOCUS

OBSERVATIONS OF THE
OCTOPUS-MOUNTAIN

Thom Gunn

It was obvious from the first that Marianne Moore's poetry had charm. What becomes steadily more apparent is that it has also the kind of scope and power that set it beside that of contemporaries like Stevens, Eliot and Pound.

Like them she wrote about poetry in her poetry, perhaps even more than they did. For where Stevens wrote about the imagination, Pound about the work in progress, Eliot about the struggle with language, she wrote about all three, and also about the nature of reading ("Literature is a phase of life", begins "Picking and Choosing"), about criticism (the critic as connoisseur, the critic as steamroller) and above all about the attitude of mind that makes composition possible. But she is famous too for the simultaneous gusto and exactness with which she presented the things of the world: animals, places, artefacts, people. Imagism was, for all her contemporaries, as A. Walton Litz has noted while speaking of Stevens, a stage of their apprenticeship, and it was for her too, though she never owned that it was, for she seems to have felt uneasy with the subject.

Certainly for concision and vividness of imagery not even William Carlos Williams could approach her. In her poem "New York", choosing to speak of one aspect of that city – as the centre of the fur trade – she evokes the look of different kinds of fur with a sensory sharpness – to make the reader gasp. She shows us a Manhattan

> starred with tepees of ermine and peopled with foxes,
> the long guard-hairs waving two inches beyond the body
> > > of the pelt;
> the ground dotted with deer-skins – white with white spots,
> "as satin needlework in a single colour may carry a
> > > varied pattern",

Marianne Moore: The Complete Prose, ed. by Patricia C. Willis. *Marianne Moore: Subversive Modernist*, by Taffy Martin. *The Savage's Romance: The Poetry of Marianne Moore*, by John M. Slatin [February 6, 1987]

and wilting eagle's-down compacted by the wind;
and picardels of beaver-skin; white ones alert with snow.

(Picardels were apparently small river-barges.) The compressed
activity in the detail about the guard-hairs and in such words as
"compacted" and "alert" has a kind of poignancy that takes them
beyond simple accuracy and vividness. Her delight in the physical
aspect is bounded by the awareness that the potency still apparent
in the pelts should be sacrificed to the commercial demands of
humans. It *is* delight, nevertheless – she pictures here a scene of
great beauty and not a slaughterhouse. But she will not abandon
herself to the details in themselves. Later in the same poem,
speaking about ancient New York as an island of forested
wilderness, she cautions that it is necessary to stay outside, "since
to go in is to be lost"; that is, to lose your powers of discrimination.
She ends by saying that what attracts her about New York,
whether in past or present, "is not the plunder,/but 'accessibility to
experience'".

To enter the wilderness of specifics is to encounter the great
danger of Imagism, where the subject of any one Imagist poem is as
important as that of any other: they are all important and somehow
equivalent, the station of the Métro the same as the oread. She loves
those specifics, but they are not enough in themselves. The poet
may emerge with plunder, and here perhaps she thinks of the other
great poet of Manhattan, Walt Whitman, for whom she apparently
felt much distaste: what did somebody like him give us but
plunder, she seems to ask, the indefatigable lists with which so
many of his poems are crowded? No, for all her wide appreciation
of the physical world of, say, New York, it is more than the
specifics, the furs, the facts, the bustle in the street, the incident and
variety of a huge city that attracts her, it is "accessibility to
experience". The phrase is from Henry James, the object of
probably her greatest admiration; and accessibility is for her, as for
James, the great value, the proof of the consciousness that is fully
alive, and finally worth more than the succession of experiences to
which it is the doorway.

She is not, then, like Whitman as he wanted to be, the poet of
mass-acceptance (though he is more than that); she is the poet of
the door which is opened discriminately. For all the gusto of her
acceptances, she makes plenty of rejections: she can be thoroughly

unkind about the "pedantic literalist", about the young dilettanti who "write the sort of thing that would in their judgment interest a lady", or about the ugly elaboration of the giant pinecone with holes for the water to spurt from, carved and put up by the Romans as a fountain. Accessibility is a door that may be closed when necessary. Thus her gusto is sharply defined by the discriminations to be made. She does not exclude her vivid intelligence from access to her vivid imagery, and – certainly until the late 1930s – each ignites the other, to produce a poetry radiant yet complex, informal yet splendid.

Throughout her long career Marianne Moore also wrote occasional prose – in a quantity that many of her later-born admirers have never dreamed of. It is here collected in *The Complete Prose*, a handsome yet formidable book of some seven hundred pages. It starts with short stories resurrected in all their juvenile oddity from undergraduate magazines and ends with complete collections of blurbs, responses to questionnaires, and other forms of opinionatedness from that old age in which Marianne Moore had become a media myth, rather like Grandma Moses, and in which oddity was an expected reflex. Between these extremes comes all the material of interest, divided by the editor, Patricia C. Willis, into the *Dial* years – the period in the 1920s in which she wrote for and edited the *Dial*, one of the seminal literary magazines of the century – and the "Middle" and "Later" years. The kinds of prose are various, and include, besides those already mentioned, film reviews, obituaries, idiosyncratic articles on everything from knives to baseball, editorials for the *Dial* on subjects of topical interest, single-paragraph reviews of books received by the *Dial*, and lectures to university audiences; but the greater part consists of reviews and essays dealing with recent literature.

It will surprise no reader of her poetry that the prose too is dotted with epigrams. At times she can be very funny, as when she says that in Charles Cotton's poems we may find, "as Coleridge says, 'the milder muse' – even the mindless muse"; or, of new novels in 1926, "We have, and in most cases it amounts to not having them, novels about discontented youth, unadvantaged middle age, American materialism." However, what she does supremely well is to go straight to the heart of a writer's activity in a single sentence, or sometimes in a single word. Thus, she points to the feeling behind the poetry of William Carlos Williams as "considerate"; she speaks of Mina Loy's use of words as "sliced and cylindrical"; she calls *Esther Waters* "wolf-lean". Of Emily Dickinson, she says: "She understood the sudden experience of unvaluable leisure by which death is able to make one 'homeless at home'." It would be easy to compile pages of her memorable apophthegms, about H. D., Samuel Johnson, Whistler, Henry James, Gertrude Stein, etc, but I will add only this one, describing the contents of the *Cantos* as "arranged in the style of the grasshopper-wing for contrast, half the fold against the other half, the rarefied effect against a grayer one". This surely exemplifies one of her great talents, that of translating physical observation into intellectual observation, and vice versa. Her comment sums up both the technique of the *Cantos* and the purpose of that technique with an admirable accuracy and compression. It is sentences like this that make you recollect that for Moore, reading is an activity in no way divorced from the rest of her life: the Canto and the grasshopper-wing exist side by side in the same part of her mind, and reference between the two of them is a matter of course.

After all this, it is disappointing to report that she is usually a brilliant critic only in short passages: her command over the whole essay is a different matter. If the 1934 essay on Williams shows her at her best, her most cogent and connected, then the 1931 essay on Pound (not the one with the grasshopper, but another), which she chose to reprint in book form twice, is more characteristic of her mature critical writing – and of that writing, I suspect, as she wanted it to be. The structure here bears a not fortuitous resemblance to that of her poems, as Taffy Martin points out in her *Marianne Moore: Subversive modernist*, and Ms Martin goes on to suggest, with a good deal of plausibility, that in some of her reviews – of Stein, of Pound, of Cummings – she was moreover indulging in a kind of conceit by imitating the form of the work she is discussing, as it were "quoting" their style for her own purposes. The Pound essay, in any case, consists of a kind of scrap-book of favourite quotations interspersed by her own comments, with a minimum of connectives. (The connectives that are *implied* are associative, as in Pound's poetry and some of her own.) The structure of the whole is hard to make out, and indeed the piece makes exhausting reading, as much for one familiar with the first thirty *Cantos* as for one new to them (it was written as a review, after all). She does not seem to have been unhappy about the rambling nature of much of her prose. Certainly I do not detect regret in her remark of 1951: "my observations cannot be regularized".

I take an extreme example; there is much straightforward and practical reviewing elsewhere. The best of the book is in the essays written between about 1920 and 1937, after which the prose falls off in much the same way as the poetry does. There are still some good things to be found, notably an obituary of Wallace Stevens, but somehow in these later years the mind behind it all is less discerning and less lively. Perhaps it was unfortunate that she should have been accepted so completely into the literary establishment towards which she had at first been defiant. Now she melted into it altogether too easily, accepting standard judgments (about the most hackneyed lines of de la Mare, for instance), and in a magazine called *Seventeen* exhorting the teenagers: "Whatever it is, do it with all your might."

Though there is an obvious continuity between her prose and her poetry, it does not follow that her prose is as much worth reading as her poetry. Sharp as her critical mind was at its best, this immense book does not constitute the same kind of discovery for me that thirty-five pages of criticism by Basil Bunting did a few years ago. Bunting had her perceptiveness, but he also chose to keep control over the form of the essay (his observations are "regularized") and he says more, finally, about Pound and Eliot in a very few pages than Moore does in the course of her many articles and reviews to do with them. *The Complete Prose of Marianne Moore*, then, is not a book I would recommend to a reader to slog through systematically; rather it would make a good bedside book, where it might last you for years.

To speak so is to make, as we used to say, a limiting judgment, and grateful as I am for the appearance of this book, I shall be far more so for the publication of her complete poetry, which has not yet occurred. The volume in print called the *Complete Poems* (305pp. Faber. Paperback, £3.95. 0 571 13306 1) is really a severe selection, in which Moore favoured the products of her old age and discriminated against the achievement of her youth by omitting such magnificent poems as "Roses Only", "Dock Rats" and "Dark Earth". The matter is complicated by the fact that she revised constantly, nervously and at times ruthlessly, now for the better and now for the worse. I suppose that eventually there will be a variorum edition, but it will be unreadable: what I *would* like to see, and as soon as possible, is an omnibus edition of all her books of poetry, restoring not only the omissions but also all the revised versions of individual poems (for example, "Poetry" in all its five versions – or is it six?) Then we shall have, returned to circulation, some powerful poetry which is at present unavailable.

It is not always easy to put your finger on what constitutes its power. She called her first authorized collection *Observations* (possibly taking a hint from Eliot's title *Prufrock and Other Observations*), and clearly the word is still an important one for her in 1951, meaning as it does both "perceptions" and "comments". The comment, as I have already implied, in some manner derives from the perception, and often amounts to an epigram, a *sententia*. Thus in the middle of the poem to the snail we read, "Contractility is a virtue/as modesty is a virtue". But the derivation is not always so straightforward, for if she is on the one hand attracted to the condensed wisdom of the maxim she is also attracted to the "beautiful element of unreason". Her poetry fascinates, but its plain sense is often harder to arrive at than those traditional-looking summings-up would seem to indicate, and we continue wondering about it, annotating, considering, memorizing, searching out its obscure corners, because it still fascinates even when it bewilders us. What looks like a *sententia* doesn't usually clinch a poem as we expect it to – as it would have, for example, an Elizabethan poem. Most readers must have been struck by the fact that it is difficult to relate every detail clearly to every other, not only in a long and complex poem like "Marriage" but even in some of the early short poems. You feel that each word is properly there, but you can't quite fit it all together. There is a slight, mysterious and unsettling discontinuity.

Both Taffy Martin and John M. Slatin react to such difficulties with pleasure. Their pleasure dissociates them from "New Critics" such as R. P. Blackmur and Morton Dauwen Zabel, between whom and themselves they wish to put as much distance as possible. About a fifth of Ms Martin's book deals with Moore's prose. She makes a large claim for the importance of her four-year editorship of the *Dial*: that by her actual arrangement of the contributions in the magazine and also by the variety in subject-matter of her monthly editorials she was trying to demonstrate by example the fragmentation of both America and modernism. I am not really convinced: in the arrangement of the items, Moore may have been simply trying to make lively contrasts, as many other editors do; and she surely wrote an editorial about whatever interested her in that particular month. After all, we know that her mind had a wide "capacity for fact" and that she had almost unlimited interests. Thus we find her writing, connectedly and elegantly as befits an editor, about maps of New York, exhibitions of Dürer and of Soviet art, children's books, Hardy's death, the salutations of letters (does one start "Dear So-and-so" or not?) There are moments when the editorial manner reminds me a little of *Times* Fourth Leaders. Martin, however, sees Moore as making a statement, through her editing, that is a "prophetically post-modern definition of American modernism". Maybe one of these days someone will claim Charles Lamb as a post-modernist too.

Martin overstresses the degree of discontinuity in the poems as well. She starts from a genuine perception – that the poems don't, all of them, add up neatly – but she does not know what to do with it, and her book consists of a number of fresh starts, leading away from it into remarks like this: "Moore's poems achieve their identity and integrity by being deceptively elusive and unfathomable." Achieve? integrity? deceptively? unfathomable? While trying to exercise the utmost charity I cannot extract much meaning from such a sentence. One can love discontinuity too much, it seems.

Slatin's book *The Savage's Romance: The Poetry of Marianne Moore* is to be taken more seriously. He does not like the idea of poetry as "autonomous", and so endeavours to show in what ways Moore's may be better understood with reference to other literature or to the details of her own life. His book, like its subject, is complicated, exasperating and often rewarding. Some of his discoveries and consequent interpretations are hard to accept, but some of them are admirably suggestive, as when for example he argues that the ending of Moore's "Novices", an assemblage of phrases quoted from different sources, "responds to" another such assemblage, the ending of *The Waste Land* published a few months before. The contrast in syntax and effect between the two only adds to the value of the comparison.

Slatin's considerable abilities as a scholar are matched by his critical gifts. When he chooses to stick to "the words on the page"

he is as sound as any of the previous generation, as you can see from
his stringent but surely accurate reading of "What Are Years".
Stringent, for unlike Martin he discriminates between better and
worse in the poetry, and reveals a degree of taste not always found
among Moore's critics.

The triumph of the book is a rich chapter about Moore's second-
longest poem, "An Octopus". As any reader may determine, the
poem is really about a mountain, an octopus of ice, and that
mountain, though she calls it by other names, is actually Mount
Rainier, which she visited with her brother in 1922. Further, as
Patricia C. Willis has discovered, they stayed near a mountain-
meadow called Paradise. This is not mentioned in the poem, but
Slatin concludes that for Moore the mountain is also an image of
America as Paradise. He then goes on to treat the poem as at least
partly allegorical, and relates it to many writers, not all of whom are
mentioned in it, one of them being Henry James, who is. And in a
splendid attempt at describing Moore's procedure, he says:

> Thus reading "An Octopus" is something like reading *The
> Golden Bowl*: just as James confines us within the limits of
> the prince's awareness, or the princess's, so Moore confines
> us within a perspective which is far too limited to
> comprehend the full significance of the scene it presents in
> such profuse detail. It is not until the very end of the poem –
> not until we have been "summarily removed" from it by
> "the avalanche", in fact – that we realize that we have been
> in Paradise.

Such an argument (and I have greatly simplified it) is of practical
help to a reader having trouble with a difficult poem, and thus it
performs the main function of criticism: it helps us to read.
Nevertheless "we" would not be able to come to such a realization
as he describes unless we had first read this chapter. I cannot but
wish that Slatin had gone further and speculated about what Moore
can have been up to when she suppressed all mention of the
meadow Paradise? Or has the critic made a poem more perfectly co-
ordinated than the one the poet wrote?

I am not sure about the answers to these questions, but they
trouble me a good deal, and I think they ought to trouble Slatin.
Another case of biographical material used to reinterpret a poem
comes earlier in his book, in his discussion of "The Fish", one of

the best-known poems. It is "a war poem", he tells us, "most likely prompted by the assignment of Moore's brother, a Navy chaplain, to sea duty in the North Atlantic late in 1917". Likelihood in Mr Slatin's mind is then replaced by certainty: in "The Fish", he asserts later, Moore imagines "the tragedy of a torpedoed troop ship with a gaping 'chasm' in its 'dead' side". According to this astonishing reading, the "bodies" that I always assumed to be those of living sea-creatures, with which the ocean is packed, are really those of drowned troops and in the last phrase of the poem – "the sea grows old in it" – *it* refers to the torpedoed ship's hold. I simply cannot accept this: Slatin has completely confused a poem's possible source with the poem itself. There is indeed a mysterious intensity of vision to Moore's view of the ocean and a violence of tone in the way she speaks of it in this poem, and Moore's anxiety about her brother may well be the source of both intensity and violence, but that is not to say that for all these years we have been missing in the imagery a story about torpedoed troop-ships. Again, Slatin fails to ask obvious questions: about intention, for example, or about ways in which contemporary readers might have read the poem. His book is far better than Martin's, but his critical powers separate from his scholarly powers like oil from water, and if she was too much in love with discontinuity, he is too easily satisfied with obscurity.

But whatever the failures in the working out of these two critical books, one can easily grant their premises, that Marianne Moore is not the orderly poet some have taken her to be. It is a sign of her stature that she can so well absorb the shock of such a new emphasis. Of course her writing can be broken and ambiguous, we agree, turning from the straightforwardness of "Sojourn in the Whale" to "An Octopus". But Blackmur and Zabel were not therefore wrong in having discussed another side to her, the side typified by continuity and "neatness of finish". The emphasis made by Martin and Slatin does not replace the old, it merely supplements it. Marianne Moore doesn't belong to any of them exclusively, after all: she is too massive a property, like the octopus-mountain itself, which can never be entirely seen from one point of view.

PEACH PIE AND
CUSTARD:
THE TWO LIVES OF
WALLACE STEVENS

Roy Fuller

Writing to the editor of *The Dial* in 1922 Wallace Stevens said: "Do, please, excuse me from the biographical note. I am a lawyer and live in Hartford. But such facts are neither gay nor instructive." However, the literary world has always found the facts enigmatic and fascinating, and his letters have long been anticipated in the expectation of their illuminating or explaining the supposed irreconcilability of his two modes of existence, as poet and successful man of affairs. What in fact comes out of them is the reverse of anything journalistically quirky or sensational; instead, the book draws a portrait sufficiently full and coherent to allay for ever the crude questionings, and one of far greater interest and subtlety than some no doubt imagined from the sparse lines previously available to view. Nothing from the archives of the Hartford insurance group of companies (which employed Stevens from 1916 until his death in 1955) is included here, but enough details emerge from Stevens's private correspondence to fix the routine of his life as a lawyer, his relations with his stenographer, the companies' coloured chauffeurs, and other colleagues, and his own attitude to his professional work. As might have been deduced – for Stevens, far from trying to escape from the Hartford, went on working for it five years beyond the compulsory retirement age – the tensions experienced by the poet were quite outside any mere clash of human types or division of time between office hours and art. The Hartford and its employees obviously held Stevens in respect and, when eventually his poetic reputation became public property, pride: on his side, there was no undue strain in his evolvement of a dignified and sometimes facetious affection, never false or condescending.

Letters of Wallace Stevens, selected and ed. by Holly Stevens [March 30, 1967]

Nearly 3,300 of Stevens's letters were available for publication when his daughter compiled this book. Not many more than a quarter of this number have been printed here, and even from these some passages have been omitted. A critic in *The New York Review of Books* has hinted that Miss Stevens's unexpressed purpose in this procedure was to remove evidence of some indiscretions and to spotlight her own filial devotion, but there is little indication of the former and none of the latter, and in reducing the enormous mass of material to reasonably saleable proportions and at so short a period from Stevens's death a modest degree of discretion can scarcely be complained of. In fact, Miss Stevens has included a number of letters which show the realities of her own marital affairs as well as some worn places in her relations with her father: besides, her omission of inessentials has almost certainly contributed to the book's compulsive readability and her footnotes and linking narrations are adequate and unobtrusive, quite admirably so.

Stevens was born in Pennsylvania in 1879, the son of a successful though not wealthy country town lawyer. The earliest letters here are a few he wrote to his mother from a summer camp at the age of fifteen. Amusing that the second letter actually contains one of those verbal imitations of non-human sounds that were such a persistent and curious feature of his verse; significant that they are full of observation; the syntax and vocabulary are already brilliant. He went to Harvard in 1897, but only one letter has survived from his years there. Miss Stevens has resourcefully filled the gap with extracts from a journal he began to keep in 1898 and with some letters from his father. The journal is full of observation, too, and of a Ruskinian precision: the letters from his father are quite remarkable. Both father and son grasp the issues of life that was to follow, and the opposition between them was far from simply conventional. The father is urging an orthodox career, though is in no doubt of his son's talent ("but for eccentricities in your genius you may be fitted for a Chair"). The son realizes that the father is holding him "in check" but has few illusions about his own character or the realities of material existence. "I am certainly a domestic creature, par excellence," he writes; and

> I should be quite content to work and be practical – but I hate the conflict whether it "avails" or not. I want my powers to be put to their fullest use – to be exhausted when

I am done with them. On the other hand I do not want to make a petty struggle for existence – physical or literary. I must try not to be dilettante – half dream, half deed. I must be all dream or all deed.

In a sense his life was aimed to disprove what his father puts in so forcible, so Stevensian a way:

One never thinks out a destiny – If a fellow takes Peach Pie – he often wishes he had chosen the Custard ... The only trouble is that since we cannot have both Pie and custard – it is oft too late to repent.

After Harvard, Stevens worked as a journalist for a short period, neither successfully nor congenially. He had the notion of resigning from his newspaper and devoting himself to writing, but quite soon he fell in with his father's urging and took up the law. In 1904 he had passed his bar examinations and was admitted to practice. In the same year he met and fell in love with his future wife. Following Stevens's death she destroyed a number of his letters to her of this period (after first copying extracts she thought might be of interest), but this is probably no great loss. The letters of the long courtship are curiously pointless, a parallel to Stevens's career as a lawyer – and, indeed, as a writer – during the same epoch. He started a law firm but it was a failure, and then worked in several practices without apparently making any mark. Lone wolf business skill, the flair for acquiring clients, are not qualities possessed by shy men, and Stevens was certainly shy. He was big and (judging by the photographs here) at all stages of his life handsome, but the formidability noted by many arose almost certainly quite unconsciously from his brain-power, his lack of ease in direct personal contacts and, no doubt, his occasional exasperation at other men's disorder and importunity (what he characterized as his "pretty well-developed mean streak"). His sexual desires were from the outset directed towards uxoriousness. And the *fin de siècle* literary tradition his adolescence inherited persisted with him for a very long time: as late as 1907 he is quoting Andrew Lang's Odyssey sonnet with approval.

But in 1908 he was freed from the antipathies of private practice by becoming employed as a lawyer by an insurance company. The following year he was earning enough to be able to marry. His father died in 1911 and his mother a year later (a sentence from his journal about his dying mother – "the beating of her heart in the veins of her throat was as rapid as water running from a bottle" – is one of the few indications in his correspondence and journal of this time of his future literary power). And then quite out of the blue so far as the reader is concerned come the letters of November 6, 1914, and June 6, 1915 (which follow without intervening material), to the editor of *Poetry*, the first another laconic response to a request for a biographical note, the second discussing the order of the sections of "Sunday Morning". Somehow Stevens had become a modern poet.

Ex post facto it can be seen that apart from the change in and hardening of the bases of his personal life, Stevens was enabled to write the early poems of *Harmonium* by the liberation from explicit meaning arrived at through his reading of the French symbolists, a process similar to that undergone by Eliot. A large part of his initial power resides in his extraordinary talent for iambic verse, his feeling for and interest in vocabulary; freed from the compulsion to narrate in any prose sense, these flourish in startling, evocative, exotic and disturbing style. Later in his life he was quite patient with correspondents who asked him to "explain" passages in his poetry, particularly the famous pieces in *Harmonium*, and his further inexplicitness is often amusing. The "nonsense" side of the modern movement in poetry – the arbitrary symbols, the private references, the unexplained personae and fragmentary plots – persisted with him, indeed, until the end and accounts for a large part of that growth sector of the American literary economy, the Stevens critical industry. But, of course, if there were no more to him than this he would merely share a place with a score of others. As it is, the conviction grows that he must be placed with the two or three greatest English-speaking poets of the twentieth century.

It is a sense uncontradicted by the letters, though the epochs they mainly record are unsensational indeed. Stevens moved to Hartford in 1916, having followed a former associate to join the Hartford group of insurance companies. His early years with them involved a fair amount of travel, including trips to Florida, which subsequently became a favourite vacation place, and this experience gave concreteness to the Americanness of his verse and in particular established the important polarity of rigorous New England and the lush tropics. He observed flora and fauna (in gardens and zoos as well as at large) with the old Ruskinian intensity. The first edition of *Harmonium* was published in 1923 and the following year his first and only child was born (about the possibility of a second child he characteristically said later: "There is nothing I should have liked more, but I was afraid of it"). Between that time and the second, enlarged edition of *Harmonium* in 1931 he clearly worked harder at his professional career than at poetry. But once again a more settled background, the opportunity to become more comfortably "a domestic creature", provided the conditions for a renewal of creativity. In 1932 he bought the spacious house he was to live in for the rest of his life (previously he had been a tenant in far from luxurious conditions) and, soon after, he was established in an impregnable position with his company, his travelling on business infrequent. From this time the typed letter becomes the rule rather than the exception as his office status enables him to use his stenographer to dictate his private correspondence, and a characteristic tone of voice emerges. There follows the larger part of his correspondence, and absorbing it is, even heroic. He sustains with a succession of correspondents an intercourse sometimes ironic, often subtly affectionate, always astonishingly polished and intelligent. Even what came to be the immutable routines of his existence are made continually fresh, and only in the last few years of his life did he himself seem to find them arduous: "I begin to feel at the end of the day that I am through for that day", he wrote in his seventieth year. "It is not that I grow tired but that my elan seems somewhat bent. I should much rather stroll home looking at the girls than anything else." His continued response to nature and paintings, to new poets and periodicals and correspondents, is remarkable. "I have never been bored in any general sense", he once observed, and we can unhesitatingly believe him.

This is not the place to try to give any account of what is the most important theme of his letters as it is of his verse – the relationship between poetry and reality. Nor to more than mention the interesting but less important question of how his devoting so much of his working time to an occupation and society removed from his art contributed to – or conceivably hindered – his working out of that theme. Almost from the outset he was seen to be a great master of language: increasingly he is being recognized as a poet of organic development and Rilkean penetration who had important things to say about the human condition of his time. How pathetic is the sparse evidence here of English interest in his work – for example, an appreciative letter in 1938 on being noticed in the little magazine *Twentieth Century Verse*, some negotiations with the Fortune Press, a comment on the notorious "Stuffed Goldfinch" review in *New Verse* – "What you say about the Pulitzer Prize is interesting. After all, there are people who think that IDEAS OF ORDER is not only bad but rotten" – a comment all the more ironical now because it can be seen to occur in a truly distinguished series of letters about poetry to Ronald Lane Latimer. Of course, wise after the event, we cannot begin to understand how the book that Stevens's more ribald business friends called *Ordeals of Ida* seemed to Geoffrey Grigson finicky, rhythmless, unreal, inhuman and to observe nothing –

> ... Children,
> Still weaving budded aureoles,
> Will speak our speech and never know,
> Will say of the mansion that it seems
> As if he that lived there left behind
> A spirit storming in blank walls,
> A dirty house in a gutted world,
> A tatter of shadows peaked to white,
> Smeared with the gold of the opulent sun.

An operation Stevens underwent on April 26, 1955, showed that he was suffering from an inevitably fatal cancer. The fact was kept from him, and he made a sufficient recovery from the surgery to go to Yale to receive an honorary degree and actually return, at the end of June and into July, to his office for a few hours a day. Only a phrase from the last letter here, dated July 15, reveals any real slackening of his hold on the two preoccupations of his life – "Considering my present condition, I can neither concentrate on poetry nor enjoy poetry". These are harrowing words following the long years of asserting, in so many different ways, poetry to be life's only sanction, and of striving so elaborately to show in his art the nature of existence. But they come, after all, in a note written to try to help a young poet quite unknown to him. By August 2 he was dead.

EMPIRE IN TIME AND SPACE

Ernst Kaiser

Robert Musil, the most imporant novelist writing in German in this half-century, is one of the least known writers of the age. Only two modern novelists compare with him in range and intelligence – Proust and Joyce; and the indirect light they cast on him also illuminates "the cultural situation." The popularity that Proust has attained suggests that modern Europe finds it easier to acknowledge the greatness that is sick. Joyce, whose private language made his later work even less accessible than was the autobiographical subjectivity of Proust, is also the object of a cult; and this although both men reckoned with the world's indifference. Musil must have reckoned with it too, but for different reasons; his writing is not exclusive and not bitter. Above all it is not sick. That his chief work, *Der Mann ohne Eigenschaften*, with its inimitable ring of authority, its strength and lucidity, remains out of print, except for a privately published posthumous third volume, is a disgrace to German publishing.

*   *   *

Robert Edler von Musil was born in Klagenfurt, Carinthia, on November 6, 1880, and educated at a cadet school. At the age of 26, after the success of his first novel and when he had already given up a lectureship in civil engineering, he abandoned an academic career in philosophy to devote himself entirely to writing. When he went voluntarily into exile after the *Anschluss*, his books were banned in Germany; he continued writing *Der Mann ohne Eigenschaften* in Switzerland, until his sudden death in 1942. This book, on which he spent twenty years, is of enormous length; twenty unrevised chapters will be included in a definitive edition.

In spite of the general disadvantage of comparing unique works – and comparison with Joyce did, understandably, exasperate Musil himself – the practice can be useful. For thus to compare two

Der Mann ohne Eigenschaften, by Robert Musil [October 28, 1949]

contraries is to disengage peculiarities and common qualities that place the writer not merely at the head of his contemporaries but, as Hazlitt said of Wordsworth, "in a totally distinct class of excellence." Work like Joyce's and Musil's is on a borderline; comprehension and comprehensiveness have been strained to the limits of what can be said. Both the book that ends "A way a lone a last a loved a long the" and the book that begins "There was an atmospheric depression over the Atlantic ..." are gigantic fragments corresponding to an element in the nature of their time. In literature, as in history, we are on a frontier, perhaps passing under the singing statues on the range above Samuel Butler's Nowhere. The greatest works of art are expeditions into unexplored territory, and in trying to reach the ultimate they may arrive only at a last possibility, their absolute intention summed up by Scott's words from the Antarctic: "Pretence is useless." The result may look like failure, above all in literature, where the heroic often counts for less than the smooth face of success; the message may sound, in the ears of the world, like the cries of dying men. But the world's reaction is like that of a body confusing the pain that the healer causes with the pain of the disease. Once we recognize where the torment lies, we suddenly grasp a fundamental similarity between such writers: the true artist's resemblance to the physician, exquisite in observation, intuitive in diagnosis and causing pain for the sake of healing only.

*   *   *

The richness and largeness common to the work of both writers, the architectural control of design, the preoccupation with history as it exists in the eternal present – all this, analysed further, reveals the differences between them. Joyce, a philosophic artist, in his over-lifesize day and night packed history into a nutshell: a gigantic nut, too hard for most teeth to crack. The huge day is one in which it is easy to get lost, as in a world. How big is a day in reality? And what sort of day is it that contains all history, including the present day? Musil, a philosopher turned artist, did not use mythological means; he treated reality not as something to pack back into the Yggdrasilian pod, but like those Japanese paper pellets which when laid on water slowly unfold in delicate and astonishing patterns. Musil's method is an unfolding, with a transparent depth as of still water under the floating pictures. A witness to the decline and fall of an ancient empire, he records not only historical events and social habits but illumines layer after layer of the causes underlying them. Here time is not twenty-four hours but one year ; the scene not a decaying outpost of another civilization but the imperial heart of Europe; the hero not the "enemy" always on the fringe, but the elect man born at the centre of things and shedding his "properties." Musil, expert in two kinds of abstraction both inadequate as art itself is, turns imperfection to imaginative account; in his third quality, that of the artist, he makes a world of irony and tragedy. It is a whole world in terms of a single year, and it poses the menacing questions: How long is one day of such a year? How long is that which seems to be only a year? The achievements of Joyce and of Musil – so closely related and yet so different – are like two hemispheres trying to join, but unable to do so. They do not combine to form the whole unity, a comprehensible world. But the defeat to which such books witness is only partial. In so far as it is the reader's defeat, and not the writer's, it is the defeat inherent in life.

*   *   *

A half-conscious, uneasy awareness of the fact that life is too much for man to cope with single-handed is the main cause of a modern tendency to keep great works of literature on the shelf unread. Where German writing is concerned, furthermore, the English are justifiably nervous; for since the Bismarckian era what has been called important has too often combined the awe-inspiringly idealistic with the ponderous, glum and uncouth. Robert Musil was not that sort of German writer. The explanation lies to a large extent in the fact that he was an Austrian; and it is well known that while the German situation may be "serious but not desperate," the Austrian situation is always "desperate but not serious." Similarities between this attitude to life and our own have often been remarked, and to English readers much of *Der Mann ohne Eigenschaften* must seem startlingly in tune. Apart from the fact that its social premise is that of satiety, saturation and completeness, in vivid contrast to the German *Drang*, its approach is utterly un-German: Musil wears the manner of one who is relaxed and at ease, who can afford to take even the most appalling circumstances easily. His writing has a wit, restraint and understatement that recall passages of Butler rather than of *The Egoist*, to which this book has been compared. For Meredith's style is diamond, Musil's plate glass: it is for looking through. But *Der Mann ohne Eigenschaften* is both an extraordinarily amusing and an extraordinarily difficult book. Its sheer length demands unusual powers of intellectual endurance from the reader if he is to enter into the experience, which is as large and dazzling as life. For it was not written for the reader any more than it was written against him; it was simply written in disregard of the average. Hence in its very likeness to life it is so steep that the reader who goes up the rock face needs, in every sense, a good head. That it is both edifying and entertaining is incidental. Musil sought to get right to the bottom – or rather, to the top – of life. As in life itself, the work's difficulty and danger is intrinsic; like everyday life, acceptance makes it finally endurable; its weight is, after all, in proportion to its bulk, it is intense and manifold, informative and reflective, refreshing in its exactitude, reconciling in its long-sighted humour.

* * *

These are high claims, but not too high. The book's length is not only horizontal, in pages; it is also vertical, each page being capable of such extension and elaboration that the implicit number of the whole rises into infinity. Just as Musil's training as a technician made him well aware of the strain that a given material will stand, so his studies in positivism made him able to consider the unanswerable nature of ultimate questions. Thus he was immune from ecstatic muddle, a vice endemic in modern German literature; he could concentrate his strength on the territory and keep his survey, for all its vast extent, economically spare, lucid and plain. The territory is one year of destiny, 1913–14; but each cross-section of a life, among all the lives merging and mingling with each other, also opens a vista of other years, making a panorama of a whole epoch, an empire in time as in space.

This gift for defining and calculating, the highly evolved mind's capacity to reduce everything to essentials and relate everything to principles, applies not only to the material but to the texture of the book. There is no artificial restriction, apparently no "construction"; there are no distinct threads of plot and sub-plot, any more than there are in life. Everything is alive; therefore everything is, as if in spite of itself, a living symbol of life itself. The result is a work of art, a world created by an artist; and it is a real world because it is limited by its own nature, by time and the fact that it is seen from one point, grouped round one man. Musil recognized his own method as clearly as he foresaw the reader's natural reaction. In a Notebook (1932) he says: "Readers expect one to tell them of life itself, not of life as it is reflected inside the heads of literature and of men. But that is justifiable only in so far as that reflection is merely a faint transfer, a worn convention. I am trying to give them the original...." And to the reader who expects art to offer him an escape from life he says, a shade sardonically: "What the story in this novel comes to is that the story supposed to be told in it is not told at all."

Just as the hero who has shed his qualities and become a man without properties is a man potentially with all properties, so, logically enough, the book contains all actions and no action – the cancelling out of action in its own futility. The son of an eminent lawyer in the State service, Ulrich, an ex-cavalry officer, almost an ex-mathematician, after long absence returns home to Vienna. His lack of "properties" is no mere witticism; it is an idea, born of experience, and so itself an experience. With a name meaning "lord of the manor" (his family name is never mentioned), Ulrich is so impersonal as to be a sublimation. He is all of us; but whereas H. C. Earwicker is an overflowing abundance, Here Comes Everybody, Ulrich is a withdrawal, his face not a sum of generalized features but a deliberate and total blank. Summing up all qualities in himself, he becomes colourless, as the spectrum in motion appears white.

> And one day Ulrich stopped wanting to be a coming man. Even in those days people had begun to talk of footballers and boxers of genius, but for at least every ten geniuses in the way of explorers, tenors or writers the newspapers were still producing no more than, at the most, one genius of a centre-half or one great tactician on the tennis-court.... But then ... Ulrich suddenly came across the phrase: "race-horse of genius." It was in an account of a sensational race, and the writer may not at all have guessed the magnitude of the idea.... But Ulrich instantly realized how inextricably his whole career was bound up with this genius among race-horses. For the horse was always a sacred animal to the cavalry; in his young days in barracks

Ulrich had hardly heard anything talked of but horses and women, and he had fled in order to become a man of importance. And now . . . when he might have begun to feel he was near the summit of his aspirations, he was greeted from on high by the horse, which had got there first.

* * *

Two main themes run side by side, an abyss between them: the *Parallelaktion*, the activities of the campaign committee organizing the Emperor's seventieth jubilee (to be held in 1918, concurrently with Wilhelm II's thirtieth), and the case of the sexual maniac Moosbrugger, on trial for murder. The *Parallelaktion* embodies the real action, or rather, inaction – a campaign that never gets started, symptomatic of that Austria where the feeling always was "es muss etwas geschehen" ("something must be done") and where what happened was usually only what could not be helped, in other words "es ist passiert" ("it just happened"). The counterbalance to all this latent eventfulness is personified by Ulrich, who becomes the committee's honorary secretary. He is a passive philosopher of a style that can only be the product of a centuries-old culture, and perhaps only in its last hours: himself a finishing touch to a way of life that has a doubting smile for everything, knowing that life itself is something that always slips beyond the scope of human planning and "ist passiert."

Figures from many sections of society are involved in the jubilee campaign, which sets out to show the world that there are not only brand-new, spit-and-polish empires, but venerable ones that can look on their cracks as on honourable scars. For one endless, breathless, feckless year the campaign, a gigantic symbol of human foolishness, an enterprise like a dinosaur, becoming more and more desperately idealistic, ambles on towards 1914 and Sarajevo. The inevitability of its failure is apparent in every feature of those who, having created it, are unable to live up to their own idea, now prismatically split into innumerable ideas.

The story that is not told might be compared to a dry, invisible river that is yet intensely perceptible as a current of will. Musil dug a wide bed for this spectral river of life; and while no liberating waters flow, the bathers crowd on the banks, explaining away the phenomenon but unable to solve the difficulty. From Graf Leinsdorf, the Austrian aristocrat *par excellence*, with his daring little theories such as that "a social-democratic republic with a strong ruler at the head might well be a far from impossible form of government," to Tuzzi, the permanent secretary, and his wife Diotima, Ulrich's cousin, who has a salon; from the banker Fischel, the poet Feuermaul, the prophet Meingast, to intense and gifted artists like the pianist Walter who "seemed to have within himself a very melodious amplifier for small happiness and unhappiness" and "always paid out emotional small-change in gold and silver, while Ulrich operated more on a large scale, with intellectual cheques" – all these and many more, with their families, servants, offices, parties, ambitions, seductions, their lack of sincerity ripped by outbursts of candour, like three-dimensional people have their Jamesian subtleties and frustrations, their Dostoevskian intoxication, their Dickensian and their Proustian aspects – they have it all, because they are, in fact, the world. Musil had the gift of universality that only the greatest novelists have possessed: what may best be called complete presence of mind. The trained philosopher, instead of reducing reality to a system of ideas, for once acts as a mirror, flashing reality straight back into the mind of the beholder. That is what Musil meant by saying he had given "the original."

And while all these people hover, longing to make their phantom plunge into the waves of the spirit, not dreaming of the river of blood that is really coming, a solitary figure approaches, walking up the dry river-bed. He is tiny at first, so long as everything surrounding him is tiny and bright-coloured, seen through the wrong end of the telescope; then gradually coming closer, growing, in an environment that grows and changes, with the inexorable logic of advancing time, the "nonattached" man is the focal point. It is hard to define the peculiar nature of this gradual enlargement and change, which is first hinted at in the dark secondary theme.

*   *   *

Sombre and terrible in the background is Moosbrugger, whose trial is a national sensation, taking on a symbolic quality as compulsively as things in reality do: the shadow-side, the lurking terror that night must fall. The paradox behind Moosbrugger is that he is the first movingly human figure to rise beside the hero: his is the child's soul innocently taking on itself the maniac's act of blood. Moosbrugger often feels the world grow "too tight" for him; if he is not to stifle, he must destroy, and instinctively he identifies pain with woman. At other times he identifies himself with the essence of being; then he dances the planetary dance of life's eternal motion. But although he is a bogy, a threat to the existence of society, he is not repulsive. It is strange how touching this grisly figure is, how at the very end, after incarceration and escape from an asylum and in the midst of a drunken, brawling life, he seems to be a large, sad animal, always behind bars and made vicious by the presence of the bars. He is the "I" against "Them," the others who for all their sharp and subtle differentiation make up a collective total. A society of Moosbruggers is unthinkable; and the essence of the case against him is, of course, that he forces society to see the Moosbrugger in itself. To escape this awareness they all take refuge in law, crown, country, "the spirit of the age" and the *Parallelaktion*, their own version of the rhythm of life.

The meaninglessness of the social game, of the dance of rain-makers who have lost their magic, is something they have not yet recognized. They still take a certain comfort in the historical brilliance of their city, their national tradition. The wasteland metaphor is not used in the book, which makes no play with symbols, never labours a point, never talks for the sake of talking. Musil, like Ulrich, is above all a scientist, eliminating, or at least isolating, the subjective element; and the feeling of waterless, riverless, hopeless territory is a feeling only. Then in the second volume Ulrich's solitude is interrupted; and the reader realizes that the man of no properties has drawn much closer. His father's death brings him into contact with his sister Agathe, whom he has not seen for many years. She is the second human figure with a hunger for truth; she is Ulrich's "self-love," as he tells her. Now the clarity of the pure colours blurs; distances are shortened; the satirical element often gives way to the grotesque. Only Ulrich remains unchanged; the white light intensifies, that is all.

But the two figures in the foreground do not occupy all the space. In the third volume the reader feels the closeness of the impending war, the menace of it in everything, though particularly in the unrelieved erotic tension between brother and sister. In the last chapter, which Musil was writing on the day of his death, Ulrich and Agathe lounge in deck-chairs on the lawn of the high-walled garden all day, moving round with the sun, in utter solitude, like mysterious substances in the alchemist's retort from which the miracle is hoped for. The chapter breaks off with the words:

> "Why aren't we realists?" Ulrich wondered. They had both long ceased to be realists, he and she; their thoughts and actions had made that quite clear for a long time. But they were nihilists and activists, now one, now the other, according to the way things came.

*   *   *

Although the surface is satire on a society in decay, and under that one system of knowledge after another, one manner of life after another, is dissected and discarded, many readers will also apprehend an esoteric pattern lying deeper still. Paradoxically, negatively, the book is an *Entwicklungsroman*, an adventure of quest and initiation, operated by stripping off skin after skin of illusion. But like every great work of art it is more than its creator consciously intended. In one of the last dialogues the banker Fischel utters deceptively simple words which in their context cause a tremor of shock: "Money has a mind of its own." So have books. It is fascinating to see the novel's shape looming out, making its own way ahead, independent, alive and growing. Yet Musil worked not like a mystic, but like an abnormally well-equipped anthropologist, with a mind as accurate as a spirit-level. It is the mind of the Man of No Properties, from whom the lines of light radiate to the other figures, showing by contrast how inessential properties and dignities of every kind are. When it becomes possible to stand back from the book and see it as a whole, characters and events suddenly turn out to be elements in a new myth, built upon a very ancient order. The reader realizes that Walter and Meingast, for instance, show how art and mysticism are not enough, that a valid interpretation of life grows out of an understanding of its most everyday ordinariness, not out of attempts to escape from reality. Arnheim, the Prussian millionaire industrialist, "the *universal* specialist," involved in speculations among ideals as in the Galician oilfields, so nearly Diotima's lover, perhaps the Tsar's confidant, personifies the conflict between mind and matter. In his conception of the "superman of letters" the world of literary brilliance is driven to its own logical conclusion; and his feints, his juggling with wealth and culture, are shown to be in the last resort no more than stock-exchange manoeuvres. Arnheim almost recognizes this when he tries to make Ulrich his friend and so subordinate him, playing the tempter who offers temporal power in return for renunciation of a chosen condition. The immanent mythical pattern is an inevitable result of the book's organic unity.

A friend of Musil's said of *Der Mann ohne Eigenschaften*: "All formal truth has its complement on the mythological side, but myth cannot be manufactured; it is something one recognizes later." If this great work can be regarded as something like a miracle play in which the mystery is indicated by the very lack of anything mysterious, the explanation lies in Musil's own words: "This book has one passion that is nowadays somewhat out of place in the realm of *belles lettres*: the passion for rightness, precision."

MODERN, TRIESTINE
AND TRUE

Anthony Burgess

Aron Hector (or Ettore) Schmitz wrote under the pseudonyms of Ettore Samigli and, more memorably, Italo Svevo. He told James Joyce that he felt sorry for the single thin vowel choked by aggressive consonants in his real name and sought a certain vocalic expansion in the ones he chose for his pen. That was typical of the man's whimsicality. At a party, surrounded, as he always was, by guests who liked his ironic brand of humour, he said that he had a bad memory: "There are three things I can't remember – names, addresses, and I forget the third." There was, however, no true whimsicality in the choice of "Italo Svevo" – Swabian Italian, or it may be the other way round. Though the Schmitz family was, like Bloom's, Hungarian Jewish and had settled in a maritime city not unlike Dublin, Svevo's early education was at Würzburg: he felt an affinity for German culture, especially if it was Austrian. He read

Italo Svevo. A Double Life, by John Gatt-Rutter. *Italo Svevo*, by Beno Weiss [May 13, 1988]

Freud and translated *Über der Traum* into Italian. The name Italo Svevo expresses two of the elements in the racial and cultural composition of Trieste, the Dublin of the Adriatic – the others were Slavonic and international Jewish. Of course, Trieste, where Svevo was born and lived most of his life, was greater than Dublin: it was the major port of the Austro-Hungarian Empire but also a part of the Italian peninsula. The irredentist movement that sought the political absorption of Trieste into the Kingdom of Italy was strong when Svevo, in 1892, published his first novel, *Una vita*, and the pseudonym suggested a reactionary stance, though, in the Bloomian manner, it merely asserted the unimportance of race and nationality. If the novel failed to impress, one of the reasons was, despite its Trieste setting, its lack of interest in Triestine politics.

When we visit Trieste today, we have no doubt that it is an Italian city, but this is only in the sense that it sees Raffaella Carrà and Mike Buongiorno on television, drinks Campari and eats the products of Motta and Alemagna. Italian is the official language, but the Triestines speak a dialect unintelligible to the Milanese and Romans. A postcard survives written by the young Lucia Joyce, in which she tells her father *"Go una bella balla"*, that *g* standing for the dead aspirate of Latin. We find the same thing in Veneto. It is like Russians enquiring into the gomosexuality of Gemingway. The dialect was never believed to have any literary potential, and it was assumed in metropolitan Italy, that if a book was published in Trieste, this was the last resort of a failed author. Trieste, in the time of Svevo, and of Joyce, was Austrian territory. Italian troops marched in in 1918, and the cover of John Gatt-Rutter's biography shows a smiling Svevo watching the city becoming Italian. He is also smoking his last cigarette. He was always smoking his last cigarette, like the hero of *La coscienza di Zeno*. At the end of the Second World War Trieste became briefly independent – a *stato Topolino* or Mickey Mouse state – and American and British troops held it against the threat of Tito's tanks. It is undoubtedly Italian now, but Italian with a difference. Any author born in it and memorializing it in his work is chiefly acceptable further south because of the example of Svevo. Svevo struggled not only for his own acceptance but for that of his literary successors. The struggle was arduous.

Beno Weiss gives briefly, and Gatt-Rutter at length, the story of a literary ambition perpetually foiled. Svevo wrote articles for the local newspaper *L'Indipendente* and attempted plays which were doomed never to be produced, working meanwhile at the Unionbank. He married his cousin Livia Veneziani when he was *nel mezzo del cammin* and started working for the Veneziani paint firm. This had a virtual monopoly of a paint formula for ships' hulls which resisted corrosion (Svevo said, straightfaced, that the painting was an under-water job). There was a branch of the firm in Charlton which Svevo was responsible for setting up and managing, and this necessitated his doing something about his English. In 1906 James Joyce had returned to Trieste from a bank clerkship in Rome and was resuming the teaching of English at the Berlitz School as well as to private pupils. The two authors, the one failed, the other a mere minor poet, though a published one, had occluded ambitions in common and, so it emerged, cognate approaches to literature. Joyce was encouraged by Svevo to push on with *A Portrait of the Artist as a Young Man*; Joyce, in his turn, admired *Una vita* and *Senilità* and, with the critical assurance he always had, pronounced Svevo a neglected author. "There are passages in *Senilità* that even Anatole France could not have improved." He then quoted some of these passages without benefit of the book. Svevo was encouraged to resume writing but he did not learn much of the kind of English he needed for a paint factory in Charlton. Nor could the Charlton workers understand his Dublin accent.

In fact, Stanislaus, Joyce's brother, could have equipped Svevo with the kind of quotidian English that he needed, while Joyce, though his pupil called him *il mercante di gerundi*, was bored with grammar and not helpful as regards lexis. When Svevo asked him what Shakespeare meant by "brass eternal slave to mortal rage", Joyce replied that he was probably thinking of German bands. Which author got the more from the other? Svevo gained encouragement, but Joyce was virtually unique, certainly in Italy, in practising and promoting literary modernism. Svevo was in some ways ahead of him. Joyce the poet was bound to be impressed by the rhetoric of Gabriele D'Annunzio, but Svevo gave practical demonstrations of how empty much of that rhetoric was. It was the anti-rhetorical, the straight ironic statements of Svevo's two neglected novels, that the Italians interpreted as the kind of linguistic clumsiness to be expected from a Triestine. But Joyce had already written *Dubliners*, and both Italo and Livia Svevo heard him read "The Dead". Livia picked him a bouquet. Expunge the *fin-de-siècle* poet in Joyce, and Joyce is seen to be not unsvevian. But *Ulysses* was to go far beyond Svevo.

It is not fanciful to see something of Leopold Bloom in this Hungarian Jew, tied to commerce but with more than something of the artist in him, walking a city of ships, bending under the onslaught of the *Bora*. The age-gap between Joyce and Svevo was twenty years, almost the same as that between Bloom and Stephen. Svevo's Jewishness was ancestral, and he had married in the Catholic Church, as he was to be buried in a Catholic cemetery. Joyce certainly probed him for Jewish lore and liturgy, to an extent that made Svevo threaten to catechize him about Ireland. In *Finnegans Wake* Livia's name is attached to the river-heroine, and her long reddish-brown hair becomes the Liffey tainted by effluent. Joyce used both the Svevos, as he was to use everybody, but Svevo could not use Joyce. It was only with the publication of *La coscienza di Zeno* in 1923, when Svevo was sixty-two, that Joyce's Paris connections seemed likely to help a neglected Triestine gain a minimal international audience, if not an Italian one. Joyce, now famous, received a copy of the novel in 1924; the author followed his book to Paris in the following year and was introduced to Crémieux and Larbaud. But in that same year Italy's finest poet, Eugenio Montale, wrote a long article on Svevo for the Italian press, following it with a further article in 1926. Also in 1926 *Le Navire d'Argent* devoted almost an entire issue to Svevo. He was not merely accepted as an Italian writer but lauded as a neglected one of European significance. Back in Trieste he met Pirandello and Marta Abba. In 1927, intending to lecture on himself in the offices of *Il Convegno* in Milan, he spoke about Joyce instead. He recognized Joyce's magnetism but could not accord him all the credit for drawing the literary world's attention to works too long disregarded. He owed to Montale his acceptance as an Italian writer, one whose stylistic achievement had previously looked like incompetence.

In 1928 Svevo was honoured by the PEN Club in Paris. The guests included Ehrenburg and Babel, Shaw, Prezzolini, James and Nora Joyce, Giraudoux and Jules Romains. He had at last achieved the literary fame he had always coveted, and it came at the right time, when the work was done and there was no danger of the falling off that drove Scott Fitzgerald to his final misery or Ernest

Hemingway to suicide. It was in this year of his triumph that Svevo was injured in a car accident and died three days later. Trieste has named a street after him, but it has named one after Joyce too. To the world of international literature Svevo must always seem to stand in the shadow of Joyce, but Italy has at last been taught to think differently. A film was made of *Senilità* and high school students are made to read the books. His stature is still perhaps in doubt. Beno Weiss, who was born in Abbazia but now teaches at Pennsylvania State University, rates him as high as Joyce, Pirandello, Kafka, Musil, Proust, Lawrence, Gide and Mann on account of "his distinctive originality, his sensitivity to the new currents that dominated his time, his wealth of interests, and his initiative capacity to probe into the inner motivations of man". John Gatt-Rutter, who teaches at Griffith University in Brisbane, says that Svevo is "an uncannily representative writer. He writes about contemporary man at his most ordinary, the man in the street" – or, if we like, the man in the paint factory. Svevo was also a Freudian, which Joyce was not, or pretended not to be. His modernity, however, was not in doubt even before he first read Freud. *Senilità*, though published in 1898, reads like a modern novel.

Joyce misled its Anglophone readers by giving it the title *As a Man Grows Older*, but Svevo's own title is misleading too. *Senilità* has not to be taken literally as meaning age and, the primary connotation, sexual impotence. It means rather, as Gatt-Rutter puts it, "an impotence to realize new human relationships based on affection rather than domination". It is about Emilio Brentani, a thirty-five-year-old bachelor working in a Trieste insurance company and living with his sister Amalia. Emilio, like his creator, has written a novel noticed in the local press but quickly forgotten. He has sunk into inertia abetted by Amalia's awareness that life has passed them both by. Emilio envies the sculptor Stefano Balli, who, though an artistic failure like himself, has great success with women.

But Emilio meets Angiolina Zarri, a girl of the working class, a slut easily recognized as such by the experienced Stefano, but to Emilio the innocent a Galatea to be remoulded in his own refined image. At first he never gets beyond chastely kissing her, but, discovering that she is freely giving herself to men less scrupulous, he sleeps with her at her invitation, not in love but in hate. Amalia,

divining the glow of sexual fulfilment about him, herself craves a
similar fulfilment for herself and falls in love with Stefano, though
she speaks his name with ardour only in her sleep. Emilio knows
that Stefano finds her unattractive and, fearing the consequences of
her infatuation, makes Stefano stay away. Amalia becomes an
alcoholic, secretly sipping scented ether, falls ill and promotes
remorse in Emilio, who brings back Stefano to see her. Stefano
admires her for the first time in his capacity as an artist, fascinated
by her physical agony. Emilio sees Angiolina for the last time, calls
her a whore, and determines to devote his life to caring for his
sister. But it is too late. Amalia dies and Emilio's drab existence
resumes, sweetened only by a dream image in which the chaste
sister and the unreformable slut combine as an impossible ideal.
The past is transfigured and casts a consolatory light over a
resigned and monotonous future:

> His love of images led him to see his life as a straight,
> uneventful road leading across a quiet valley; from the
> point at which he had first met Angiolina the road branched
> off, and led him through a varied landscape of trees,
> flowers, and hills. But only for a short while; after that it
> dropped to the valley, and became again the straight high
> road, easy and secure, but less tedious now because it was
> refreshed by memories of that enchanting, vivid interlude,
> full of colour and perhaps too of fatigues.

The novel was not well understood by a public that required
rhetoric and melodrama in its fiction. The Nobel Prizeman Paul
von Heyse, who had praised the less mature *Una vita*, approved the
sharpness of the observation and the exactness of the psychological
analysis but accused Svevo of wasting his time on a "repugnant"
subject: his characters lacked health and strength and what the
fictional tradition regarded as "normality". It was this judgment
that broke Svevo's ambition. He accepted glumly "a unanimous
judgement (there is no more perfect unanimity than silence) and for
twenty-five years I abstained from writing. If it was a mistake it was
mine." He did in fact go on writing but did not publish. *La coscienza
di Zeno* was a long time gestating.

   Confessions of Zeno can be regarded as a seminal modernist novel
not only in its psychoanalytical theme but in a narrative technique
that eschews traditional linearity. Zeno Cosini is a fifty-six-year-old

Triestine businessman, outwardly prosperous but inwardly tormented by a psychoneurotic disorder that expresses itself in aches
and pains real and imagined and, above all, an incurable addiction
to cigarettes. He visits an analyst, Dr S. (Sigmund? Svevo?
Schmitz? Samigli?), probably based on Edoardo Weiss, the
Triestine Freudian and a good friend of Svevo's. Dr S. asks Zeno
to keep a diary in which, using free association, he may release
material from his unconscious. Thus the technique of the novel
allows past and present time to cohabit. As with Ford Madox
Ford's *The Good Soldier* the narration is unreliable, and the reader is
warned about this in a brief preamble. Along with the unreliability
of memory goes the deeper unreliability of the paradoxes of Zeno
of Eleas, which form the metaphysical substructure of the work. If,
says Eleatic Zeno, we have to cross an infinite number of points to
travel from A to B in finite time, we can never arrive at our
destination. This seems to justify Zeno of Trieste's paradox of the
last cigarette never being the last. The fusion of earnestness and
humour is remarkable, though the comedy of the *ultima sigaretta*
may be less apparent to an age that is giving up smoking than to
Svevo's own. Yet Zeno's comic addiction has a wider symbolism
than could properly be appreciated in 1923. Svevo, aware of the gas
or poisonous smoke of the First World War, grants Zeno an
apocalyptical vision of the world's end, in which everything goes
up in smoke.

Svevo was as ahead of his time as was Joyce, and it is only since
the Second World War that he has found a true audience. Italy,
bemused by Ciceronian prose and the fireworks of D'Annunzio,
was slow to understand Svevo's narrative flatness, irony and
psychological penetration. It has been left to Anglophonia to
celebrate his strange life and complex personality. John Gatt-
Rutter's book is fuller than, but does not really supersede, P. N.
Furbank's biography of 1966. Weiss's little book, which comes in
Twayne's World Authors Series, does much in a small space.
Richard Ellmann's life of Joyce has still to be consulted,
nevertheless, for an authoritative picture of the pre-war Trieste in
which Schmitz flourished but Svevo languished and in which
destiny contrived a mutual literary encouragement that produced
two of the masterpieces of modernism.

FURY AND ELEGANCE

John Bayley

No woman in English poetry has written like Blake, or like Eliot. Nor, for that matter, could either Blake or Eliot have written with the conscience and the fury of a sibyl, the status of a society beauty, the experiences of a divorced wife, terrorized widow and persecuted mother. No other woman poet has had the opportunities given to Anna Akhmatova, and it may be that such opportunities – the kind not vouchsafed to Emily Brontë, or to Sylvia Plath – are what a great female artist requires and can make best use of. Akhmatova was a very unselfconscious poet in many ways; she had qualities of elemental force, utterance haunted and Delphic; yet these went together with elegance and sophistication, even a certain kind of mirror-gazing and a cunning which is *chétif*, or, as the Russians say, *zloi*. She is not in the least like Blake or Eliot, and yet those are the English poets – different as they are – who offer some sort of parallel with her finest work. The incongruity in coupling such names shows how exceptional is her own poetic being.

Her individuality was not likely to recommend her to the men at the top – nor did it. At the time of her expulsion from the Writers' Union, Zhdanov called her "a nun and a whore". Sound archetypes for a great poet, observes D. M. Thomas, in the introduction to his translation of her two greatest poems, *Requiem* and *Poem Without a Hero* (his is the first complete version of the latter in English).

But though it is nice to think the party hack uttered praise without knowing it, such a description is in fact wholly incongruous with the kinds of contrast in Akhmatova's personality. Strangely enough she has as a poet more in common with what are – in a degraded form – Soviet ideals: restraint, correctness, propriety. Her poetry is dignified in the grandest sense without pretending to dignity, an equivalent in art of what she called the severe and shapely spirit of Russian orthodoxy.

Requiem, and *Poem Without a Hero*, by Anna Akhmatova, translated by D. M. Thomas [April 16, 1976]

Blok, or Yeats, would have been delighted to see themselves as archetypes of nun or harlot, libertine or sage – it would be a part of the methodical build-up of their poetic selves. She was herself in a more absolute sense. Though full of admiration, her attitude to Blok was as to some sort of unstable demon or actor in a seductive but dangerously wicked farce. The majesty of her own being seems to declare: "One doesn't behave like that"; and she says the same thing in the same tone to state tyranny, to the horrors of the *Yezhovschina*, to all the destructive convictions of inhuman conceit. She knows – none better – that offence comes, but woe unto them by whom it cometh, whether it be the perverse and deliberate invocation of madness and violence, or the policy of cruelty and persecution in the name of some abstract good. A curious feature of *Poem Without a Hero*, which irritated some of her friends and well-wishers as it did the priests of the new regime, is the resurrection and expiation of old St Petersburg sins as if they were one with the new torments of Leningrad.

The central part of the poem's "triptych" bears the epigraph "My Future is in my Past", a version of the device of Mary Queen of Scots: "In my beginning is my End." Thomas's notes point out that she refers to Eliot as the source for this, and only discovered that it was Mary's motto just before her death. Probably she knew of the *Four Quartets*, and their provenance in besieged London. Certainly the passage in "Little Gidding" that begins "In the uncertain hour before the morning" gives a more direct impression of the tone and movement of her poem than any translation can do.

One does not believe like that; one does not do such things. If one is tempted, if one is compromised or guilty, one is haunted by the dead and devoured by conscience. To meet throughout life, as in a mirror, one's image or double – an idea which constantly recurs in her poetry – is not for her a way in which the artist escapes himself or by which he profits: such an identification may be with a great fellow-spirit in suffering, as was Akhmatova's with Mandelshtam, but it was more often like a warning, an admonition of sin and shortcoming. The role of conscience in her poetry reminds us how unfamiliar such a possession is to most poets, whose natural tendency in the Nietzschean and modern era is to say that "such as I cast out remorse". She was deeply religious, and religion – as Dr Johnson noted – does not come over in poetry, but conscience, its precursor and attendant, can and does.

It figures largely, and strangely, in *Poem Without a Hero*, whose title itself suggests the collapse of a Nietzschean world in which men of action, or the hero as poet and seer, could play a part. Its denizens, including Blok, including the poet herself, are in one sense poor creatures, not the heroic figures into whom an intense vision of the past transmutes so many. For this is a poem about remorse, and about a past "in which the future is rotting".

Thus although it is arbitrary to attach a single life and its interior shaping, as Akhmatova does, to the ordeal of Russia in the revolution, to the years of terror and invasion, the theme of remorse – for one and for all – unites these things as they could not have been united in any artificial poem in which such events were directly lamented or celebrated. She refused to be "melted to a state hymn"; hers is not a "public" poem as is, for example, Margarita Aliger's moving *Spring in Leningrad*.

Poem Without a Hero was more than twenty years in the writing, and appeared to the poet, during that time, as a recurrent and inescapable malady. On its smaller scale *The Waste Land* had the same characteristic of a visitation, painful to suffer, more painful to evade. And another phenomenon is significantly true of both poems: they derive their status from the reality of the *fait accompli*. Though critics may seek to demonstrate after the event their underlying "unity" and so forth, such poems only now seem so inevitable and so public because they made a total success of being so private and so arbitrary.

As might be expected of Akhmatova, however, *Poem Without a Hero* is extremely literal, as concerned with place and event as a Hardy poem, and closely connected to the poet's life in pre-war St Petersburg. A child of the professional middle classes – her father was a naval architect – she grew up in the capital at a time when its artistic life was at its most febrile and brilliant, the height of the "Silver Age", not only in poetry but in painting, ballet, music; and her poem makes full choreographic use of these forms. She married the poet Gumilev, and together with Mandelshtam they began the Acmeist movement, which best defines itself negatively as a reaction against Blok and the Symbolist poets, a kind of classicism which their admiration for Dante links with the nascent notions of Hulme and Eliot. Her poetry at this time has an unstylized purity, sometimes simplistic, absorbed in what might be called the moral nature of things, and assuming its own kind of confidence from them.

But Akhmatova was also assiduously of the fashionable artistic coterie. Like other poets she recited her poems at the Stray Dog, a cabaret decorated by the leading stage designer Sudeikin, whose wife Olga Glebova-Sudeikina performed there in productions such as Belayev's *Blundering Psyche* and danced in the Fauns ballet half naked and wearing horns a "goat-legged nymph" as Akhmatova calls her. Blok was a revered member of the group, as was Mikhail Kuzmin, a poet and homosexual whom Akhmatova deeply distrusted, and who makes appearances, though briefly, as the evil genius in her poem.

He was probably in love with Vsevolod Knyazev, a young dragoon officer and apprentice poet, the Petruchka of the poem and its "senseless sacrifice", who was himself romantically devoted to the fascinating Sudeikina. When he discovered that Blok – handsome, famous, and a great womanizer – was his successful rival for her affections, he shot himself on the landing of her flat, after seeing her return home in the small hours with Blok, as related at the end of the poem's first section. By that time estranged from her husband, Akhmatova was sharing the flat with Sudeikina, and she herself went round to the young officer's quarters to look for compromising evidence, as the poem suggests: she leaves the place "on tip-toe". She refers to herself as Sudeikina's "ancient conscience", and is obsessed with her as a double or mirror-image of herself, an empty-headed, amiable but amoral beauty. A photograph in the French *édition bilingue* of the poem shows the two statuesquely handsome women together, with clasped hands.

After the war and the terror and starvation of the revolutionary years Sudeikina fled to Paris; Akhmatova stayed in what had become Leningrad. The poems of this period are grim, spare and laconic, but it was not till the mid-1930s, when the Yezhov terror began and Mandelshtam was arrested, that the full horror of what was in store became apparent. Her son Lev Gumilev was arrested, solely because of his father's name; sent from Siberia to fight in the war, he was then rearrested and not finally released till after Stalin's death. At the time of his first arrest Akhmatova joined every day for months the queue waiting outside the prison for news of relatives, and from this experience came the poem *Requiem*, written between 1935 and 1940, or rather committed during that time to memory and to the memories of friends – it was not published until

1963, and then outside Russia and without the author's consent.

The theme of *Poem Without a Hero* came to her, she tells us, on a night in December 1940. Much was written before the German invasion and the siege. She was later evacuated with other artists, including Shostakovich, to Tashkent, where the poem was completed. There is a certain irony in this Soviet solicitude for intellectuals, which probably saved her life: but it is consistent with persecution. They were an asset of the state, and the state, since Pushkin's time, had set a high value on the power of poetry. Her popular status grew in the war years and became an embarrassment to the authorities, who withdrew permission for her collected poems to be published and subjected her to increasing degrees of persecution, including constant escort by the secret police. After Stalin's death came a degree of rehabilitation, a visit to the West, a great and growing reverence on the part of all intellectuals and lovers of Russian verse, for whom she was its voice and conscience.

The action of *Poem Without a Hero* opens on New Year's Eve 1940, the moment when its conception took place. The scene is a house on the Fontanka canal, a white room full of mirrors, in which "instead of the expected guests, the author is visited by shadows from the year 1913, disguised as mummers":

> From childhood I have feared mummers.
>   It always seemed to me that someone,
>   A kind of extra shade
>   "Without face or name", had slipped in
>   Among them....

The phantoms play roles from the old St Petersburg world, notably Don Juan, from Mozart and Byron, Pushkin's Stone Guest, one of Blok's most famous poems "The Steps of the Commander", and from Molière's version, which was staged in 1910 by "Dapertutto" – Vsevolod Meyerhold. The multiple references are typical of the poem's method but – as in *The Waste Land* again – the clarity and trenchancy of the verse makes its immediate impact without any need of notation.

These roles were associated with Sudeikina, and Blok is there "in motley stripes of a milepost", an image that recalls through Pushkin's poem about devils in a snowstorm the blizzard of *The Twelve*, the literal correlative being the verst marks of a Russian high road striped black and white. Then a parenthetic passage refers to the actual "expected guest":

> Guest from the future, will he really come
> Taking the left turn across the bridge?

That was the way to Akhmatova's apartment near the Fontanka; and though he is not named, the "guest from the future" is Isaiah Berlin, who visited there shortly after the war and talked all night, giving her encouragement at a time when the state, which during the war had maintained her as if she had been some potentially valuable asset or machine, had apparently decided to phase her out and consign her to silence.

An intermezzo gives snatches of talk and laughter from the past – in the next scene a voice is reading in Sudeikina's bedroom. Knyazev haunts the movement, his cry "I am ready for death" coinciding with Mandelshtam's words to Akhmatova at the time of his arrest:

> Is this the guest from behind the mirror,
> The shape that flitted past the pane?
> Is the new moon playing a joke, or
> – Between the cupboard and the stove – is
> Somebody standing again?

His shape now that of the self-hanged Kirillov standing "in a terribly strange manner" in *The Possessed*. But for all its macabre images (the capital is called Dostoyevskian) the poem here is full of a vital gaiety and conveys the same animated celebration that Pushkin did in his "sad tale" "The Bronze Horseman", a line from whose prologue – "I love you, Peter's creation" – is the heading of Akhmatova's epilogue.

Part 2 is headed *Reshka*, i.e., "tails", the obverse of the coin, with a further significance of defeat and, in its variant, of prison bars. An editor complains about the poem and its obscurities; the author disowns interpretation and the idea of state or public recognition. Her intimacies will remain her own, and her poem's, and the muse informs her that the poem has no traditional romantic ancestry, no kinship with the heroes of the nineteenth-century pantheon. The third and last part begins with a brief prose evocation of Leningrad under siege, breaking off into poetry, spoken by the author's voice, 7,000 kilometres away. At no point does the poem become "public", even when the poet remembers her friends

who stayed to perish
In an iceblink of waters, a glitter of spires

and not even when in flight she sees below the road to Siberia, along which her son and so many others have been driven. The end is a vision of Russia herself, "knowing the hour of vengeance", walking eastward before the poet, with clenched hands and dry eyes. "Vengeance" refers to the German invaders, but the image of suffering Russia has a wider significance. This is confirmed, it seems to me, by the more singly and conventionally "wartime" conclusion written and then taken out (the poem was never "finished", but the intention seems clear here) in which "young Russia" is seen emerging from Ural and Altai, and advancing, like a mirror reflection, to the faithful defence of Moscow.

Such an account cannot by itself carry conviction of the poem's authority and grandeur; like most such masterpieces it is about as non-international as could be, and it is saturated, besides, in the communal references of generations of Russian art. *Requiem* is much more simple, generically moving; a number of reasonably adequate versions have already appeared, and D. M. Thomas's, to my mind the best so far, has much less to persuade us of than in the case of *Poem Without a Hero*. Persuasion is the point. Auden, characteristically honest, said that he could not feel Mandelshtam was a great poet, "because the translations I have seen don't convince me of it". Thomas's version of *Poem Without a Hero* is not of course itself a great poem: but it makes us feel the original is one, and that is a remarkable achievement. For the translation is itself a good poem: in writing poetry as a translation rather than translating poetry, Thomas shows that it need not be, as Nabokov said, "a parrot's screech, a monkey's chatter". [...]

Of course his sedulous skill cannot convey Akhmatova's simple atavism, plunging excitement and drooping pathos. [...] And the "difficulties" of the poem seem more formidable in English, more saturated and obscure, because the reader is not carried on by the brio of the narrative. Sudeikina, for instance, had been taking part in a show at the Stray Dog called *The Road from Damascus*, which is the point of the reference to her return – a return *into* sin, the opposite of Paul's – but the beat of the Russian makes this evident subliminally, without the need of pausing and pondering.

Not that the poem is anything but arcane. Akhmatova calls it a

Chinese box "with a triple base", and its numerological patterning is as complex as its references to real people, events, works of art. But it is essentially a voice poem, in that tradition which Pushkin stylized in the figure of the "Improvisatore" in *Egyptian Nights*, who denies any idea of how complex verse comes to him suddenly, rhymed and in regular feet, so that it can be instantly declaimed. Like so many Russian masterpieces the poem has the form of an open secret, at once spontaneous and enigmatic. "I frequently hear of certain absurd interpretations of *Poem Without a Hero*", writes Akhmatova in her foreword. "And I have been advised to make it clearer. This I decline to do. It contains no third, seventh, or twenty-ninth thoughts. I shall neither explain nor change anything. What is written is written."

And she ends with a dedication to "its first audience", the fellow-citizens who died in Leningrad during the siege, which reveals the deep source of her simplicity and her greatness, both in this poem and in *Requiem*. "Their voices I hear, and I remember them, when I read my poem aloud, and for me this secret chorus has become a permanent justification of the work."

PAPER TIGERS

John Sturrock

In one of the earliest and most lastingly provocative of his stories, "Pierre Menard, autor del Quijote", Jorge Luis Borges conceived a writer of remote and intriguing trifles whose ambition it is to write a book that will coincide in every particular with one already in existence, *Don Quijote*. The coincidence would be a much more glamorous feat than it sounds, because Menard soon realizes that he cannot backdate his memory and start thinking spontaneous seventeenth-century thoughts; instead of a copy of Cervantes's novel he will have to produce a premeditated, twentieth-century re-creation of it. The impediment is not any lack of talent for the task, only the time for its accomplishment; he has chosen, perversely, to fulfil himself on a scale compatible only with

Jorge Luis Borges: A Personal Anthology, ed. by Anthony Kerrigan [November 14, 1968]

eternity, the dimension set aside by Borges for lofty games of escape from chance like fiction or metaphysics. But however ample the facilities for play may be in eternity, time remains a problem somatically, and Menard completes only two chapters and a bit of his novel before his death.

*   *   *

The impulse for his project comes from Borges's proposition that all ideas are compossible for the mind whose modesty is god-like enough to accommodate them, a proposition which, whatever flaws it may have for a neurologist, is particularly bracing for the writer, since it means that there are no limits to his mental freedom, beyond syntactical ones. It is rather less bracing for literary critics, who like to believe that a determinate personality conditions each written word of the work they are studying and renders it expressive. But what contortions such critics would be faced with, says Borges, if they found out that L.-F. Céline had written the *Imitatio Christi*. His own theorem is more liberal: the greater the creator – God, let us say, or Shakespeare – the more smudged the personality. Thus when Borges calls on God he can please himself whether he addresses him as Someone or Nobody.

One of the ideas which the divinely self-effacing Pierre Menard finds himself forced into sharing with Cervantes is that fighting men are superior to writing men, a priority laid down in Don Quijote's famous "Discourse on Arms and Letters". But unlike Cervantes, the veteran of the Turkish wars, Menard does not find it easy to sustain a belief so comically out of keeping with a life's practice of literary annotation in provincial France. As an antidote to his reading of Julien Benda and Bertrand Russell, and to acquire the necessary stiffening, he turns to Nietzsche; the point is, in fact, that his *Quijote* is not a rewriting of Cervantes's *Quijote* at all but a reading of it; it is Cervantes read, say, by a contemporary reader who has previously taken in something of *Also sprach Zarathustra*. The function of Menard's story is to make clear that it is the order we read books in that decides their meaning for us, not the order they were written in.

Menard's defence, after Cervantes, of an active and errant principle against a sedentary one is more than just a cunning exploration by Borges into his theory of analogy, because it relates closely to a bifid tradition within his own ancestry. From his father's family he has been stocked with contemplative genes, from his mother's with heroic ones, and Borges has taken the opportunity of presenting himself as the meeting-point of these rival urges, whose reconciliation takes place in his fictions.

He has been free enough, largely and fittingly in his poems, in celebrating the gallantry of certain of his maternal ancestors in the defence of Argentinian causes of the nineteenth century. But he has been freer still in owning up to his extreme bookishness, having been brought up among (largely English) books as a child and having later returned to care for them as a librarian in Buenos Aires. Thus, when he writes, as he has done, "few things have happened to me and many have I read" or "life and death have been lacking in my life", he is slanging reality for falling short of some ideal epic, fit for the descendant of a warlike family. Indeed, Borges cannot help identifying himself in his stories as a writing man: in one of the briefest and most sympathetic of his self-portraits he turns up as a Jewish newspaper editor, "short-sighted, atheist and very shy" – such condensation ought to spur us on to estimating what the exact degree of kinship is between these three attributes.

Having inherited his father's poor sight, Borges is now almost wholly blind, a deterioration which may have offered him a cruel proof of the Schopenhauerian doctrine he has so lovingly underwritten, that everything which happens to us is a dark enactment of our own will. For Borges is one of those Romantics who have defined writing as an activity that should take place with the eyes closed. What he has displayed above all is fiction's considerable capacity for transforming the mournful contingencies of direct observation.

*   *   *

One story which he has said is among those he likes best, and which has been placed third in his *Personal Anthology*, is "El Sur" (The South), where the autobiographical pressures are less diffuse than they are elsewhere and well worth the uncovering. The hero of "El Sur", Juan Dahlmann, is a third-generation Argentinian and also a point of uneasy confluence between conflicting strains, theological on his father's side, military on his mother's. The story is of his quest to recover the image of his maternal grandfather, who had been killed in battle, the image, in fact of a "romantic death" (to romanticize death is quite certainly the highest of the pen's possibilities for Borges). Dahlmann wants to travel south, the compass-point of colour and vitality, and reoccupy the ruin of a ranch belonging to his mother's family. Instead he falls victim – though his death does not take place on the page – to a destiny rank with the essential themes of Argentinian literature. Having been challenged to a knife fight by a stranger in a bar he is supplied with a weapon in his moment of need by an ancient gaucho.

*   *   *

Yet the whole of the second half of "El Sur" is blatantly spurious for anyone reading the story with the degree of care needed to keep fully in contact with Borges, because there is a "hinge" at the moment where an acceptable reality is exchanged for fantasy or nightmare. Tiny symmetries between the two halves of the story betray Borges's literal duplicity, notably a slight head-wound first inflicted on Dahlmann when he walks into a door left carelessly ajar – by an "accident", in fact, which is also an invitation to penetrate to the other side of the décor. This wound develops, excessively, into septicaemia and an operation in hospital involving an anaesthetic, i.e., a rational moment for reality to be abandoned. The wound is later taken up and used again when the challenge to Dahlmann is issued, bizarrely, in the form of a volley of paper pellets hitting him on the forehead – the paper no doubt being an indication of the purely literary nature of his imminent glorification.

"El Sur" is a privileged guide to Borges's philosophy of fiction because he has said that he turned to writing fictions having been a poet, essayist and critic, after an attack of septicaemia and as a challenge to a mind he feared might have been sterilized by his illness.

This same elevation of the banal into the mythical often takes a more moralistic form than it does in "El Sur", since Borges is also fond of showing how a literary transposition of events is enough to make a villain into a hero. In "Tema del traidor y del héroe" the Irish patriot Fergus Kilpatrick, a traitor to his own cause, becomes the much-mourned talisman of that same cause thanks to the stupendous efforts made in the stage management of his death by the well-read investigator, Nolan; in an adjacent story, "La Forma de la espada", another Irishman, John Vincent Moon, is a hero in his own narrative but a coward in inescapable fact, and given away by the scar on his face; in "La Otra muerte" an Argentinian countryman is allowed to make up for his frailty in battle many years before by a delirious projection of valour in the hour of his death.

These stories not only act out the urge to buy back weakness with strength, they also expose this urge for what it is, a fiction. Whatever intimate inadequacy may have set Borges to oscillating between the real world and his own makeweight one, there is also the public fact that, as an Argentinian writer, he started writing fiction against a tradition of another kind, the tradition of *Martin Fierro*, which he himself has faithfully analysed with its "religion of courage", its "generous" knife-fights, and so on. And perhaps because of his seven years in Europe, between 1914 and 1921, Borges has remained highly sensitive towards what he calls the "ciphers" of Argentinian culture, the gaucho, the *compadrito*, the tango – a dance so debased in its export version that the rest of us are more likely to decipher it as the bent-kneed prowl of Groucho Marx.

Ever since he returned to Argentina, after periods of callow poetastery in Geneva and Madrid, Borges has been a townsman of Buenos Aires, yet the pampas have gone on lapping round his urban consciousness. All idea of local colour as such has become abhorrent to him, but he has taken over the endless plains, the *llanura*, for his metaphysical fantasies. Such topography as he has bothered to preserve in his writing, at any rate since he left behind the gaudier manner of his early years, has tended morosely towards the barren and the flat, to the point where even Cornwall, in one story, has been equipped with some "sandy hills", preparatory to the erection there of a labyrinth and the introduction into it of some murderous and implausible orientals. The relationship of labyrinth to landscape is the relationship of literature to life: as he creates, Borges is defending his right to deal with universal themes rather than more recognizably "Argentinian" ones, as well as bringing imagination into the style of a country seen as badly in need of *asombro*.

It is because he has restricted himself to supplying imagination to his country's literature, rather than its political or social institutions, that Borges has been deplored by a number of his continent's younger and more committed writers. In the massive compilation put out in his honour by the Cahiers de l'Herne in 1964 he was paid the guarded insult at one point of being told that he had taught his successors to appreciate many forms of writing but not his own. Certainly his political postures have been indecisive, though he aroused Perón sufficiently to be sacked from his job as a librarian and put in charge of chicken sales in Buenos Aires market. (Friends saved him from this degradation and turned him into a teacher and lecturer on English and American literature, a fall and resurrection which Borges himself has yoked ironically together as cause and effect.)

There has also been an escapologist's wit about his rare statements of social policy: a rejection of Marxism in its guise of historical inevitability, on the grounds that a gentleman likes to be associated only with lost causes: a recent subscription of the conservative, anti-Castro line, as being the appropriate decision for a political sceptic. Such ideological levity makes it a nice paradox that Borges should have become, in Paris, one of the feted predecessors of the critical guerrillas of *Tel Quel*, who have taken him over as a writer opposed, like themselves, to the damaging fallacy that writing is expression and not creation. Some of these young lions have dismantled Borges's stories with a finesse that has daunted even their author, but they have had to insist too heavily on suppressing all indication in them that they were born from the circumstances of Borges's life. However deafening the cosmic overtones in his fiction, or however persuasively it can be interpreted as dramatizing the creative process, it does have roots in his biography.

*   *   *

Appropriately, it was in France, during the series of radio interviews he gave to Georges Charbonnier and of which the texts were later published, that Borges chose to play up the affective element in his stories and so defend them, by implication, against the extremists who believe that an intellectual interpretation of them can be exhaustive. This affective element is one of anxiety and solitude. Solitude is, as Borges makes clear, the condition of creativity: where should his own creature, Ts'ui Pen, be found – English-speaking readers at least can take the hint in his given name and recognize the wily Chinaman as a writer – working away at his labyrinthine novel, if not in a very willow-patterned outhouse called the Pavilion of Limpid Solitude? Others again of

Borges's canny self-projections wrestle with the decipherment of the universe in actual captivity, and, their focal length thus shortened, these prisoners degenerate into helpless fantasists. One, a Muslim fakir, sets out to draw himself a map of the world in his prison cell but ends up covering the walls with tigers – the "dreamtigers" that are a persistent image in Borges and figure the writer's forced suppression of physical reality:

> but still, the act of naming it, of guessing
> what is its nature and its circumstances
> creates a fiction, not a living creature,
> not one of those who wander on the earth

The poem from which these lines come, "El Otro tigre", starts off in a library, a reminder that the solitary creator, unable to be forever dashing outside to check the promptings of his imagination against the reality, is not deprived of mental stereotypes; he invents against a tradition of such inventions and so puts in his own claim for admission to the literary community. In a book of spoof detective stories, which he wrote together with another Argentinian dabbler in the infinite, Adolfo Bioy Casares, Borges introduced a detective who is actually under sentence of death and copes with a series of mysteries without ever emerging from the death cell. This is certainly out-Poeing Poe, but it is also a grim reminder of the limits of the literary. The name of the detective is Parodi, a pun which proves that true originality lies not with man the unraveller but with Time the mystagogue.

*   *   *

No one has worked more wholesomely than Borges to cut the modern writer down to size, and challenge the orphic labels often pinned to him. (Diligent readers of "La Lotería en Babilonia" might, for example, find fleeting relief in a "sacred latrine" called Qaphqa.) He has said that of all his books it is *El Hacedor* that he likes the best, a flimsy collection of "reflections" and "interpolations", some of them brief pieces of prose, others poems, defined for the most part by their modest divergence from some existing literary model or philosophical idea. There is something excessive about this self-denial, and the corresponding promotion of traditional tropes above personal ones, as in the essay on the *kenningar* of the northern Sagas; and the fact is that Borges himself, as a young man, was a committed *ultraist* and involved as such in the hunt for wild and telling personal images à la Gomez de la Serna.

Yet the theory he has developed in reaction against this expressionism is not by any means as sterile as it may seem, since to quote an expression from the past does not mean denying or demeaning the present. This theory is best expounded in a story (included in the *Personal Anthology*) called "La Busca de Averroes". Here, the Andalusian Arab commentator of Aristotle is in quest of the meaning of two unknown terms he has just come across in the Greek, Comedy and Tragedy; he concludes that the first is a satire or anathema, the second a panegyric. This conclusion is followed by Borges's own, that his story is the narrative of a defeat, the defeat of Averroes's attempt to understand Aristotle and the defeat of his own attempts to understand Averroes:

> I sensed that Averroes, striving to imagine a drama without ever having suspected what a theatre was, was no more absurd than I, who strove to imagine Averroes with no material other than some fragments from Renan, Lane and Asín Palacios.

Thus Borges, the algebraist, works to a strict formula: Borges is to Averroes as Averroes is to Aristotle. But how serious is he being when he says that the story represents a defeat for both of them? Satire and panegyric can be taken as contradictory attitudes towards a given text, the first depending on a retreat from it, the second on an identification with it. Shortly before he at last feels that he has understood what Aristotle means by his terms, Averroes is recorded as defending in conversation the literary repetition of a poetic figure from earlier centuries, comparing Destiny with a blind camel. The repetition, as he maintains, establishes a relationship with four terms: it expresses the sadness of the man who repeats it as well as fusing his sadness with that of the poet who said it before him. A vast interval of time, full of unique and largely unrecorded circumstances, separates the first event from the second, but the repetition spans it with a formula of generic identity.

*   *   *

This Platonic (or Proustian) snub to the march of time is, for Borges, nothing more final than a literary device, and one whose acceptance, as he knows, is especially difficult now that we are all such convinced nominalists – the English he picks out as being even more nominalist than most. But if he is always turning back to Berkeley or Schopenhauer for support, this is only because their seamless idealism makes them the patron thinkers of the man who subtends a fictive world in print. Borges does not propose them as guides for living by, and is, indeed, given to quoting Hume's verdict, that Berkeley's position was irrefutable but unacceptable.

Measured against a thoroughgoing nominalism all literature tends more or less to the generic, so that, by tending much more vigorously than others in this direction, Borges is, as ever, performing helpful exercises in literary criticism. Indeed, he has written a story, "Funes el memorioso", to exhibit the fate of the nominalist, since Funes is a young man unable to forget anything, so fact-bound that he cannot even achieve the humble level of generalization required to share humanity's system of numeration. Funes, who dies a dismally premature death, is suffocated by circumstances, whereas Borges planes so high above them that, in his terms, it is the circumstantial detail that makes his narrative *un*real.

Thus the whole process of literary invention (or discovery) is exposed – Plato again – as being one not of inclusion but of omission, modelled on a life that Borges has appraised as an "education in forgetting". The higher the writer hoists himself out of the empirical slough the more imposing are his allegories. Condensation and discontinuity, as in the Freudian "dream-work", become instruments for achieving shock and intensity (Borges, who knows he has been influenced by the techniques of the cinema in this respect, has never managed to get his own scenarios produced).

The "education in forgetting" goes through three stages: first there are events, then memories of events, then words representing the memories of events. In the end "only words remain". But if most of us resent oblivion Borges sees it as a blessing. In a line of poetry that is unusually direct he has asked for the sort of eternal life which belongs to the animals, the life of the ever-punctual now: "to be for ever, but never to have been". Thus his stories, which deny this now so heartily, are really invocations of the Void, and the trivial circumstance that threatens them with conclusion a merciful release – it is striking how often the solution of a Borges mystery comes pat upon a shower of rain.

*   *   *

Because of the abnormal dissociation he has practised between the real world and the fictive one Borges asks to belong, like one of his heroes, Herbert Quain, "not to art but to the history of art". (Quain, a novelist with a rare line in the narrative uses of bifurcation, is granted an obituary in the *TLS*, a specially reinforced example of the detail that makes for unreality, since this journal does not print obituaries!) Borges's writings are full of the idea of the world's literature as a cumulative adventure, as the slow but continuing conquest of chance by human laws, like in his fictional Babylon where the two finally become co-extensive. And the function of the Babylonian scribes is interpolation, variation, omission. Obsessed with theology Borges may be, but not with its orthodox forms – he is the student of those who have extended or diverted theological tradition by their heresies. His firm assumption of his own place on the lengthening book-shelves of the human race, and his insistence that all books are one book, all writers one writer, are beliefs, moreover, which lay unusual store by the physical preservation of the literature of the past. There is, in Borges, no getting away from the preoccupations of the librarian.

The only one of his books to have appeared in this country before the *Personal Anthology* was *Fictions*, published by Weidenfeld and Nicolson in 1964. The result is that we now have some of his stories available twice, and the bulk of his writing still not available in English at all. The translations in this *Personal Anthology* read fluently enough, but Anthony Kerrigan's introduction is eccentric and the exchange of letters between him and a fellow-translator included at the end of the volume an unforgivable editorial liberty.

English readers have every reason to hope that the rest of Borges's fiction, and a selection at least of his essays, should appear over here. He had read, re-read and related to the present a whole mausoleum of English writers whom few of us today ever pick up at all, and some bumptious modernists might be startled and improved by coming across a sophisticated comment on the art of narrative illustrated from William Morris, G. K. Chesterton being quoted on the Death of the Novel, or what amounts to an equation between the practice of Robbe-Grillet and that of Joseph Addison.

DIGGING IN
ALEXANDRIA

Henry Gifford

Constantine Cavafy became one of this century's leading poets against all the odds. Born in 1863, he grew up when one tide of poetry, the Romantic, was beginning to run out, and its successor, the modernist, would not come in until he was nearly fifty. In many ways he was disadvantaged, especially in the lack of any obvious poetic talent. Alexandria had its own literary world; but even to that he came unprepared, after seven years of his early adolescence in England, so that to the end of his days he spoke Greek with something of an English accent, and the earlier poems show him not to have been altogether at ease in his native language. It was unfortunate too that he came from a Phanariot family. The Phanariots had often held high office in the Ottoman Empire; theirs was a natural allegiance to the stilted and mainly sterile tradition of the *katharevousa* or "purified" idiom. Cavafy took pride in his aristocratic past. His father's export business had declined with the fortunes of Alexandria itself when the Suez Canal undermined its prosperity. Constantine was obliged to work for thirty years as a "temporary" clerk of the Third Circle of Irrigation, eking out his salary with occasional flutters on the stock exchange. In literature he had to make his own way, and it was only after long years of struggling probation that he found a distinct voice and a domain which proved to have been brilliantly chosen for his needs. On entering the second decade of the century he found himself to be a genuine master, and a modern, though general recognition was still delayed.

The poems left behind on Cavafy's death in 1933 fall into three categories. The "canon" selected by himself consists of 153 poems, plus one other completed in the last months but still then unpublished. These make up the collected edition of 1935 by Timos Malanis. Cavafy had published his poems either in

The Greek Poems, by C. P. Cavafy, translated by Memas Kolaitis. *C. P. Cavafy: Collected Poems*, translated by Edmund Keeley and Philip Sherrard [August 24, 1990]

periodicals or small pamphlets, or as broadsheets later to be collected in a folder. In his peculiar way he anticipated *samizdat* – not however mainly for reasons of censorship, though as a homosexual he needed to tread very carefully in a city where a scandal like that of Oscar Wilde would have ruined his life. Cavafy was highly circumspect in choosing the right people to whom these poems could be entrusted. A further total of seventy-five poems, the "hidden" or "unissued" ones, was held in reserve, and some of these, after reworking, might have joined the canon. Finally there are twenty-four poems "repudiated" by Cavafy himself, which had been published between 1886 and 1898 during his apprenticeship.

Certainly the "unissued" poems deserve some attention, the more so because a number of these are even more outspoken than what he was bold enough to place in the canon, on the love that he termed "Greek" or "anomalous" or "robust". The "repudiated" poems are in the main embarrassingly weak. At least they serve to show what difficulties he had to surmount, and how necessary it was for him to face up to his predicament with entire honesty.

George Seferis, the second Greek poet of this century to achieve international fame, which Cavafy earned only after his death, "came", in his words, "late to the Alexandrian". His real encounter with Cavafy's work (which can be followed in *O Kavafis tou Seferi* (The Cavafy of Seferis), edited by G. P. Savidis, Athens, 1984) had to wait until 1941, when he was evacuated from Crete to Alexandria with the government he served. This event reawakened his curiosity about a poet not hitherto very congenial to him. Malanis soon led him on a tour round the old part of the city. Its close alleys with overhanging houses, the cafés where young Egyptians were smoking languidly and the air reeked of hashish, the little oriental shops, all brought him to a feeling of desperation. He could imagine Cavafy

> slowly gathering his impressions from these trifles, in every corner, and making his four or five poems a year. You have to go to Alexandria in order to understand how Cavafy worked.

Where else, he asked himself, could you obtain "such a sense of stagnant dissolution"?

Later that year, in South Africa with the Greek government in

exile, he settled to a close study of the poems. It is unusual for a
poet, already of considerable note, to write a detailed commentary
on the work of his most challenging predecessor in the generation
before, especially when they belong to opposed traditions. Seferis's
father had been a prominent champion of the demotic, which his
son wrote with exceptional grace and point. But Cavafy, as he
observed, when gradually moving towards the demotic – in itself
surprising for one from his origins – handled it with a pair of tongs.
Seferis by now had recognized that at least Cavafy's later poetry
spoke to this time of crisis in which the fate of Greece and of the
European civilization once nurtured by it now hung in the balance.
He thought much during these months about the meaning of
Hellenism, and Cavafy did something to enlarge his view. But what
he most prized in the older poet was an example of self-knowledge
and poetic discipline.

One of the *Three Secret Poems* Seferis published in 1966 contains
an admonition to himself which seems to recall his experience of
Cavafy:

> The poem
> do not drown it in the deep planetrees
> nourish it with what earth and rock you have
> For anything more –
> dig in the same place to find it.

Cavafy had been forced to see that only through acknowledging –
and then exploiting – his limitations could he become the poet he
aspired to be. As Seferis put it:

> Cavafy could do nothing but write the language that was
> his reality and his *necessity* ... [Seferis's italics]
>
> It is very instructive to watch this poet who seems
> initially to have no talent, apart from the talent of a
> peculiar persistence, gather up slowly the living elements
> that he can save, to combine them, turning an obstacle
> into a stair, so as to proceed at the slow pace of his
> accumulated experiences.

The "earth" for Cavafy, as for any poet, was his milieu.
Eavesdropping on the *petits bourgeois*, so an Alexandrian friend
expressed it to Seferis, he catches their "common speech" in the
café or the stock exchange, "at dynamic moments when they break

the bonds of syntax and grammar and shape the language anarchically". In fact, like Wordsworth he makes his own "selection of the real language of men in a state of vivid sensation", even though in low-lying Alexandria these townsmen are not elevated by "the mountain's outline and its steady form". The "rock" for Cavafy had to be his own determination to achieve an entire sincerity in his art, however evasive or disingenuous he may have been in his anxious daily life. And by digging in the same place – the Alexandria he so rarely left – he would arrive at the subsoil of Greek history, that dimension in which his imagination would find perfect freedom.

Cavafy defined himself as a historical poet. One who has the historical sense in the way Eliot understood it recognizes the past in the present, and judges the present against the past. Cavafy's imagination did not move freely over the whole range of Greek history, still less of Roman. Seferis with some justice calls "pseudo-historical" those poems before Cavafy's mature period from 1911 – his own dividing line – where he cannot truly identify with his subjects. It took him twenty-five years to realize that his journey had led him full circle to Alexandria, and to choose as his territory the Hellenistic age following Alexander the Great's death in 323 BC, in its initial splendour and then the later decline under the Romans, and also certain episodes from Byzantine history down to its latest times. Classical Greece was too remote for Cavafy. It is suggested by Seferis that his few poems on Homeric themes are related to the appearance of Pallis's renowned demotic version of the *Iliad* in 1893, and David Ricks in *The Shade of Homer* (reviewed in the *TLS* of April 27-May 3) argues persuasively that "The Horses of Achilles" shows clear traces of Pope's rendering, and that Cavafy sees this episode from *Iliad* XVII in the light of comments by Arnold, Pater and especially Ruskin. But in the Hellenistic age he felt truly at home. This was already the world of the Greek diaspora, with its mingling of races, the transient kingdoms in oriental lands, the dangers and calamities of a prolonged time of troubles.

Cavafy defined his position as follows: "I too am Hellenic . . . not Greek, nor Hellenized, but Hellenic". That is to say, he felt little affinity with mainland Greece. Seferis believed it was not until the overthrow of Smyrna (Seferis's own birthplace) in 1922 that Cavafy took notice of events across the Aegean. Edmund Keeley in discussing his Hellenism has quoted approvingly what E. M. Forster wrote in a review of the translations of Cavafy by John Mavrogordato (1951):

> He was a loyal Greek, but Greece for him was not territorial. It was rather the influence that has flowed from his race this way and that through the ages, and that (since Alexander the Great) has never disdained to mix with barbarism, has indeed desired to mix .... Racial purity bored him .... The civilization he respected was a bastardy in which the Greek strain prevailed, and into which, age after age, outsiders would push, to modify and be modified.

It is the Greeks of ancient Syria, of its main cities Antioch, Beirut, Seleuceia, and also of Alexandria, who interest Cavafy, and their sensibility, subtle, luxurious, and already becoming nostalgic, is his own. Seferis, whose lost Smyrna in many respects he recognized in Alexandria (soon itself to be lost), could draw on the Greek popular tradition, embodied for him in the forthright Makryannis, a general of peasant stock in the Greek war of liberation. Cavafy, wholly urban and from a cosmopolitan city, lacked that support. This makes him, in his marginal position and essential solitude, a poet for the late twentieth century.

"The first English translation of Cavafy", says Forster, "was made by Cavafy." He was not aware that "Constantine's first inadequate translator", according to the Cavafy scholar George P. Savidis, was his elder brother John, who "wrote frigid poems in English". Forster came to know Cavafy in Alexandria during the First World War. Visiting him one day in that over-furnished flat at 10 rue Lepsius where Cavafy spent his last twenty-five years, he was told by him: "You could never understand my poetry, my dear Forster, never." Then he brought out his poem "The God Abandons Antony" – dated 1911, it marks his imaginative return to his own ground, Alexandria – and read it aloud. When Forster was able to "detect some coincidences between its Greek and public school Greek", Cavafy was "amazed", or with his usual politeness pretended to be. He then went through the poem for Forster's benefit. "It was not my knowledge that touched him but my desire to know and to receive." This little episode tells much about Cavafy's longing to communicate through his poetry, and the despair he felt of ever being understood by a foreigner, however cultivated. His initial disclaimer may have been faintly coquettish, but behind it there lurks a genuine frustration.

Few readers today have even school Greek to call upon, but fortunately, from Mavrogordato on, Cavafy has been well served by translators. Auden maintained that "any poem" of Cavafy's in a competent translation would convey "a tone of voice" that you immediately recognized as unique. The truth of this remark appears to be borne out by the many admirers he has found abroad, who, one may infer, read him only in translation, such as Montale, Czeslaw Milosz and Joseph Brodsky. All of them respond to that "tone of voice". Brodsky has written "Every poet loses in translation, and Cavafy is not an exception. What is exceptional is that he also gains . . ." – gains because once he "began to strip his poems of all poetic paraphernalia", the "deliberately 'poor' means" he adopted actually give the reader's imagination more play. One should point out that the "poor" means are used with a great deal of subtle artistry. The governing tone of his voice is dry, the idiom precise, laconic, and the music – for music does exist in his verse – subdued. Cavafy claimed that, while it would have been impossible for him to write novels or plays, "I sense within me 125 voices that tell me I could have written history". And all these voices are differentiated. [. . .]

III

T. S. ELIOT AND
VIRGINIA WOOLF
REVIEW . . .

BRUCE LYTTELTON
RICHMOND

T. S. Eliot

It was Richard Aldington who took me to Bruce Richmond's office in Printing House Square, I believe at Richmond's request, probably in 1920. Aldington was at that time reviewing French literature regularly for *The Times Literary Supplement*, and Richmond knew of our acquaintance. Richmond had seen articles and reviews of mine in *The Athenaeum* (edited by Middleton Murry) in which they had been appearing for a year or more past. At that time I was still a clerk in Lloyds Bank: but whether my presentation at *The Times* took place in my lunchtime, or after bank hours, or on a Saturday afternoon, I cannot now remember. Nor do I remember what was said at this (for me) memorable meeting. There is still a picture of the scene in my mind: the chief figure a man with a kind of bird-like quality, a bird-like alertness of eye, body and mind. I remember his quickness to put the newcomer at ease; and the suggestion in his mien and movement of an underlying strength of character and tenacity of purpose. But to be summoned to the presence of the Editor of *The Times Literary Supplement* and to be invited to write for it was to have reached the top rung of the ladder of literary journalism: I was overawed, by *The Times* offices themselves, by the importance of the occasion, and in spite of the cordial warmth of the greeting, by the great editor himself.

For Bruce Richmond was a great editor. To him I owe a double debt, first for the work he gave me to do and for the discipline of writing for him, and second for illustrating, in his conduct of the weekly, what editorial standards should be – a lesson I tried to apply when I came to edit *The Criterion*. Richmond took a personal interest in the men and women who wrote for him: I remember many a pleasant luncheon as his guest, when his next suggestion for an article or review would be put forward; and incidentally I learnt to appreciate the merits of Russian Stout and Double Gloucester cheese. The province assigned to me in the *Literary Supplement* was

[Article] [January 13, 1961]

Elizabethan and Jacobean poetry, but chiefly dramatic poetry. The result of our first meeting was my leading article on Ben Jonson; and nearly all of my essays on the drama of that period – perhaps all of my best ones – started as suggestions by Richmond. A book was forthcoming to "serve as a peg" for an article; a book for review was usually designated as "my pigeon". In this way, one gradually became an authority in the field allotted. But once a writer was established among his reviewers and leader-writers, Richmond was ready to let him make excursions outside of the original area. Thus, a chance remark in conversation revealed that I was an ardent admirer of Bishop Lancelot Andrewes, and I was at once commissioned to write the leader which appears among my collected essays.

One lesson that I learnt from writing for *The Times Literary Supplement* under Richmond was that of the discipline of anonymity. I had served my apprenticeship as a reviewer in *The Athenaeum* under Murry, but there all the articles and reviews were signed. I am firmly convinced that every young literary critic should learn to write for some periodical in which his contributions will be anonymous. Richmond did not hesitate to object or delete, and I had always to admit that he was right. I learnt to moderate my dislikes and crotchets, to write in a temperate and impartial way; I learnt that some things are permissible when they appear over one's name, which become tasteless eccentricity or unseemly violence when unsigned. The writer of the anonymous article or review must subdue himself to his editor – but the editor must be a man to whom the writer can subdue himself and preserve his self-respect. It is also necessary that the editor should read every word of what he prints; for he is much more deeply inculpated in what he prints anonymously, than in what he prints over the writer's name.

This brings me to my second point. I have said that it was from Bruce Richmond that I learnt editorial standards, and that I endeavoured to apply them in editing *The Criterion*. Of course it is far easier to edit a literary quarterly than to edit a literary weekly. But apart from this, there was one quality of Bruce Richmond as an editor which I could not emulate, and that is his own anonymity. His name never appeared; he wrote nothing; he did not give lectures or public addresses. Yet, and all the more because he remained in the background, he *was* the *Literary Supplement* in a way impossible to an editor who was primarily or even secondarily a writer. I believe Richmond kept his name out of *Who's Who* for years and was only obliged to yield to that moderate degree of publicity when his University made him a Doctor of Letters *honoris causa*.

Though I could not, and naturally would not, devote my life to *The Criterion* as Richmond devoted his to *The Times Literary Supplement*, I did try to model my conduct on his to some respects. I learnt from him that it is the business of an editor to know his contributors personally, to keep in touch with them and to make suggestions to them. I tried to form a nucleus of writers (some of them, indeed, recruited from *The Times Literary Supplement*, and introduced to me by Richmond) on whom I could depend, differing from each other in many things, but not in love of literature and seriousness of purpose. And I learnt from Richmond that I must read every word of what was to appear in print – even though, in *The Criterion*, all contributions were signed or initialled.

It is a final tribute to Richmond's genius as an editor that some of his troupe of regular contributors (I am thinking of myself as well as of others) produced some of their most distinguished critical essays as leaders for the *Literary Supplement*. For Bruce Richmond we wanted to do our best. Good literary criticism requires good editors as well as good critics. And Bruce Richmond was a great editor: fortunate those critics who wrote for him.

CREATIVE CRITICISM

T. S. Eliot

Mr J. E. Spingarn is the author of an excellent informative book on the literary criticism of the Italian Renaissance; he is a scholarly critic who is entitled to be listened to with respect. In this book, however, it would seem that Mr Spingarn, who at one time was professor of literature in an American university, was determined to assert, even a little boisterously, his emancipation from the scholastic and academic point of view. Dedication to Croce, "the

Creative Criticism: Essays on the Unity of Genius and Taste, by J. E. Spingarn [August 12, 1926]

most original of all modern thinkers on art," and the motto from
Barbey d'Aurevilly, "who can doubt that criticism, as well as
poetry, can have wings?" are both significant. Mr Spingarn, after
Croce, is also an original "thinker on art"; but "freedom" is not, as
Mr Spingarn, seems to think, the one thing needful for criticism.
Mr Spingarn's criticism has certainly realized the possibility
suggested by Barbey d'Aurevilly: it has wings; unfortunately, like
the fabulous bird of paradise it has wings but no feet, and can never
settle. Mr Spingarn's first essay, on "The New Criticism," is a
recitation of all the distinctions and classifications which art and
criticism are now to repudiate. For Mr Spingarn the phrase "self-
expression" appears to be completely adequate.

> What has the poet tried to do, and how has he fulfilled his
> intention? What is he striving to express and how has he
> expressed it? What impression does his work make on me,
> and how can I best express this impression?

The dogmas of "The New Criticism" (for dogmas they are) run
somewhat as follows, in extracts from Mr Spingarn's essay:

> we have done with all the old rules . . . We have done with
> the *genres*, or literary kinds . . . there are as many kinds as
> there are individual poets . . . All art is lyrical . . . We have
> done with the theory of style, with metaphor, simile, and all
> the paraphernalia of Græco-Roman rhetoric . . . We have
> done with all moral judgment of literature . . .

Mr Spingarn has what is called "infectious high spirits." The
test, of course, of any critical programme or platform, such as his, is
the sort of criticism which it produces. Unfortunately, all of the
essays in this small book are of the same general order, and with
some variety of gesture hail the dawn of "creative criticism"
without providing any specimens of it. Mr Spingarn has scholarship and some taste, and this book is by no means a fair
representative of his work; it is to be hoped that he will support his
theories, or his faiths, by a work of concrete criticism.

We must take exception, however, to his term "The New
Criticism," which seems a misnomer. It implies that this is the
creed of the youngest critics of importance, which is far from being
the case. The younger critics, or some of them – witness Mr Ramon
Fernandez in France and Mr Herbert Read in this country – have by

no means done with "all moral judgment of literature"; on the contrary, they seem to be resuscitating it to a new and different life.

NICOLO MACHIAVELLI,
1469–1527

T. S. Eliot

[. . .] We have therefore to inquire what there is about Machiavelli to impress the mind of Europe so prodigiously and so curiously, and why the European mind felt it necessary to deform his doctrine so absurdly. There are certainly contributing causes. The reputation of Italy as the home of fantastic, wanton and diabolical crime filled the French, and still more the English, imagination as they are now filled by the glories of Chicago or Los Angeles, and predisposed imagination toward the creation of a mythical representative for this criminality. But still more the growth of Protestantism – and France, as well as England, was then largely a Protestant country – created a disposition against a man who accepted in his own fashion the orthodox view of original sin. Calvin, whose view of humanity was far more extreme, and certainly more false, than that of Machiavelli, was never treated to such opprobrium; but when the inevitable reaction against Calvinism came out of Calvinism, and from Geneva, in the doctrine of Rousseau, that too was hostile to Machiavelli. For Machiavelli is a doctor of the mean, and the mean is always insupportable to partisans of the extreme. A fanatic can be tolerated. The failure of a fanaticism such as Savonarola's ensures its toleration by posterity, and even approving patronage. But Machiavelli was no fanatic; he merely told the truth about humanity. The world of human motives which he depicts is true – that is to say, it is humanity without the addition of superhuman Grace. It is therefore tolerable only to persons who have also a definite religious belief; to the effort of the last three centuries to supply religious belief by belief in Humanity the creed of Machiavelli is insupportable. Lord Morley voices the usual

[Article] [June 16, 1927]

modern hostile admiration of Machiavelli when he intimates that Machiavelli saw very clearly what he did see, but that he saw only half of the truth about human nature. What Machiavelli did not see about human nature is the myth of human goodness which for liberal thought replaces the belief in Divine Grace.

It is easy to admire Machiavelli in a sentimental way. It is only one of the sentimental and histrionic poses of human nature – and human nature is incorrigibly histrionic – to pose as a "realist," a person of "no nonsense," to admire the "brutal frankness" or the "cynicism" of Machiavelli. This is a form of self-satisfaction and self-deception which merely propagates the Jew of Malta-Nietzsche myth of Machiavelli. In Elizabethan England the reputation of Machiavelli was merely manipulated unconsciously to feed the perpetually recurring tendency to Manichæan heresy: the desire for a devil to worship. The heretical impulses remain fairly constant; they recur in the Satan of Milton and the Cain of Byron. But with these indulgences of human frailties Machiavelli has no traffic. He had none of the instinct to pose; and therefore human beings, in order to accept him at all, had to make him into a dramatic figure. His reputation is the history of the attempt of humanity to protect itself, by secreting a coating of falsehood, against any statement of the truth.

It has been said, in a tone of reproach, that Machiavelli makes no attempt "to persuade." Certainly he was no prophet. For he was concerned first of all with truth, not with persuasion, which is one reason why his prose is great prose, not only of Italian but a model of style for any language. He is a partial Aristotle of politics. But he is partial not because his vision is distorted or his judgement biased, or because of any lack of moral interest, but because of his passion for his country. What makes him a great writer, and for ever a solitary figure, is the purity and single-mindedness of his passion. No one was ever less "Machiavellian" than Machiavelli. Only the pure in heart can blow the gaff on human nature as Machiavelli has done. The cynic can never do it; for the cynic is always impure and sentimental. But it is easy to understand why Machiavelli was not himself a successful politician. For one thing, he had no capacity for self-deception or self-dramatization. The recipe *dors ton sommeil de brute* is applied in many forms, of which Calvin and Rousseau give two variations; but the utility of Machiavelli is his perpetual summons to examination of the weakness and impurity of the soul. We are not likely to forget his political lessons, but his examination of conscience may be too easily overlooked.

ELIZABETH AND ESSEX

T. S. Eliot

When Mr Strachey published his "Eminent Victorians" there arose a myth about him which neither his earlier nor his later works have been able to dissipate. He was received as the mocking iconoclast of the Victorian Pantheon, a stripper of reputation, a master of the art of reducing the great to the small. Even his "Queen Victoria" did not succeed in correcting this impression, though it revealed clearly Mr Strachey's genuine passion for genuine royalty and the fact that where he destroys one romance he creates another. He destroyed some myths about Victorians, no doubt; but the upshot of his work was rather to replace one romantic view which had become incredible by another more suited to reception by his own generation. Irony and mockery are not Mr Strachey's product, but merely his tools, which he uses slyly to allow us the luxury of sentiment without being ashamed of it. The great difference, indeed, between Mr Strachey's methods and those of his imitators is that the latter are often limited to mere derision, whereas in Mr Strachey there is always affection, and often strong admiration, for his prey.

In this book there is less of the ironic or amusing than even the most intelligent reader might expect; and what little there is appears incidentally, and perhaps merely to give that flavour of realism which we like in our romance. It is a "tragic history"; and it is not only of dramatic material, but is treated with dramatic skill. So dramatic is it that we forget at times that it is history at all. Yet it has its perfectly correct historical face. Dialogue is restricted to a minimum – only words actually reported, and quotations of letters skilfully embroidered into the text. It is only occasionally, with what is one of Mr Strachey's characteristic devices – one which is dangerous for him and fatal for anyone else – the reverie, the

Elizabeth and Essex, by Lytton Strachey [December 6, 1928]

thoughts and dreams which some person may be supposed to have indulged at some critical moment, as of death, that we are reminded that this is drama, of a peculiar kind, more than history.

The author's presentation of his chief figures, however, is, we believe, as near to the right historical judgment as posterity can ever arrive. The chief figures are three: the Queen, Robert Devereux Earl of Essex, and Francis Bacon. Like some other dramatists, Mr Strachey is more fascinated by his villain (Bacon) than by his hero (Essex). His Bacon is the twentieth-century equivalent for the Ignatian Machiavel of Elizabethan drama. He appears in higher relief, and with greater economy of words, than in the essay by Macaulay. Bacon serves, indeed, as his example of his view of the Elizabethan character. To Mr Strachey the Elizabethan age appears remote and strange. "With very few exceptions – possibly with the single exception of Shakespeare – the creatures in it meet us without intimacy; they are exterior visions, which we know but do not truly understand." This inscrutability Mr Strachey is too wise to try to explain, and is content to insist upon.

> Human beings, no doubt, would cease to be human beings unless they were inconsistent; but the inconsistency of the Elizabethans exceeds the limits permitted to man. Their elements fly off from one another wildly; we seize them; we struggle hard to shake them together into a single compound, and the retort bursts. How is it possible to give a coherent account of their subtlety and their *naïveté*, their delicacy and their brutality, their piety and their lust? Wherever we look, it is the same. By what perverse magic were intellectual ingenuity and theological ingenuousness intertwined in John Donne? Who has ever explained Francis Bacon? How is it conceivable that the puritans were the brothers of the dramatists?

Now it is quite true that at this distance the actions of Elizabethans appear often more inconsistent than our own. It is also true that in Elizabethan drama, even in the plays of Shakespeare, consistency of conduct in characters was obviously of much less importance to the dramatist and to the audience than it is to our contemporaries. As Mr Mario Praz has pointed out in his admirable essay on the Machiavellian tradition in England, inconsistency and contrast were admired more than consistency and unity. But it is necessary to draw a distinction between fundamental differences of human nature at different times – if there are any – and differences due to different ideas held by man as to what he is and as to what is admirable. To our mind the difference between the Elizabethans and ourselves is more a difference of fashion than a difference of nature. They allowed their inconsistencies to flourish and exulted in them; we have a morality, or a psychological theory (which is the same thing) which makes us ashamed of them.

It is not altogether certain either that Mr Strachey, with this view of Elizabethan inconsistency, does not tend to exaggerate and even exploit it. The apparent inconsistencies of Donne, which he cites, would not even be interesting unless we felt them latent in ourselves. And there never was a time, and probably never will be, when piety and lust might not be found side by side. We have only to examine the literature of India. What is piquant about Mr Strachey's attitude is that it combines the reasonableness of the eighteenth century with the romanticism of the nineteenth. He criticizes like an eighteenth-century rationalist, and admires like a nineteenth-century romantic.

But having adopted this view, Mr Strachey is able to make the most of Bacon as a dramatic figure, flashing and glittering before us.

> Francis Bacon has been described more than once with the crude vigour of antithesis; but in truth such methods are singularly inappropriate to his most unusual case. It was not by the juxtaposition of a few opposites, but by the infiltration of a multitude of highly varied elements, that his mental composition was made up. He was no striped frieze; he was shot silk. The detachment of speculation, the intensity of personal pride, the uneasiness of nervous sensibility, the urgency of ambition, the opulence of superb taste – these qualities, blending, twisting, flashing together, gave to his secret spirit the subtle and glittering superficies of a serpent. A serpent, indeed, might well have been his chosen emblem – the wise, sinuous, dangerous creature, offspring of mystery and the beautiful earth. The music sounds, and the great snake rises, and spreads its hood, and leans and hearkens, swaying in ecstasy; and even so the sage

Lord Chancellor, in the midst of some great sentence, some high intellectual confection, seems to hold his breath in a rich beatitude, fascinated by the deliciousness of sheer style. A true child of the Renaissance, his multiplicity was not merely that of mental accomplishment, but of life itself. His mind might move with joy among altitudes and theories, but the variegated savour of temporal existence was no less dear to him – the splendours of high living – the intricacies of Court intrigue – the exquisiteness of pages – the lights reflected from small pieces of coloured glass. Like all the greatest spirits of the age, he was instinctively and profoundly an artist.

We have quoted this passage as much as a specimen of Mr Strachey's heightened style as to illustrate his character of Bacon. But as a character of Bacon it is, too, heightened through the romantic "perfumed mist" which invests the Renaissance. It is a right view of Bacon, and only misleading, if at all, by isolating the figure. Bacon was neither the first nor the last man to combine administrative ability with philosophic ability: neither the first nor the last to be swayed between several intellectual passions and to give himself alternately to one or the other. His love of public life, his legal gifts, were born and fostered of heredity and environment: his philosophic gifts were, as they always are, a freak. (Similarly, Donne's keenness for law and theology was natural, his genius for poetry a freak; and he is not the first or the last.) And finally, Francis Bacon is neither the first nor the last man to combine intellectual power with moral turpitude; examples might be found in any age. Without trespassing on modern times, might not Bolingbroke be made as much a paradox as Bacon?

But, once we have allowed Mr Strachey his dramatic licence for intensification and isolation, we must admit that his characters seem to us otherwise true to history. His character of Elizabeth is particularly just. He takes a middle path between those who represent Elizabeth as merely a puppet moved by the scheming Whig nobility created by her father – as merely a pawn in the game of spoiling the monasteries – and those who picture Elizabeth's Ministers as merely intelligent servants. The power of these intelligent servants Mr Strachey does not diminish; and indeed once of his most powerful figures is that of Robert Cecil – always kept behind the arras, and always working to one end with a consistency which seems inconsistent with Mr Strachey's Elizabethans. But he makes it quite clear that the power of these servants was always precarious, always maintained by indefatigable attention and consummate diplomacy. And had the character of Elizabeth not been a strong one, and had it been different from what it was, her Ministers could not have played the *rôle* they did play.

> A deep instinct made it almost impossible for her to come to a fixed determination upon any subject whatever. Or, if she did, she immediately proceeded to contradict her resolution with the utmost violence, and, after that, to contradict her contradiction more violently still. Such was her nature – to float, when it was calm, in a sea of indecisions, and, when the wind rose, to tack hectically from side to side. Had it been otherwise – had she possessed, according to the approved pattern of the strong man of action, the capacity for taking a line and sticking to it – she would have been lost . . . Her femininity saved her. Only a woman could have shuffled so shamelessly, only a woman could have abandoned with such unscrupulous completeness the last shreds not only of consistency, but of dignity, honour, and common decency, in order to escape the appalling necessity of having, really and truly, to make up her mind. Yet it is true that a woman's evasiveness was not enough; male courage, male energy were needed . . . Those qualities she also possessed; but their value to her – it was the final paradox of her career – was merely that they made her strong enough to turn her back, with an indomitable persistence, upon the ways of strength.

This is finely said, and illustrates, like the passage quoted about Bacon, Mr Strachey's taste for employing the cheap phrase or word: to "tack hectically," "appalling necessity," "shreds of consistency," "sheer style"; it is out of such material that Mr Strachey constructs his remarkable prose. But it is also just, and has not been so well said before.

So far we have said nothing of the narrative of the adventures of Essex and his quarrels and reconciliations with Elizabeth. One of Mr Strachey's peculiar gifts, besides that of lucidity, is his cunning ability to accelerate or reduce the speed of his narrative. It is difficult to see how, with such simple means, this is done; but it is part of his dramatic gift to be able to give us the feeling, and the impatience, of intolerable delays and shifts and changes, and the rush of sudden events as well. For this reason we want to read the book at a sitting; we could no more insert a bookmark until tomorrow than we could see a play by going to a different act each night. The account of the tumult in the city is as exciting as the brawl of a Shakespearian mob, and instils the sense of the destiny and doom of Essex. And the last paragraph of the book, after Elizabeth has expired, reads like the chorus at the end of a tragedy. The last figure on the stage is that of Robert Cecil, first Earl of Salisbury:–

> But meanwhile, in an inner chamber, at his table, alone, the Secretary sat writing. All eventualities had been foreseen, everything was arranged, only the last soft touches remained to be given. The momentous transition would come now with exquisite facility. As the hand moved, the mind moved too, ranging sadly over the vicissitudes of mortal beings, reflecting upon the revolutions of king-doms, and dreaming, with quiet clarity, of what the hours, even then, were bringing – the union of two nations – the triumph of the new rulers – success, power, and riches – a name in after-ages – a noble lineage – a great House.

AMERICAN CRITICS

T. S. Eliot

This book is a compilation of essays on related subjects, written on various occasions, but having something of the nature of a symposium, though the various authors do not criticize each other. It is of considerable general interest. The authors are chiefly of the academic world and of the younger generation; they represent the most intelligent aspect of contemporary American scholarship.

The Reinterpretation of American Literature, ed. by Norman Foerster [January 10, 1929]

During the last twenty years, and largely under the influence of Irving Babbitt at Harvard and his friends, a new type of American scholar has appeared. While the influence of President Eliot, of Harvard, dominated – roughly during the last quarter of the nineteenth century – the standards of American university scholarship were Teutonic. The degree of Doctor of Philosophy was all important; in the field of letters it was obtained by minute researches and *Forschungen*. The teacher of modern languages was well equipped with Gothic and Icelandic and Low Latin, but was often without any wide philosophic view of literature, and completely out of touch with the creative work of his own time. Now the tendency is to fly to the other extreme: no American college is without a course or two in contemporary literature, and even of contemporary American literature; and contemporary literature is perhaps given an exaggerated importance. It must be pointed out that the influence of Professor Babbitt has been to establish a just balance: not to disparage the scholarly research of such men as Kittredge and his pupils, which has borne good fruit in our time in the work of men like Professor John Livingstone Lowes, of Harvard, and, on the other hand, not to neglect contemporary literature, but to judge it by universal and severe criteria.

Mr Norman Foerster is one of the most brilliant of Mr Babbitt's disciples, and one of those nearest to the master. His recent work, "American Criticism" (which has not yet been published in England), contains, besides much sound criticism, an authoritative exposition of the "New Humanism." He has edited, with a preface, this collection of essays by colleagues of the American Literature Group of the Modern Language Association. These writers demand in unison a thorough revision of the traditional views of American literature and of the traditional methods of composing histories of American literature. As Mr Pattee's essay entitled "A Call for a Literary Historian" (reprinted from the *American Mercury*) shows, they are much in sympathy with the modern school of American history and desire to cooperate with it. They seem to belong, furthermore, to what may be called (without too much emphasis on dates and ages) the third generation of modern American criticism. The first generation is represented by Irving Babbitt and Paul Elmer More (the former little known, the latter almost completely ignored, in this country). Theirs was the first attempt to de-provincialise America, to replace the fireside criticism of men like James Russell Lowell by the harder standards of Sainte-Beuve and Taine and Renan. There followed a more impatient group of critics of America, represented in the rougher sort by Mr Mencken with his "Prejudices" and "Americana," and in the genteeler sort by Mr Van Wyck Brooks with his "Wine of the Puritans" and his "Ordeal of Mark Twain." The tendency of Mr Mencken was to exaggerate the value of everything contemporary which offended Boston – whether it offended the Puritan traditions of Beacon Hill or the views of the Irish-American bishopric; the tendency of Mr Brooks to be merely querulous. The third generation represents the disciples of the first generation: among general men of letters it is represented by Mumford, Munson, Allen Tate, among others; in the universities it is represented by Mr Foerster and his friends. It is one of the most interesting post-War phenomena of America. It could hardly exist, in its actual form, without the confidence and self-consciousness which the War aroused in America; but it represents also the sanest attempt to criticize and control this post-War America.

It is true, as these writers join in affirming, that there is no good history of American literature. It is also true, as they seem to be aware, that such a history would be very difficult to write. Barrett Wendell's monumental work, to which several of the writers refer sarcastically, is out of date; it was written from the point of view of old Boston, and was almost an admission, in a great many words, that there is no American literature. The most brilliant book, fragmentary, prejudiced, unbalanced as it is, and sometimes completely misleading, is certainly Mr D. H. Lawrence's dashing series of essays. Mr Lawrence's essay on Fenimore Cooper is the best thing ever written on Cooper; as might be expected, he is by no means so inspired about Poe and Hawthorne. What we are not sure that all the authors in this volume recognize is the isolated speciality of the task. Anyone who writes a history of American literature as *parallel* to English or French literature, or any other literature European or Asiatic, will be wrong, however moderate or just his claims for America may be. The justification for the history of American literature – instead of merely promoting the important Americans into a history of English literature – is that there is undoubtedly something American, and not English, about every American autho . There is also something English about him, even when his ancestry is Swedish, German or Italian. An American writer, to write a first-rate history of American literature, must know far more about England, and even about the rest of Europe, than an Englishman needs to write a history of English literature, or a Frenchman to write a history of French literature. The case of Henry James is in point; James is understood by very few Americans and very few Englishmen. To understand James one should know the America that he knew at least as well as he knew it, and the England that he knew (and the rest of England) perhaps better than he knew it. The authors of this volume insist rightly that the history of American literature can only be written by an American who is not limited to the point of view of Boston or New York or Philadelphia or Chicago but who is what we may call a cosmopolitan-American, with equal knowledge and understanding of the whole country. But we should add that he must have this further intimate knowledge of Europe. The genuine history of American literature will be one which shall have importance in Europe as well as in America. Perhaps these are some of the reasons why it has not yet been written, and why Mr Lawrence's book, with all its faults, is still the best. There is some repetition, and much detail of little interest in itself, in this volume. But though only the expression of a desire for a history of American literature, it contains many hints of what is to come (Poe's critical abilities are at last being recognized) and deserves the study of every English critic.

A TALKER

Virginia Woolf

When one opens a book of poetry and discovers the lines –

> In 1862 Charles publishes
> How Orchid Flowers are Fertilized by Insects,

or,

> In 1833 a man named Hallam,
> A friend of Alfred's, died at twenty-two,

The Great Valley, by Edgar Lee Masters [April 12, 1917]

one may be either delighted or annoyed; one may feel that this method is the genuine, unhumbugging speech which poets would always use if they were sincere; or one may inquire with some asperity why, if Mr Masters wants to say this sort of thing, he does not run all his lines into one, and say it in prose. But this last seems to us a stupid criticism; the lines would be no better if they were all of the same length, and, moreover, they would not be prose. The lines we have quoted are not prose; the lines that follow are not prose.

> Up there in the city
> Think sometimes of the American village and
> What may be done for conservation of
> The souls of men and women in the village.

The difficulty of describing Mr Masters lies precisely in the fact that if he is not a prose writer, still less is he a poet. And for this reason it is not necessary to consider him as a man who is making serious experiments in metre like the Imagists or the Vers Librists. He has none of the sensibility which, whether we think it irritable or perverted or inspired, is now urging them to break up the old rules and devise new ones, more arduous than the old. He seems to us to have little ear for the sound of words, and no poetic imagination. When he does an exercise in the classical style, such as "Marsyas," or "Apollo at Pherae," he is as smooth and dull and conscientious as a prize poet at one of our universities. His metaphors are then of this description:—

> And looking up he saw a slender maid
> White as gardenias, jonquil-haired, with eyes
> As blue as Peneus when he meets the sea,

or,

> And once he strove with music's alchemy
> To turn to sound the sunlight of the morn
> Which fills the senses as illuminate dew
> Quickens the ovule of the tiger-flower.

Whatever poetry may be, it is nothing at all like this; and although we very much prefer

> For when they opened him up
> They found his heart was a played out pump,
> And leaked like a rusty cup,

we doubt whether that is any more in the right direction.

But if Mr Masters is neither a poet nor a prose writer, we must, after reading 280 pages of his work, find a name for him; and on the whole we think it nearest the mark to call him a talker. His jerky, creaking style, the inconsecutiveness of his thought, his slap-dash use of language, his openness and plain speaking (the best of his poems is too frank to be quoted) all seem to mark him as a person who utters his ideas in talk, without stopping very long to think what he is saying. As the above quotations will have shown, when he stops to think he becomes the shadow of other respectable people; even the restraint of a rhyme seems to shackle him at once. But when he is most at his ease, and therefore at his best, we seem to see him in the corner of a New England public house, telling stories about Jerry Ott, Cato Braden, Malachy Degan, or Slip Shoe Lovey, with considerable shrewdness, humour, and sentimentality. In this mood he resembles a very primitive and provincial Robert Browning. And when there is a political crisis he gets upon his feet and delivers a harangue about life in general – for he is extremely didactic – more in the style of one of our village orators, save that his background is made of great advertisement hoardings, factory chimneys, and sky-scrapers, instead of ancient churches and the oaks of ancestral parks.

> Suppose you do it, Republic.
> Get some class,
> Throw out your chest, lift up your head,
> Be a ruler in the world,
> And not a hermit in regimentals with a flint-lock.
> Colossus with one foot in Europe,
> And one in China,
> Quit looking between your legs for the reappearance
> Of the star of Bethlehem –
> Stand up and be a man!

To a stranger the familiarity of this colloquial style seems to show that Mr Masters is at any rate a true son of the house. The chief interest of his work, indeed, comes from the fact that it is self-consciously and self-assertively American; and it is for that reason we suppose that the American public hails it with delight, on the principle, with which we must agree, that one native frog is of more importance than a whole grove full of sham nightingales.

BOOKS AND PERSONS

Virginia Woolf

There are two kinds of criticism – the written and the spoken. The first, when it gets into print, is said to be the cause of much suffering to those whom it concerns; but the second, we are inclined to think, is the only form of criticism that should make an author wince. This is the criticism which is expressed when, upon finishing a book, you toss it into the next armchair with an exclamation of horror or delight, adding a few phrases by way of comment, which lack polish and ignore grammar but contain the criticism which an author should strain all his forces to overhear. If criticism can ever help, he will be helped; if it can ever please, he will be enraptured; the pain, even, is salutary, for it will be severe enough either to kill or to reform. One or two writers there are who can put this criticism into prose; but for the most part the adjectives, the grammar, the logic, the inkpot – to say nothing of humanity and good manners – all conspire to take the dash and sincerity out of it, and by the time speech becomes a review there is nothing left but grammatical English.

Mr Arnold Bennett is one of the few who can catch their sayings before they are cold and enclose them all alive in very readable prose. That is why these aged reviews (some are nearly ten years old) are as vivacious and as much to the point as they were on the day of their birth. They have another claim upon our interest. They deal for the most part with writers who are still living, whose position is still an open question, about whom we feel more and probably know more than we can with honesty profess to do about those dead and acknowledged masters who are commonly the theme of our serious critics. At the time when Mr Bennett was Jacob Tonson of the *New Age*, Mr Galsworthy, Mr Montague, Mrs Elinor Glyn, Mr W. H. Hudson, Mr John Masefield, Mr

Books and Persons, by Arnold Bennett [July 5, 1917]

Conrad, Mr E. M. Forster, Mr Wells, and Mrs Humphry Ward were not exactly in the positions which they occupy to-day. The voice of Jacob Tonson had something to do with the mysterious process of settling them where, as we think, they will ultimately dwell. It is true that we are not going to rank any book of Mr Galsworthy's with "Crime and Punishment," and we dissent a little from the generosity of the praise bestowed upon the novels of Mr Wells. But these are details compared with the far more important question of Mr Bennett's point of view. We have said that his is spoken criticism; but we hasten to add that it is not at all what we are accustomed to hear spoken at dinner-tables and in drawing-rooms. It is the talk of a writer in his work-room, in his shirt-sleeves. It is the talk, as Mr Bennett is proud to insist, of a creative artist. "I am not myself a good theorizer about art," he says. "I ... speak as a creative artist, and not as a critic." The creative artist, he remarks, on another occasion, produces "the finest, and the only first-rate criticism."

We do not think that this is a book of first-rate criticism; but it is the book of an artist. Nobody could read one of these short little papers without feeling himself in the presence of the father of fifty volumes. The man who speaks knows all that there is to be known about the making of books. He remembers that a tremendous amount of work has gone to the making of them; he is versed in every side of the profession – agents and publishers, good seasons and bad seasons, the size of editions and the size of royalties, he knows it all – he loves it all. He never affects to despise the business side of the profession of writing. He will talk of high-class stuff, thinks that authors are quite right in getting every cent they can for it, and will remark that it is the business of a competent artist to please, if not *the*, certainly *a*, public. But it is not in this sense only that he is far more professional than the English writer is apt to be or to appear; he is professional in his demand that a novel shall be made absolutely seaworthy and well constructed. If he hates one sin more than another it is the sin of "intellectual sluggishness." This is not the attitude nor are these the words of "mandarins" or "dilettanti" – the professors and the cultivated people whom Mr Bennett hates much as the carpenter hates the amateur who does a little fretwork.

London swarms with the dilettanti of letters. They do not belong to the criminal classes, but their good intentions, their culture, their judiciousness, and their infernal cheek amount perhaps to worse than arson or assault.... They shine at tea, at dinner, and after dinner. They talk more easily than [the artist] does, and write more easily too. They can express themselves more readily. And they know such a deuce of a lot.

Whether we agree or disagree we are reminded by this healthy outburst of rage that the critic has not merely to deal out skilfully measured doses of praise and blame to individuals, but to keep the atmosphere in a right state for the production of works of art. The atmosphere, even seven years ago, was in a state so strange that it appears almost fantastic now. Canon Lambert was then saying, "I would just as soon send a daughter of mine to a house infected with diphtheria or typhoid fever as" let her read "Ann Veronica." About the same time Dr Barry remarked, "I never leave my house ... but I am forced to see, and solicited to buy, works flamingly advertised of which the gospel is adultery and the apocalypse the right of suicide." We must be very grateful to Mr Bennett for the pertinacity with which he went on saying in such circumstances "that the first business of a work of art is to be beautiful, and its second not to be sentimental."

But if we were asked to give a proof that Mr Bennett is something more than the extremely competent, successful, businesslike producer of literature, we would point to the paper on "Neo-Impressionism and Literature." These new pictures, he says, have wearied him of other pictures; is it not possible that some writer will come along and do in words what these men have done in paint? And suppose that happens, and Mr Bennett has to admit that he has been concerning himself unduly with inessentials, that he has been worrying himself to achieve infantile realisms? He will admit it, we are sure; and that he can ask himself such a question seems to us certain proof that he is what he claims to be – a "creative artist."

MODERN NOVELS

Virginia Woolf

In making any survey, even the freest and loosest, of modern
fiction it is difficult not to take it for granted that the modern
practice of the art is somehow an improvement upon the old. With
their simple tools and primitive materials, it might be said, Fielding
did well and Jane Austen even better, but compare their
opportunities with ours! Their masterpieces certainly have a
strange air of simplicity. And yet the analogy between literature
and the process, to choose an example, of making bicycles scarcely
holds good beyond the first glance. It is doubtful whether in the
course of the centuries, though we have learnt much about making
machines, we have learnt anything about making literature. We do
not come to write better; all that we can be said to do is to keep
moving, now a little in this direction, now in that, but with a
circular tendency should the whole course of the track be viewed
from a sufficiently lofty pinnacle. It need scarcely be said that we
make no claim to stand even momentarily upon that vantage
ground; we seem to see ourselves on the flat, in the crowd, half
blind with dust, and looking back with a sort of envy at those
happy warriors whose battle is won and whose achievements wear
so serene an air of accomplishment that in our envy we can scarcely
refrain from whispering that the prize was not so rare, nor the
battle so fierce, as our own. Let the historian of literature decide. It
is for him, too, to ascertain whether we are now at the beginning,
or middle, or end, of a great period of prose fiction; all that we
ourselves can know is that, whatever stage we have reached, we are
still in the thick of the battle. This very sense of heights reached by
others and unassailable by us, this envious belief that Fielding,
Thackeray, or Jane Austen were set an easier problem, however
triumphantly they may have solved it, is a proof, not that we have
improved upon them, still less that we have given up the game and
left them the victors, but only that we still strive and press on.

Our quarrel, then, is not with the classics, and if we speak of
quarrelling with Mr Wells, Mr Bennett, and Mr Galsworthy it is

[Article] [April 10, 1919]

partly that by the mere fact of their existence in the flesh their work
has a living, breathing, every-day imperfection which bids us take
what liberties with it we choose. But it is also true that, while we
thank them for a thousand gifts, we reserve our unconditional
gratitude for Mr Hardy, for Mr Conrad, and in a much lesser
degree for the Mr Hudson, of "The Purple Land," "Green
Mansions," and "Far Away and Long Ago." The former,
differently and in different measures, have excited so many hopes
and disappointed them so persistently that our gratitude largely
takes the form of thanking them for having shown us what it is that
we certainly could not do, but as certainly, perhaps, do not wish to
do. No single phrase will sum up the charge or grievance which we
have to bring against a mass of work so large in its volume and
embodying so many qualities, both admirable and the reverse. If
we tried to formulate our meaning in one word we should say that
these three writers are materialists, and for that reason have
disappointed us and left us with the feeling that the sooner English
fiction turns its back upon them, as politely as may be, and marches,
if only into the desert, the better for its soul. Of course, no single
word reaches the centre of three separate targets. In the case of Mr
Wells it falls notably wide of the mark. And yet even in his case it
indicates to our thinking the fatal alloy in his genius, the great clod
of clay that has got itself mixed up with the purity of his inspiration.
But Mr Bennett is perhaps the worst culprit of the three, inasmuch
as he is by far the best workman. He can make a book so well
constructed and solid in its craftsmanship that it is difficult for the
most exacting of critics to see through what chink or crevice decay
can creep in. There is not so much as a draught between the frames
of the windows, or a crack in the boards. And yet – if life should
refuse to live there? That is a risk which the creator of "The Old
Wives' Tale," George Cannon, Edwin Clayhanger, and hosts of
other figures, may well claim to have surmounted. His characters
live abundantly, even unexpectedly, but it still remains to ask how
do they live, and what do they live for? More and more they seem to
us, deserting even the well-built villa in the Five Towns, to spend
their time in some softly padded first-class railway carriage, fitted
with bells and buttons innumerable; and the destiny to which they
travel so luxuriously becomes more and more unquestionably an
eternity of bliss spent in the very best hotel in Brighton. It can
scarcely be said of Mr Wells that he is a materialist in the sense that

he takes too much delight in the solidity of his fabric. His mind is too generous in its sympathies to allow him to spend much time in making things shipshape and substantial. He is a materialist from sheer goodness of heart, taking upon his shoulders the work that ought to have been discharged by Government officials, and in the plethora of his ideas and facts scarcely having leisure to realize, or forgetting to think important, the crudity and coarseness of his human beings. Yet what more damaging criticism can there be both of his earth and of his Heaven than that they are to be inhabited here and hereafter by his Joans and Peters? Does not the inferiority of their natures tarnish whatever institutions and ideals may be provided for them by the generosity of their Creator? Nor, profoundly though we respect the integrity and humanity of Mr Galsworthy, shall we find what we seek in his pages.

We have to admit that we are exacting, and, further, that we find it difficult to justify our discontent by explaining what it is that we exact. We frame our question differently at different times. But it reappears most persistently as we drop the finished novel on the crest of a sigh – Is it worth while? What is the point of it all? Can it be that owing to one of those little deviations which the human spirit seems to make from time to time Mr Bennett has come down with his magnificent apparatus for catching life just an inch or two on the wrong side? Life escapes; and perhaps without life nothing else is worth while. It is a confession of vagueness to have to make use of such a figure as this, but we scarcely better the matter by speaking as critics are prone to do of reality. Admitting the vagueness, let us hazard the opinion that for us at this moment the form of fiction most in vogue more often misses than secures the thing we seek. Whether we call it life or spirit, truth or reality, this, the essential thing, has moved off, or on, and refuses to be contained any longer in such ill-fitting vestments as we provide. Nevertheless we go on perseveringly, conscientiously, construct-ing our thirty-two chapters after a design which more and more ceases to resemble the vision in our minds. So much of the enormous labour of proving the solidity, the likeness to life, of the story is not merely labour thrown away but labour misplaced to the extent of obscuring and blotting out the light of the conception. The mediocrity of most novels seems to arise from a conviction on the part of the writer that unless his plot provides scenes of tragedy, comedy, and excitement, an air of probability so impeccable that if all his figures were to come to life they would find themselves dressed down to the last button in the fashion of the hour, he has failed in his duty to the public. If this, roughly as we have stated it, represents his vision, his mediocrity may be said to be natural rather than imposed; but as often as not we may suspect some moment of hesitation in which the question suggests itself whether life is like this after all? Is it not possible that the accent falls a little differently, that the moment of importance came before or after, that, if one were free and could set down what one chose, there would be no plot, little probability, and a vague general confusion in which the clear-cut features of the tragic, the comic, the passionate, and the lyrical were dissolved beyond the possibility of separate recognition? The mind, exposed to the ordinary course of life, receives upon its surface a myriad impressions – trivial, fantastic, evanescent, or engraved with the sharpness of steel. From all sides they come, an incessant shower of innumerable atoms, composing in their sum what we might venture to call life itself; and to figure further as the semi-transparent envelope, or luminous halo, surrounding us from the beginning of consciousness to the end. Is it not perhaps the chief task of the novelist to convey this incessantly varying spirit with whatever stress or sudden deviation it may display, and as little admixture of the alien and external as possible? We are not pleading merely for courage and sincerity; but suggesting that the proper stuff for fiction is a little other than custom would have us believe it.

In some such fashion as this do we seek to define the element which distinguishes the work of several young writers, among whom Mr James Joyce is the most notable, from that of their predecessors. It attempts to come closer to life, and to preserve more sincerely and exactly what interests and moves them by discarding most of the conventions which are commonly observed by the novelists. Let us record the atoms as they fall upon the mind in the order in which they fall, let us trace the pattern, however disconnected and incoherent in appearance, which each sight or incident scores upon the consciousness. Let us not take it for granted that life exists more in what is commonly thought big than in what is commonly thought small. Any one who has read "The Portrait of the Artist as a Young Man" or what promises to be a far more interesting work, "Ulysses," now appearing in the *Little Review*, will have hazarded some theory of this nature as to Mr

Joyce's intention. On our part it is hazarded rather than affirmed; but whatever the exact intention there can be no question but that it is of the utmost sincerity and that the result, difficult or unpleasant as we may judge it, is undeniably distinct. In contrast to those whom we have called materialists Mr Joyce is spiritual; concerned at all costs to reveal the flickerings of that innermost flame which flashes its myriad messages through the brain, he disregards with complete courage whatever seems to him adventitious, though it be probability or coherence or any other of the handrails to which we cling for support when we set our imaginations free. Faced, as in the Cemetery scene, by so much that, in its restless scintillations, in its irrelevance, its flashes of deep significance succeeded by incoherent inanities, seems to be life itself, we have to fumble rather awkwardly if we want to say what else we wish; and for what reason a work of such originality yet fails to compare, for we must take high examples, with "Youth" or "Jude the Obscure." It fails, one might say simply, because of the comparative poverty of the writer's mind. But it is possible to press a little further and wonder whether we may not refer our sense of being in a bright and yet somehow strictly confined apartment rather than at large beneath the sky to some limitation imposed by the method as well as by the mind. Is it due to the method that we feel neither jovial nor magnanimous, but centred in a self which in spite of its tremor of susceptibility never reaches out or embraces or comprehends what is outside and beyond? Does the emphasis laid perhaps didactically upon indecency contribute to this effect of the angular and isolated? Or is it merely that in any effort of such courage the faults as well as the virtues are left naked to the view? In any case we need not attribute too much importance to the method. Any method is right, every method is right, that expresses what we wish to express. This one has the merit of giving closer shape to what we were prepared to call life itself; did not the reading of "Ulysses" suggest how much of life is excluded and ignored, and did it not come with a shock to open "Tristram Shandy" and even "Pendennis," and be by them convinced that there are other aspects of life, and larger ones into the bargain?

However this may be, the problem before the novelist at present, as we suppose it to have been in the past, is to contrive a means of being free to set down what he chooses. He has to have the courage to say that what interests him is no longer this, but that; out of "that" alone must he construct his work. The tendency of the moderns and part of their perplexity is no doubt that they find their interest more and more in the dark region of psychology. At once therefore the accent falls a little differently; it becomes apparent that the emphasis is upon something hitherto ignored or unstressed in that relation, a feeling, a point of view suggesting a different and obscure outline of form, incomprehensible to our predecessors. No one but a modern, perhaps no one but a Russian, would have felt the interest of the situation which Tchehov has made into the short story which he calls "Gusev." Some Russian soldiers are lying ill in the hospital of a ship which is taking them back to Russia. We are given scraps of their talk; a few of their thoughts; then one of the soldiers dies, and is taken away; the talk goes on among the others for a time; until Gusev himself dies and, looking "like a carrot or a radish," is thrown overboard. The emphasis is laid upon such unexpected places that at first it seems as if there were no emphasis at all; and then, as the eyes accustom themselves to twilight and discern the shapes of things in a room, we see how complete the story is, how profound, and how truly in obedience to his vision Tchehov has chosen this, that, and the other, and placed them together to compose something new. But it is impossible to say that this is humorous or that tragic, or even that it is proper to call the whole a short story, since the writer seems careless of brevity and intensity, and leaves us with the suggestion that the strange chords he has struck sound on and on. There is, perhaps, no need that a short story should be brief and intense, as there is perhaps no answer to the questions which it raises.

The most inconclusive remarks upon modern English fiction can hardly avoid some mention of the Russian influence, and if the Russians are mentioned one runs the risk of feeling that to write of any fiction save theirs is waste of time. If we want understanding of the soul and heart where else shall we find it of comparable profundity? If we are sick of our own materialism the least considerable of their novelists has by right of birth a natural reverence for the human spirit. "Learn to make yourself akin to people . . . But let this sympathy be not with the mind – for it is easy with the mind – but with the heart, with love towards them." In every great Russian writer we seem to discern the features of a saint, if sympathy for the sufferings of others, love towards them, endeavour to reach some goal worthy of the most exacting demands of the spirit constitute saintliness. It is the saint in them which confounds us with a feeling of our own irreligious triviality, and turns so many of our famous novels to tinsel and trickery. The conclusions of the Russian mind, thus comprehensive and compassionate, are inevitably perhaps of the utmost sadness. It might indeed be more true to speak of the inconclusiveness of the Russian mind. It is the sense that there is no answer, that if honestly examined life presents question after question which must be left to sound on and on after the story is over in hopeless interrogation that fills us with a deep, and finally it may be with a resentful, despair. They are right perhaps; unquestionably they see further than we do and without our gross impediments of vision. But perhaps we see something that escapes them, or why should this voice of protest mix itself with our gloom? The voice of protest is the voice of another and an ancient civilization which seems to have bred in us the instinct to enjoy and fight rather than to suffer and understand. English fiction from Sterne to Meredith bears witness to our natural delight in humour and comedy, in the beauty of earth, in the activities of the intellect, and in the splendour of the body. But any deductions that we may draw from the comparison of one fiction with another are futile, save as they flood us with a view of infinite possibilities, assure us that there is no bound to the horizon, and nothing forbidden but falsity and pretence. "The proper stuff of fiction" does not exist; everything is the proper stuff of fiction; whatever one honestly thinks, whatever one honestly feels. No perception comes amiss; every good quality whether of the mind or spirit is drawn upon and used and turned by the magic of art to something little or large, but endlessly different, everlastingly new. All that fiction asks of us is that we should break her and bully her, honour and love her, till she yields to our bidding, for so her youth is perpetually renewed and her sovereignty assured.

IV

A TLS TREASURY

MR CHURTON COLLINS
ON BLAKE*

W. B. Yeats

Sir, – Mr Churton Collins has for many years commended accurate learning and the university teaching of literature as the only certain guides to good taste. It is, therefore, interesting to know that he himself, the accuracy of whose learning is notorious, thinks Blake's lines ending "Did He who made the lamb make thee?" not only "falsetto" but, when taken from their context, "nonsense pure and absolute." When I was a boy my father was accustomed to read me passages of verse that seemed to him and to his friends great poetry, and this very stanza was among them; and now that I have edited Blake, and thought much over every line that he wrote, I cannot think that cry "Did He who made the lamb make thee?" less than a cry out of the heart of all wisdom. A recent article of Mr Churton Collins about the importance of learning as a guide to taste almost converted me to his opinion, but now I return to my own opinion that many a cultivated woman without learning is more right about these matters than all the professors.

I am, Sir, your obedient servant,

W. B. YEATS

AN AMERICAN ON
AMERICA†

Ezra Pound

Mr Fullerton seems to have written this book very easily. Easy writing makes hard reading. His views are approximately those of the minority of Americans who are accustomed to think of the

*[Letter] [May 30, 1902]
†*The American Crisis and the War*, by William Morton Fullerton [October 19, 1916]

United States as an integral part of the world. He has embedded an arraignment of President Wilson in a meandering attempt to explain the United States of to-day. [...]

Mr Fullerton's book perhaps demands closer attention than the average reader will be disposed to give it. The argument is clear only when followed very closely. There is a curious piece of rather inconsequential optimism at the end of the preface, doubtless sound enough as opinion, but not an integral part of the thesis. The writer displays, moreover, a curious and typically American tendency to think that "all may be for the best"; that although America is somewhat *déclassée*, though Mr Wilson has lost a magnificent opportunity, still the war will "wake up America," will teach her to "know herself more truly."

It is at least doubtful whether the war will have so beneficent an effect. Having escaped the rigours of war, Americans may, with exquisite optimism, regard themselves the more as the favoured of Providence. They may be more sensitive, more "touchy" about frank criticism of actual faults either by native or by foreign critics, and may still regard "breeziness" as an atonement for every shortcoming. But Mr Fullerton probably knows that his country-men do not like to read gloomy books. It is, however, difficult to say with certainty whether he has in reality written for them or for the European intellectual, who surely needs no argument to convince him that Mr Wilson has not advanced American political prestige.

THE "DADA MOVEMENT"

F. S. Flint

The "Dada Movement" was born – the metaphor is the author's own – in the Cabaret Voltaire, at Zurich, in 1916. M. Tristan Tzara is its father, its chief sponsor, and its wildest son. If we could ignore the decencies of print, as the Dadaists do, we might be tempted to give to M. Tzara a different part in the generation of this

Vingt-cinq Poèmes, by Tristan Tzara [January 29, 1920]

"movement"; for its true parent is the anarchy of the times, and M. Tzara is merely a speck that has grown into a monstrosity. The word "Dada" we are told, means nothing; it is the name given by the "Krou" negroes to the tail of a sacred cow; in a certain part of Italy, a cube and a mother, and, in Russia and Rumania, a wooden horse and a nurse are called "Dada." In England – we make M. Tzara a present of this information – "Dada" is a baby-word for "father." But, in art and literature, "Dada" means exactly nothing. It is the rallying-cry of a group of men who have discovered that our senses are no true registers of the external universe and that our actions and words, in relation to eternity, are futile. "Si je crie," says M. Tzara, in one of his numerous manifestoes (he is, on principle, against manifestoes, as he is also against principles) – "si je crie:

> Idéal, idéal, idéal,
> Connaissance, connaissance, connaissance,
> Boumboum, boumboum, boumboum,

j'ai enregistré assez exactement le progrès, la loi, la morale et toutes les autres belles qualités que de différents gens très intelligents ont discuté dans tant de livres, pour arriver, à la fin, à dire que tout de même chacun a dansé d'après son boumboum personnel.

We seem to remember that Nietzsche said much the same thing in far better language. But, since "toutes les choses sont éternelles et vaines," and the times are out of joint, and men are human, mean and bloodthirsty, and their words and actions of no more value than the gibberings and gestures of lunatics, let us, says M. Tzara, in effect, frankly be lunatics: let us abolish the family, morality, logic, common sense, memory, archæology, the prophets, the future: "Liberté: *Dada, Dada, Dada,* hurlements des couleurs crispées, entrelacement des contraires et de toutes les contradictions, des grotesques, des inconséquences: La Vie." M. Tzara appears to have missed Nietzsche's remarks on liberty. It is a pity.

The manifestoes from which the foregoing quotations have been taken were printed in "Dada, recueil littéraire et artistique"; they have the merit of occasional lucidity; sometimes, even, behind their general incoherence and their imperfect French – for M. Tzara neither writes nor spells French correctly – may be detected a glimmer of what, properly presented, might be quite good sense. This cannot be said, however, of either the "poems" or the "drawings" composed under the inspiration of M. Tzara's cry of liberty, *liberté chérie*. [. . .]

It is useless to attempt to refute these men. "Non ragioniam di lor . . ." Their principle being to have no principles, and their art to have no art, their works can be safely left to the general common sense, which will destroy them. (We read in the "Anthologie Dada" a protest against the action of the director of the Pestalozzi school of Zurich in effacing "les 2 grandes peintures murales de Van Rees et Arp, premières œuvres modernes, abstraites, sur les murs d'un grand édifice . . . Cet acte de barbarie ne fut que très vaguement condamné par la presse." For once, the much decried *bourgeois* was probably in the right). If it is asked why, demanding "des œuvres fortes droites précises et *à jamais incomprises*," the Dadaists yet publish them, the answer is that publication is similar to the act of the madman who buttonholes you, whispers a few mysterious words, and walks off cackling with laughter. Dada – cackle: the joke is against us. But we do not mind. We are much more concerned to see that, according to a "Dada" leaflet, MM Henri Bergson, J.-E. Blanche, Charlie Chaplin, Paul Claudel, André Gide, Pierre Hamp, Maurice Maeterlinck, Jules Romains, André Salmon, and Paul Valéry "ont adhéré au Mouvement Dada." Mr Chaplin, at least, might have had more sense.

DOWSON'S POEMS

T. S. Eliot

Sir. – In the interesting review of Ernest Dowson's Poems in your last issue, your reviewer suggests that I caught the phrase "Falls the shadow" from Dowson's "Cynara." This derivation had not occurred to my mind, but I believe it to be correct, because the lines he quotes have always run in my head, and because I regard Dowson as a poet whose technical innovations have been underestimated. But I do not think that I got the title "The Hollow Men" from Dowson. There is a romance of William Morris called

[Letter] [January 10, 1935]

"The Hollow Land." There is also a poem of Mr Kipling called
"The Broken Men." I combined the two.

I am, Sir, your obedient servant,

T. S. ELIOT

24, Russell Square, London, W.C.1.

EDWARD LEAR*

W. H. Auden

Left by his friend to breakfast alone on the white
Italian shore, his Terrible Demon arose
Over his shoulder; he wept to himself in the night,
A dirty landscape-painter who hated his nose.

The legions of cruel inquisitive "They"
Were so solid and strong, like dogs; he was upset
By Germans and boats; affection was miles away:
But, guided by tears, he successfully reached his Regret.

How prodigious the welcome was: flowers took his hat
And bore him off to introduce him to the tongs;
The demon's false nose made the table laugh; a cat
Invited him to dance and shyly squeezed his hand;
Words pushed him to the piano to sing comic songs.

And children swarmed to him like settlers: He became a land.

FRANZ KAFKA†

Hugh Walpole

Sir, – A reviewer must have every right to the freedom of his
opinion: therefore I make no protest against the criticism of Mr
Warner's novel "The Aerodrome," although I totally disagree
with it. But when your reviewer talks of Kafka's "world of
portentous nothings" and sneers persistently at the work of that

*[Poem] [March 25, 1939]
†[Letter] [April 19, 1941]

beautiful writer, something must be said on the other side. To many of us Kafka's "Castle" and "The Trial" are poetic allegories of moving beauty and eloquent symbolism. Rather than "portentous nothings" they are books filled with philosophy and human pity.

HUGH WALPOLE

MATTHEW ARNOLD

Wyndham Lewis

[...] Dr Arnold of Rugby was an amazing person. He was responsible for two such contradictory symbols of his energies as Hodson's Horse of Indian Mutiny fame, and "Empedocles on Etna" (or, more simply stated, his own son). Most typical was Hodson's Delhi exploit, when the king sent his three sons to surrender. Major Hodson killed all three of them on the spot. He "felt it expedient" to do this, for he had learned decision upon the playing-fields of Arnold's Rugby. Also it was Dr Arnold's habit, when there was a boys' mutiny, to employ Hodson to quell it; so the latter had plenty of practice with mutinies while still at school.

But if Dr Arnold was a many-sided man his most improbable feat was to have such a son as Matthew. There have been many instances of paradoxes of this kind, but the student of Victorian England must feel particularly puzzled by this conjunction. Yet Dr Arnold was not such a complete idiot as Lytton Strachey made him out to be. When he settled at Laleham and began to have a man-size family, he provided all his children with dog-names, and their life was ordered according to the law of the kennel. When he and his dogs moved to Fox How, he framed rules such as this.

> That Dogs Didu and Widu do not fish, nor go out rowing or sailing without a man, nor go on walks without the Elder Dogs. That all Dogs, unless there is some positive engagement, do stay within doors, and read for their canine edification, from ten o'clock to twelve. That all Dogs bear

Matthew Arnold: Poetry and Prose, ed. by John Bryson [August 6, 1954]

themselves reverently and discreetly towards Dog K – not barking, biting or otherwise molesting her, under pain of a heavy judicum with many smites.

Matthew Arnold's dog-name was Crab. This suggested disinclination in the infant Matthew to acquire the standing position.

Although Dr Arnold evidenced many symptoms of an agreeable originality, our subject, Matthew, seemed disposed to escape from the shadow of his famous father in every way he could. However, one can see how a father, who screwed one down into a ritual, re-naming one and laying down laws for one's behaviour while a child, might certainly leave an impression of an alarming pervasiveness. So we find, without surprise, the adult Matthew making himself as different as possible to look at from the man who bore him. He became a dandy. Apparently the way he wore his side whiskers marked him out as a young man inclined to the elegancies. And, to the end, we learn, his abundant chevelure remained with him, and was cut in a continental fashion. If he entered a drawing room or a restaurant, this alone would produce an "un-English" impression, which was as he wished it to be.

The natural disparity between the elegant young poet and the burly schoolmaster was not all; Matthew differed from his parent in more ways than in his head-dress. In a letter Dr Arnold deplores Matthew's moral shortcomings; which would signify the absence in him of a certain type of earnestness. He developed from the outset a gaiety of mind, combined with an airy arrogance. A gaiety adhered to with an arrogant firmness would be an uncomfortable attribute in the eyes of a father who was a professional moralist.

Matthew's mind was marvellously independent. He excelled in disagreement. His country as well as his class was the occasion for routine disagreement. At every turn in his writings one comes upon a comment like this:

> Still to be able to think, still to be irresistibly carried, if so it be, by the current of thoughts to the opposite side of the question … I know nothing more striking, and I must add that I know nothing more un-English.

Here is another example: he is writing about criticism. "Almost the last thing for which one would come to English literature is just that very thing which now Europe most desires – criticism."

In every country the most valuable men are those in disagreement – whether critical of America, critical of Germany,
critical of Russia, critical of Spain, &c. There is nothing more
valuable in a nation than a critic – a sincere upside-down man.
[...]

As a poet Matthew Arnold is in a class apart. As to his rank, no
greater poetry was ever written than the concluding song of
Callicles in "Empedocles on Etna." One could not, alas, say as
much for the entire poem, though "Empedocles on Etna" has
everywhere lines of great beauty.

A CHILD ASLEEP IN ITS
OWN LIFE*

Wallace Stevens

Among the old men that you know,
There is one, unnamed, that broods
On all the rest, in heavy thought.

They are nothing, except in the universe
Of that single mind. He regards them
Outwardly and knows them inwardly,

The sole emperor of what they are,
Distant, yet close enough to wake
The chords above your bed to-night.

HOW NOW RED HORSE?†

Ezra Pound

Sir, – The Christmas *Tatler* publishes a drawing of the Grecian
Tavern in which the owner's name is spelled without the terminal
-e used by the noble and better known family Howe.

*[Poem] [September 17, 1954]
†[Letter] [January 9, 1959]

I doubt if philological triflers will have noticed it, or whether Longfellow has left any trace in British memory outside *The Abbey*. The Oxford University Press, 1908, edition of his *Tales of a Wayside Inn* misprints the name, but the original arms of mine host of the Red Horse, Duxbury, agree in the shorter spelling. (Photographic evidence can be supplied if this is of any interest.) A good deal of discredit has been cast on New England heraldry, and it would be amusing to know whether the arms described by Longfellow are known to the College of Heralds.

> ... gules upon his shield
> A chevron argent in the field,
> With three wolf's-heads, and for crest
> A Wyvern part-per-pale addressed ...

Genealogists might speculate on the natural sequence of the profession of tavern-keeping, but there seems fair chance that some younger son of the Grecian's proprietor should have set up in the same, or approximate, line in the Colonies.

EZRA POUND

COMMENTARY

As we know from George Painter's wonderfully thorough biography, Marcel Proust was not encouraged by the little he had heard before his death about Scott-Moncrieff's translation of *A la Recherche du Temps Perdu*. His own suggestion had been that the book should be translated by Gilbert Cannan, [...] who had translated Romain Rolland's enormous *Jean Christophe*, but, as Mr Painter writes: "providentially ... Charles Scott-Moncrieff had already resolved to devote his life to the translation ...". Such a resolution was a fitting match for Proust's own fastidious but absolute determination to get his book published in France, which had kept his emissaries busy for many months in 1911–12. Scott-Moncrieff was not immediately successful either when he tried to interest London publishers in his translation: Mr Painter records his offer of *Swann's Way* as a serial to an ailing and agrarian-sounding magazine called *Land and Water* in January, 1920. But this was not his first

[Article] [November 9, 1967]

failure, as is shown by two letters which he wrote to Messrs Constable in 1919 and which are still in the firm's archives.

The first is dated October 22 and addressed from the New Oxford and Cambridge Club. Scott-Moncrieff starts it with true Pall Mall courtesy, "Gentlemen", and makes no mention of Proust until he is well into his second page. His first concern is a book of "mainly political" light verse called *Snakes in the Grass*, which he had submitted to Constable's and on which he wanted a decision. He goes into some detail over this before dropping the great name: "Meanwhile I have another book of some importance which I think is more worthy of the traditions of your house: that is a translation of M. Marcel Proust's *A La Recherche du Temps Perdu...*." The book, he explains, is being "widely read and discussed in France and England – but I have not heard of any proposal to translate it". The letter ends with the offer of a specimen of his own translation.

The publishers' answer has not survived, but it must have been a prompt and dusty one, since Scott-Moncrieff's second letter to them is dated only eight days after the first. This time he puts Proust first and *Snakes in the Grass* (which also seems to have been rejected) second. "I am flattered to learn that you have 'gone very carefully' into my suggestion", he writes, and then introduces a crucial semicolon; "I fear that my handwriting misled you. *A la Recherche du Temps Perdu* is not the work of M. Marcel Prevost but of M. PROUST, a widely different person ..." Even in 1919, when the mildly scandalous novels of Marcel Prévost were still being read, Scott-Moncrieff's amiable understatement can only have been an act of great restraint. It is followed by an excessively practical justification of his undertaking to translate Proust in the first place. Having compared the book for "bulk" with *Jean Christophe* (a similar comparison no doubt explains why Proust had decided that Gilbert Cannan was the man with the stamina to translate him as well) he goes on: "I do not think that many people will care to read it in French – the pages are very closely printed and the sentences are as long as those of Henry James." He ends by apologizing: "I am sorry to trouble you again in this matter – but your deciphering of Proust as Prevost in my former letter completely altered the circumstances of my proposal".

But the altered circumstances did not alter the publisher's refusal, and Scott-Moncrieff's translation went eventually to Chatto and Windus, where it remains. Almost fifty years after the event the most

striking feature of his two letters is their total reticence about the
aesthetic qualities he had detected in Proust; if Scott-Moncrieff had
in fact calculated that his best chance of success lay in suppressing
the enthusiasm he must have felt then this is an interesting
indication of publishing manners at the time. [...]

THE LAY OF WYSTAN

Gavin Ewart

(Two Fragments from the Icelandic)

Fragment 1
Not in the war slain, eastwards came Wystan,
Wilfully wanton with charming Chester,
Fair and young, fate to endure.
For some weeks sat they, harmonious house-guests,
Pampered and peaceful in Paulton's Square.

The weather-wise hunters, Wystan, Chester,
Returned from the hunt. Great Wystan of Wolfdale,
A Lord of London, the bane of fell dwellers[1],
Bold with his blood-worm[2] to boys of Berlin,
Now rested he fairly in 1946.

On the lone island they lay together,
Oliver the thrall who hefted them house-room,
Fair and young, fate to endure,
Free from skulduggery of the Skjöldungs.

Breakfasted they in their rueful raincoats,
Dressing-gowns as Yggdrasil undreamed-of,
Fair and young, fate to endure,
Their big white feet were gleaming wonders ...

Fragment 2

Wystan of Wolfdale, cottaged in Christ Church,
Disgusted the dons with his myths of man-love,
Bored they were, it was blatant buggery:
"Where are my boys? What has befallen them?"

[Poem] [August 20, 1982]

His speech in the din-world[3] of the Christ Church
                              Common Room
Was vivid with buggery and sweet vermouth,
Wystan the warrior lamented loudly:
"Learn me, Völund, lord of the elves:
Where are my boys? What has befallen them?"

A high-born elm, an idol of fortune,
Hailed with many a hornful of mead,
Highly and holily his runes were rated,
But Wystan of Wolfdale lay miserable, his mate gone,
On Middle Earth unmatched but by misery mastered . . .

[1] *killer of giants (an epithet of Thor)*
[2] *sword*
[3] *mortal world, world of pain*

SMALL FANTASIA
FOR W. B.

Seamus Heaney

Where does spirit live? Inside or outside
Things remembered, made things, things unmade?
What came first, the seabird's cry or the soul

Imagined in the dawn cold when it cried?
Where does it roost at last? On dungy sticks
In a jackdaw's nest up in some old stone tower

Or a marble bust commanding the parterre?
How habitable is perfected form?
And how inhabited the windy light?

What was learned from the midwife and the hangman?
What's the use of a held note or held line
That cannot be assailed for reassurance?

[Poem] [January 27, 1989]

NOTES ON CONTRIBUTORS

ROBERT M. ADAMS. American scholar and critic; his books include studies of Stendhal and Joyce.

RICHARD ALDINGTON (1892–1962). Poet, novelist, man of letters.

JOHN BAYLEY (1925–). Former Warton Professor of English literature at Oxford; author of studies of Shakespeare, Pushkin etc.

JOAN BENNETT (1896–1986). Fellow of Girton College, Cambridge; author of *Virginia Woolf: Her Art as a Novelist* (1945).

EDMUND BLUNDEN (1896–1974). Poet, author of *Undertones of War*.

SIR DENIS BROGAN (1900–74). Authority on French and American history.

CHRISTINE BROOKE-ROSE. Novelist and critic; professor of English language and literature, University of Paris, 1975–88.

ANTHONY BURGESS (1917–). Novelist and polymath.

JOHN CASEY. Fellow of Gonville and Caius College, Cambridge; author of *The Language of Criticism* (1966).

R. D. CHARQUES (1899–1959). On the editorial staff of *The Times* from 1927.

HAROLD CHILD (1869–1945). Former actor; literary and theatrical historian; member of the editorial staff of *The Times*.

AUSTIN CLARKE (1896–1974). Irish poet.

ALAN CLUTTON-BROCK (1904–76). On the staff of *The Times* from 1930; chief art critic from 1945.

ARTHUR CLUTTON-BROCK (1868–1924). Man of letters.

ANTHONY CRONIN (1926–). Irish poet and critic; author of *A Question of Modernity* (1964).

F. T. DALTON (1872–1927). Assistant editor of the *TLS* from 1902 to 1923.

DONALD DAVIE (1922–). Poet and critic.

MARY DUCLAUX, *née* Robinson (1857–1944). Poet; authority on French literature.

RICHARD ELLMANN (1918–87). American scholar, long resident in England; biographer of Joyce and Wilde.

GAVIN EWART (1916–). Poet.

CYRIL FALLS (1888–1971). Military historian.

HUGH I'ANSON FAUSSET (1895–1965). Literary journalist.

F. S. FLINT (1885–1960). Civil servant and poet.

G. S. FRASER (1915–80). Poet and critic.

ROY FULLER (1912–). Poet, Professor of Poetry, Oxford University, 1968–73).

P. N. FURBANK. Biographer of Diderot, Svevo and E. M. Forster.

S. B. GATES (1893–73). Aeronautical designer; occasional literary reviewer from the *TLS* from 1928.

HENRY GIFFORD (1913–). Former Professor of English at the University of Bristol; author of studies of Pasternak, Tolstoy etc.

A. H. GOMME. Author of *D. H. Lawrence: A Critical Study of the Major Novels* (1978).

THOM GUNN (1929–). English-born poet, long resident in the U.S.

MICHAEL HAMBURGER (1924–). Poet and translator.

PAMELA HANSFORD JOHNSON (1912–81). Novelist.

SEAMUS HEANEY (1939–). Irish poet.

ERICH HELLER (1911–90). His books include a classic study of modern German literature, *The Disinherited Mind* (1952).

RAYNER HEPPENSTALL (1911–81). Novelist, critic and historian of crime.

R. J. HOLLINGDALE (1930–). Journalist; author of studies of Nietzsche, Thomas Mann etc.

JOSEPH HONE (1882–1959). Biographer of Yeats and George Moore.

ERNST KAISER. Author of *Robert Musil* (1962).

ERIC KORN (1935–). Book dealer and literary commentator.

F. R. LEAVIS (1895–1978). Critic, Fellow of Downing College, Cambridge.

A. S. MACDOWALL (1887–1933). Essayist and member of the editorial staff of *The Times*. Fellow and for a time Sub-warden of All Souls College, Oxford.

E. E. MAVROGORDATO (1870–1946). For many years a general reviewer for the *TLS*; tennis correspondent of *The Times*.

MALCOLM MUGGERIDGE (1903–1990). Author and broadcaster.

EDWIN MUIR (1887–1959). Poet; translator of Kafka.

JOHN MIDDLETON MURRY (1889–1957). Man of letters.

ROY PASCAL (1904–80). Former professor of German at the University of Birmingham; author of studies of Goethe, the German novel, etc.

PETER PORTER (1929–). Australian-born poet.

ANTHONY POWELL (1905–). Novelist. On the staff of the *TLS* from 1947 to 1953.

CRAIG RAINE (1944–). Poet and critic.

SIR ALEC RANDALL (1892–1977). Diplomat; ambassador to Denmark, 1945–53.

CHRISTOPHER RICKS. Professor of English at Boston University since 1986; author of studies of Milton, Tennyson, T. S. Eliot etc.

EDGELL RICKWORD (1898–1982). Poet and critic.

ALAN ROSS (1922–). Poet; editor of the *London Magazine*.

PETER RUSSELL. Editor of *Ezra Pound: A Collection of Essays to be presented to him on his Sixty-Fifth Birthday* (1950).

R. A. SCOTT-JAMES (1878–1959). Journalist; author of *The Making of Literature* (1928).

EDWARD SHANKS (1892–1953). Poet and critic.

N. C. SMITH (1871–1961). Headmaster of Sherborne School. Published books on Robert Bridges and Sydney Smith.

HAROLD STANNARD (1883–1947). Political journalist; member of the editorial staff of *The Times*.

J. P. STERN (1920–92). Professor of German at the University of London; author of studies of Nietzsche, Kafka etc.

JULIAN SYMONS (1912–). Novelist, critic and biographer.

PHILIP TOMLINSON (1882–1955). Joined the editorial staff of *The Times*, 1928; assistant editor of the *TLS*, 1939–47.

MARTIN TURNELL (1908–). Author of *The Novel in France* (1950).

SIR HUGH WALPOLE (1884–1941). Novelist.

ORLO WILLIAMS (1883–1967). Author; Clerk of Committees, House of Commons.

INDEX OF CONTRIBUTORS
AND OF BOOKS AND AUTHORS
REVIEWED

The TLS Companions

The projected series includes
COMMUNISM edited by Ferdinand Mount
MODERN POETRY edited by Alan Jenkins
THE ARTS edited by Peter Porter